MAN of GOD

Essays of the Life and Work of the Preacher

Shawn D. Mathis, General Editor

Associate Editors
Larry D. Mathis
Stan Smith
J..J. Turner

McDONOUGH CHURCH OF CHRIST
P.O. Box 1290
McDonough, Georgia 30253
(404) 954-1337

Gospel Advocate Company
P.O. Box 150
Nashville, Tennessee 37202

Published by Gospel Advocate Company
P.O. Box 150, Nashville, TN 37202

ISBN 0-89225-459-9

Table of Contents

Preface

Shawn D. ￼

Ministry is a precious gift of God. Answering the call to preach the Word provides a man with unique opportunities and challenges. Although we are all God's children, those who serve as ministers have a unique position as men of God. The man of God has the special privilege and responsibility of serving as a faithful spokesman for God.

There are many aspects to the work of the minister: teacher, mentor, counselor, comforter, administrator, and more. We have the special blessing of sharing important moments in the lives of God's people — marriages, births, illnesses, achievements, sorrows, death. But the apex of the preacher's work is the presentation of the Gospel of Jesus Christ.

G. Campbell Morgan once said, "In the true sermon there must always be passion. But the passion must be something created by no conscious effort. It must come out of what we are declaring and out of our consciousness of it." This passion for sharing the message of Christ and what He has done for us is the moving force in the man of God.

The purpose of this collection of essays is to help focus our attention on many of the basic principles underlying the life and work of the preacher. The contributors to this anthology represent an incredible resource of knowledge and experience. They are all dedicated proclaimers of the

Gospel. Their contributions represent perhaps the largest cooperative effort on a written work that has been undertaken in our fellowship. It is their hope that current ministers will be encouraged in their work, those considering preaching will be motivated to pursue that call, and members of the church will gain deeper insight into the role of the minister.

As editor of this anthology, I would like to recognize the special contributions of several individuals. My deepest thanks go to Larry D. Mathis, J.J. Turner and Stan Smith. As associate editors, these men were instrumental in the initial planning of this project and in the many hours of editorial work required to prepare it for publication. They have also been constant encouragers, friends and partners in ministry.

I would also like to express my appreciation to: Jimmie Gordon and Marvin Torbett, who encouraged this work from its conception; the Flanders Road Church of Christ in Toledo, Ohio, who has supported me in both this work and my daily ministry; Dee Rutherford, for her secretarial and grammatical help; Chris Zember, for his editorial work; Robert V. Nowlin Jr., for compiling the biographical information; Becky Mathis; F. LaGard Smith; Greg Tidwell; and Kerry Anderson.

I am always thankful for my gentle wife, Vida. She is compassionate and understanding and has been constantly supportive through the many hours this project required.

Finally, I would like to dedicate my efforts on this volume in honor of my parents, Larry and Sharon Mathis. They encouraged me and showed me how to become a man of God. May God bless them with robes of white and victors' wreaths.

Man of God

F. LaGard S

Desiderius Erasmus said, "If it is possible to train ele-
phants to dance, lions to play, and leopards to hunt, it should
be possible to teach preachers to preach." Considering the
number of preachers who enthusiastically flail away in the
pulpit yet rarely usher us to the portals of heaven, Erasmus
may have been overly optimistic. Yet if there is ever to be
any hope for teaching preachers to preach, this anthology —
written to preachers by preachers — will offer a significant
contribution to the cause.

Though practical at every turn, this volume is not just
another "how to" book for the eager homiletics student. The
title itself, *Man of God*, gives it away: No man preaches well
who is not himself transformed by the very words he has
been called to proclaim. As William A. Quale has so well
captured it, "Preaching is not the art of making a sermon
and delivering it. Preaching is the art of making a preacher
and delivering that." Thus, section by section, it is only after
exploring the man of God — his life, ministry and study —
that the book directly addresses the central subject of
preaching. It's the right order.

As one whose lineage includes four generations of gospel
preachers, I have great respect for those who publicly proclaim the Word. As far as I can tell, my forebearers on the
American frontier were men not only of the Book, but more

importantly, men of the God of the Book. Certainly that was true of my father who, though never formally educated, committed great portions of Scripture to memory, and the entirety of it to his heart.

At my father's feet, I learned the crucial difference between merely getting up a sermon and preaching the Word with passion. It isn't just a matter of histrionics, but more akin to what Abraham Lincoln once delightfully described: "I don't like to hear cut-and-dried sermons. When I hear a man preach, I like to see him act as if he were fighting bees."

I don't know about fighting bees, but I think I know what Jeremiah felt when he said, "His word is in my heart like a fire, a fire shut up in my bones. I am weary of holding it in; indeed, I cannot." That's exactly how I feel as a Christian author. And that's exactly what I want — no, desperately need — from those who would preach to me. Not outlines, not overheads, not three points and a poem, but a God-sent, heartfelt fire in their bones!

That, too, is the challenge of this welcome volume: Worthy sermons from worthy men impelled by worthy motives from on high. It's about better exposing the text and about living lives that have nothing to fear from exposure. It's about scholarship and discipleship, meditation and dedication. It's about you and your God, you and your family, you and your elders, you and all those who look to you — both to your life and to your preaching — to lead them to Christ.

Never in our lifetime has the challenge of preaching been so great. In this relativistic, nonjudgmental age, the message of sin and salvation couldn't be more foreign to our thinking. Even in the Lord's church, it's only theological fast food that most Christians want to carry away. For most, being warmed, if not filled, is quite enough. Or so they believe, until their spiritual emptiness leads to shattered lives which finally send them running to the preacher in the hope that he will put on a different hat and somehow counsel them back to wholeness apart from the Word.

Many forces are challenging the authority of God's revealed will. Whether it be from cultural influences on doctrine, or the kind of church growth theories that demand a gospel of pragmatism, the dire need for courageous gospel preaching couldn't be clearer. Who will proclaim the Word in its fullness? Who will stand against the tide of contemporary shallowness? Indeed, who will take us by the hand and show us the kind of transcendence of which God's ancient preachers spoke?

If the writers of this book are correct — and they are — only the true man of God is able to accomplish so noble a task. Are you such a man? Do you want to be? Then read on and be greatly encouraged, just as I have been.

The message throughout is unmistakable: Men of God, preach the Word!

F. LaGard Smith is professor of law at Pepperdine University in Malibu, California, and is author of more than a dozen books including *ACLU: The Devil's Advocate*, *Baptism: The Believer's Wedding Ceremony*, *The Narrated Bible*, *The Daily Bible*, *Meeting God in Quiet Places*, *What Most Women Want*, *The Cultural Church*, *When Choice Becomes God* and *Sodom's Second Coming*.

MAN of GOD

Part 1 — A Man of God

The Call to Preach

David Phar

It is important for the man who is preaching, and for the student who is considering the ministry, to understand the biblical basis for a call to preach.

This chapter is concerned with the process by which one decides to be a preacher, especially in regard to divine influence, along with the commitment and faithfulness that must follow that decision. Becoming a preacher is something that one must decide within himself, but it is not something that he should decide alone. God must be a part of the decision. If God is involved in the decision it cannot be an option, it becomes an imperative.

There is a sense in which one is called to preach. To preach or not to preach is not left to whim, convenience, or personal advantage. When one has accepted the responsibilities of preaching, is he at liberty before God simply to decide to change to another profession? Paul wrote, "Yea, woe is unto me, if I preach not the gospel" (1 Cor. 9:16). Is it possible that there might be placed upon us the same kind of obligation when we accept the call?

Wrong Motives

Some become preachers for wrong reasons. Various worldly issues may make the ministry attractive: the desire to be in the limelight, approval from others, exemption from military service, income tax advantages, professional status, or the perception that ministry is a relatively easy job.

While it is true that from a practical perspective preaching may be considered a profession — it may be one's occupation and livelihood — few things have been so harmful to the church as the view of ministry as a mere profession. There is an eternity of difference between the preacher who preaches and is paid and the one who preaches for pay. "The hireling fleeth, because he is an hireling, and careth not for the sheep" (John 10:13).

Biblical Guidance

God communicates to us through the Bible. Thus no aspect of life should be without direction from the principles of Scripture. Certainly any consideration to preach should involve careful study of God's Word. The Bible is the canon to define preaching and preachers. Those who decide to preach must prepare for the task by private and formal education in the Word. Those already preaching must make the study of the Word a lifelong pursuit. Yet without first having a basic understanding of what God has revealed about preaching one can hardly make a legitimate decision to be a preacher. While it would be presumptuous to set some required standard of biblical literacy before one could say he has decided to preach, it is likewise presumptuous for one to decide he ought to preach without having given thoughtful attention to what God has revealed about preaching.

The Bible alone can determine what kind of men should be preachers. There are specific character requirements. "Be thou an example of the believers, in word, in conversation, in charity, in spirit, in faith, in purity" (1 Tim. 4:12). Actually all instructions regarding godly conduct apply, but one who would instruct others in righteousness must give particular attention to his influence on others (cf. Matt. 23:3). The vessel that serves the Gospel must be one of honor. Only by purging himself of worldly dross can one be "a vessel unto honor, sanctified, and meet for the master's use, and prepared unto every good work." Thus he must flee from sin and follow after all that is good (2 Tim. 2:20ff). "And the servant of the Lord must not strive; but be gentle unto all men, apt to teach, patient, in meekness instructing those that oppose themselves" (2 Tim. 2:24-25).

Character studies through the Bible can be particularly helpful. From Enoch to John we can see the qualities that have made men useful as heralds of God's truth. Henry Ward Beecher's definition of preaching was: "Truth through personality."[2] The personalities of the preachers we find in both Testaments have considerable variety. There is no single style, no uniform temperament, and no exclusive approach. This assures us that God can use a great variety of men. There is, however, singularity of character, purpose, faithfulness, courage and steadfastness. One who is wrestling with the decision to preach should contemplate the great preachers of the Bible — Moses, Elijah, Jeremiah, and John the Baptist — examining whether he has a similar character.

The Bible shows what is expected of preachers. Local congregations may expect the performance of certain duties, but only God can outline the work of an evangelist. How many hours to be spent in the office, visitations required, and many like duties may have their degree of importance, but they are trivial compared to heaven's requirements. It may be that God's requirements are thought to be so obvious that they need little attention. Or maybe they are so sublime that some feel more comfortable with more mundane aspects of a minister's work. Surely, though, every preacher must know that God expects his servants to have a commitment that says, "What the Lord saith unto me, that will I speak" (1 Kings 22:14). One's deliberations over preaching must not focus on whether he can live on a preacher's pay, but on whether he can die for what is right as did Stephen, Zacharias, John and other martyrs.

Biblical teaching about the lostness of humanity, the gospel as the only hope of the world, and the need for laborers will surely have an influence on one's decision to preach. Jesus said, "Lift up your eyes, and look on the fields; for they are white already to harvest" (John 4:35). Paul sensed a debt that could only be paid by preaching (Rom. 1:14ff) When the world's need and God's grace have filled one's soul, the time may come when the sublime charge to "preach the word" rises off the page and takes hold of a man's heart.

The call of Isaiah provides a useful example (Isa. 6:1-11). Though involving miraculous elements, the principles are applicable to the call of the man of God. There must be a majestic view of God, a sensitive view of redemption, a realistic view of the world, and a confident view of truth. With such a vision arising from the Scriptures, one can rightly respond to God's call: "Here am I, send me."[3]

God's Purpose

While questioning various traditions of what it means to be called, God does indeed exercise influence. There is a sense in which God calls some men to the ministry of the Word and does not call others.

God has a purpose for every life and His purpose for some is that they preach. This does not negate the responsibility every Christian has to spread the Gospel as he has opportunity; it recognizes that God expects more of certain ones who minister especially in edification and evangelism (Luke 12:48). It is helpful to remember that a preacher is only an ordinary member of the Lord's church who has a higher degree of responsibility in the ministry of the Word.[4]

In his autobiography, Batsell Barrett Baxter begins with his theology of God having a plan for every person's life. After reviewing how God directed the lives of various Bible persons by both miraculous and providential influences, Baxter observed that while it may not be in some grand and spectacular role God does have a place for us in His plan. He further explains that God's plan for each of us may not be as clearly defined as in the case of Saul of Tarsus: "But we do believe that if we yield our lives to God's will He will open doors of opportunity in very natural, unspectacular ways through which each of us can play an important part in His plan."[5]

The parable of the talents shows that ability plus opportunity equals responsibility (Matt. 25:14ff). Different people have different abilities and opportunities; therefore, different responsibilities. This is an especially important principle in the consideration of who ought to be preachers. Has God given an individual the talent and opportunity to serve Him in this capacity? "And he gave some, apostles; and some prophets; and some evangelists; and some, pastors and teachers" (Eph. 4:11). While this text has a particular application to the apostolic age, it illustrates different roles for different persons as determined by the provisions of the Lord.

It would seem obvious then that in seeking to discover God's will as to whether one should preach we must consider His providence in giving enabling talents and encouraging opportunities. Every Christian should have a keen appreciation of what it means to be a steward: "Moreover it is required in stewards, that a man be found faithful" (1 Cor. 4:2). Faithfulness in stewardship means making the proper use of that which is provided. The stewardship of talents and opportunities means using them in a manner most pleasing to God; the way God expects them to be used. The question is, "Does God expect me to use the talents He has given me in the preaching of the word?" The call to preach involves evaluation of what the Lord has placed in our hands.

There are certain personal endowments that would ordinarily seem essential. One should examine, for example, whether he has the ability to communicate; whether he has the self-discipline to make effective use of his time and resources; and whether he has the intellectual ability to adequately understand and explain a broad range of both religious and secular concepts. As Nederhood emphasizes, one must have "the gift of judgment, the gift of wisdom ... He must have the ability to understand what is really happening among the people he is closely related to, and he must be able to respond to the situation in such a way that does not make it worse, but better."[6]

One may increase his ability, of course, and many have been very effective who started with seemingly little likelihood of success. It is not expected, that one begin with the same ability to communicate that he would have after training and experience. While the absence of certain native abilities might be reason for being cautious before committing oneself, our purpose is not so much to discourage those who may seen incapable as it is to emphasize the stewardship responsibility of those who have such talents.

God's Providence

Believers do not see the unfolding of life's circumstances as mere accidents of fate. We may not understand how, we may not understand why, but we believe that God is at work in our lives (cf. James. 4:13ff). As relates to this study, what the Lord provides may be an open door into the ministry of the word. It might be an opportunity for education. It might be the needs of a mission field. It might be changes in the family, economic circumstances, encouragement from others, or numerous other things. The point is that providence may be moving one in this direction.

We must exercise caution in our interpretation of providence. The emergence of what seems to be a positive opportunity may not by itself indicate that one ought to become a preacher. On the other hand, some of life's reversals may serve to bring one into the ministry. For example, one should not decide to be a preacher because he lost a job; but losing his job might be the providential push needed to give a more useful direction for his life.

God-given potentials and opportunities should not be ignored. These things help one see his God-given responsibilities. This is not to imply that the only way to share God's truth is as a full-time preacher. It is to affirm plainly, however, that every person should make conscientious decisions regarding what to do with his life.

Paul names grace as the foundation upon which his ministry was built. He said, "By the grace of God I am what I am; and his grace which was bestowed upon me was not in vain; but I labored more abundantly than they all; yet not I, but the grace of God which was with me" (1 Cor. 15:10). Obviously Paul had marvelous talents, but such were always minimized as he emphasized instead the place of Christ (1 Cor. 1:29, 31; 2:1-5). What Christ had done for him became the compelling force behind all that he did for Christ (2 Cor. 5:13). The point that must not be missed is that it is never God's will for a man to be a preacher unless that man has had an overwhelming appreciation of what the Lord has done for him. Stated positively, the more one is obsessed with the impact of heavenly grace in his own life, the more he will be ready to preach it to others.

Of first importance is one's personal relationship with the Lord. He must know Christ. Spiritual mediocrity will not suffice. There can be no casual commitment to God. One must be crucified with Christ and live by faith (Gal. 2:20). That faith must be a compulsion, so that he does not speak just to get others to believe, but because he believes and cannot keep from speaking (2 Cor. 4:13). Before preaching, one must be settled in his convictions and fully persuaded of his own hope. There is no substitute for spiritual maturity.

Obviously one must be experienced in prayer. Every thought and action that leads one toward the decision to preach should involve fervent petitions. We could hardly imagine that God is calling one into the ministry who has not been calling for God's guidance. Our attention here, though, is on how much prayer has already been a part of his life. The decision to preach should not be made without prayer.

Thy Will Be Done

We have approached the call to preach as a decision one makes because he believes it is God's purpose for his life. No one should presume to be a preacher unless he believes this is what God wants him to do. If preaching is what God wants him to do, it must follow that "having put his hand to the plow," there is no looking or turning back (Luke 9:62). Those who enlist in this service are expected to enlist for life (cf. 2 Tim. 2:3).

This is not to indict those who because of unavoidable circumstances must give up full-time ministries. Neither should we be critical of one who simply finds that he is not able to be effective. What is being emphasized is that preaching is not merely a profession; it is not a profession which can be adopted or abandoned at our convenience. If one is called to preach, if he is convinced that this is the best way that he can serve Christ and humanity, he should expect to continue in the fight, keeping the faith, until he has finished the course (2 Tim. 4:7).

Endnotes

1. Alfred P. Gibbs. *The Preacher and His Preaching*. (Kansas City: Walterick Pub., 1964) 86.

2. Gibbs 28.

3. David R. Pharr. "Who Will Go?" *The Messenger*. Oct. 1990: 6.

4. Joel Nederhood. "The Minister's Call," *The Preacher and Preaching*, Ed. Samuel T. Logan, Jr., 1986: 39.

5. Batsell Barrett Baxter. *Every Life a Plan of God*. (Abilene: Zachary Associates, 1983) 8ff.

6. Nederhood 53.

David Pharr attended Freed-Hardeman University, Rio Grande College and Alabama Christian School of Religion. He has been preaching the Gospel for 25 years. He has served as the director of East Tennessee School of Preaching in Knoxville, Tennessee. In addition to local ministry, he has served as editor of Carolina Christian and has written extensively.

Jesus As an Example for Preachers

Hugo McC

Any preacher does well to emulate Paul, but Paul would have every preacher look beyond him to the supreme example: "Be ye imitators of me, even as I also am of Christ" (1 Cor. 11:1). Jesus, as a heaven-sent proclaimer, could assert that Jehovah anointed Him to preach the Gospel (Luke 4:18).

A boy will not stumble as much when he puts his feet in his father's snow-tracks. So a preacher, when he steadily keeps his eyes on Jesus, will stumble less. One reason the Lord came into the world was to make tracks: "Leaving you an example, that you should follow his steps" (1 Peter 2:21).

Five Ways Jesus Is Not An Example

First, His miracles (from the virgin birth to the ascension) were necessary to implement the Divine plan of redemption (1 Tim. 3:16). They are faith-begetters (John 5:36), but they were not designed as examples that preachers today might duplicate. Unfortunately some preachers have misused the statement, "Jesus Christ is the same yesterday and today and forever." They use it to try and prove that they are to perform miracles as did Jesus; they never seem to get to the point of demonstration (Heb. 13:8).

Second, Jesus was a sinless man unlike any other man who ever lived. It is important that the great model for preachers should have no defect or missing of the mark and should be "holy, blameless, pure, [and] set apart from sinners" (Heb. 7:26). Practically speaking such a standard is too high for preachers. With the right attitude men of God will die trying to be sinless, but nobody other than Jesus will ever reached that goal.

Third, His fasting 40 days and nights is not a task for the modern preacher to attempt. The Lord's abstaining from food for nearly six weeks apparently shows physical and spiritual preparation for forthcoming temptations from Satan. But that abstinence is not set forth as an example for today's preachers. Through the centuries some ascetics and extremists have emulated the Lord with little or no profit for themselves or anybody else.

Occasional fasting is beneficial as long as it does not result in "harsh treatment of the body" (Matt. 9:15; Col. 2:23). Incidentally, as one notices that Jesus' lengthy fast did not incapacitate Him or put Him in a sick bed, one learns how strong He was physically and how He took care of His health.

Fourth, Jesus kept the Law. Though Jesus perfectly observed Moses' Law His example in this regard is only by way of a parallel (Luke 4:16; 22:8). Preachers are not under the Law of Moses but under Christ's law (Rom. 7:6; Gal. 3:25; 6:2). In this matter then His example teaches gospel preachers to be as respectful and obedient to New Testament commandments as Jesus was to the Old Testament Law (Matt. 5:19; 1 John 2:4).

Fifth, His lack of formal schooling is not an example. The necessity of schooling, even for those preachers of the first century with Holy Spirit inspiration, is evident in that Jesus placed His apostles in a three-year training program (Matt. 10:19-20). Formally or informally, every gospel preacher must go to school. Paul, on death row and knowing he had only a few months left to preach, believed that he should continue to study. He requested Timothy to bring him "his scrolls, especially the parchments" (2 Tim. 4:13). Many gospel preachers are doing better work for the Master because of education.

Five Ways Jesus Is an Example

First, His respect for Scripture is an example. To Jesus the Old Testament was no ordinary book. A lawyer once inquired, "Teacher, what shall I do to inherit eternal life?" The Lord replied with a question, "What is written in the law? How readest thou?" (Luke 10:25-26). Jesus called the Old Testament "the word of God," affirming that the "scripture cannot be broken" (John 10:35). In Jesus' estimation men are foolish and "slow of heart" who do not "believe in all that the prophets have spoken" (Luke 24:25). Ministers of the Word must have the same regard for the whole Bible as Jesus did for the Old Testament, a high view of Spirit-inspiration resulting from the inerrant Word of God (2 Tim. 3:16-17).

Second, His knowledge of Scripture is an example. Even as a boy Jesus grew in "wisdom" (Luke 2:52). Since the greatest source of wisdom is that which is a light to one's path, the holy Scripture, one knows what Jesus studied (Psalm 119:105). His first 30 years were learning years. Like Ezra, He "set his heart to seek the law of Jehovah" (Ezra 7:10). Because of studious application He had on His tongue a scripture quotation to meet every temptation Satan offered (Matt. 4:1-11).

Third, His schedule is an example. Jesus' custom was to enter the synagogue on the Sabbath (Luke 4:16). More is implied than is seen on the surface. Apparently Jesus followed a schedule including at least four items, and sometimes five. He studied the Scriptures, prayed, went to Sabbath worship, went about doing good, and enjoyed social visits in the homes of His friends (Luke 2:52; 4:16; 10:38-42; Mark 1:35; Acts 10:38).

Every preacher who accomplishes anything worthwhile sets a time pattern for his daily activities and does his best to follow it. His hours are never unplanned. The pressure of so many calls to serve people hinders preachers from following a rigid schedule, but they must make one and keep it in mind if, from the pulpit and from house to house, they are going to be able to nourish men's souls. John Banister, for 25 years at Skillman Avenue church in Dallas, secluded himself in his study from 8 o'clock until 12 five days a week for prayer and application of the Scripture. He left word with the church secretary to call him only in an emergency. As a result his sermons abound with Scripture.

Fourth, His simplicity is an example. Affectation and sophistication were foreign to Jesus who would sit on a mountain side to preach (Matt. 5:1). The boat of a commercial fisherman was not noted for its pleasant odor, yet Jesus would use such for a pulpit (Matt. 13:2). He did not originate clergymen's apparel as "the cloth of the ministry." His attire was no different from that of other men. Judas identified Him, not by clothes but by a kiss (Matt. 26:48). The simplicity of Jesus no doubt is one of the reasons why the common people were drawn to Him and "heard him gladly" (Mark 12:37).

To be effective a preacher must be understood. Once when a preacher with many long words in his sermon had finished, a brother leading the dismissal prayer, said "Lord, we hope you understood this sermon, because we did not." It is the power of the Word, not ornate language, that will change lives.

Fifth, His commitment is an example. Jesus loved His Father (John 14:31). One is not surprised that, among the 613 commandments in the law of Moses, Jesus selected one as above all the others: "Thou shalt love Jehovah thy God with all thy heart, and with all thy soul, and with all thy might" (Deut. 6:5). With Him those beautiful words were not simply a memory verse, they necessarily included doing what the object of love would say.

In Jesus' thinking, love for God cannot be separated from obedience to the Father's commandments (John 14:15, 31). Before He left heaven He told His Father, "I delight to do thy will, O my God; yea, thy law is within my heart" (Psalm 40:8; Heb. 10:7). Then, on this earth, a commitment to His Father's will was uppermost in His mind. When only 12 years old, Jesus was surprised that His mother and step-father did not understand that He must be about His Father's business ("house" Luke 2:49, NIV). Even when tired and hungry, to Him something was more important than eating: "My meat is to do the will of him that sent me, and to accomplish his work" (John 4:34).

As true commitment demands, He always put away personal desires: "I seek not mine own will, but the will of Him that sent me" (John 5:30). That sentiment dominated His thinking, and He repeated it: "I am come down from heaven, not to do mine own will, but the will of him that sent me" (John 6:38). This mind-set kept Him in an urgency: "I must work the works of him that sent me, while it is day; the night cometh, when no man can work" (John 9:4). By way of anticipation, on the night before black Friday's blood-letting and death, that total commitment to the will of God was on Jesus' mind is evident in His prayer: "I glorified thee on the earth, having accomplished the work which thou hast given me to do" (John 17:4). On the cross in His last hour the same controlling obsession was apparently on His mind as He exclaimed, "It is finished" (John 19:30). He knew He had left nothing undone in His messianic mission to earth.

Jesus' mind-set not only determined His deeds but also His choice of words: "I spake not from myself; but the Father that sent me, he hath given me a commandment, what I should say, and what I should speak" (John 12:49).

As Jesus knew He was heaven sent (John 12:49), so His preachers should have the consciousness that they too are on divine assignments (Rom. 10:15). It is bound to have strengthened Jesus to know that the one who sent Him was always with Him (John 8:29). This assurance also braces Jesus' preachers today (Phil. 4:5). One of the assurances enjoyed by Jesus, "I do always the things that are pleasing to him" (John 8:29), gospel preachers can only approximate. But it is their highest pleasure to do what pleases God their Father. In the true sense of a misused statement, "love and do as you please," both Jesus and His preachers only please to do God's will.

As love for God and for His will was Jesus' first priority, His second was love for mankind and human service. The second commandment, "Thou shalt love thy neighbor as thyself" (Lev. 19:18), typified Jesus. The example He set, going "about doing good" (Acts 10:38), is attainable by all His preachers. Such a mind-set in His ministers will automatically kill any tendency toward laziness and prevent their spending too much time in their studies with books.

When two men wanting to visit with Jesus asked where He was staying, the people-loving Lord understood and courteously invited them, saying, "Come and see" (John 1:39). Those two (Andrew and probably John, Zebedee's son) undoubtedly never forgot their getting to spend several hours with the Lord. When people were "distressed and scattered" (Matt. 9:36), the Lord's heart was touched, and He solicited prayers in their behalf. When people had continued with Jesus three days with nothing to eat, He saw to it that a meal was provided because He was filled with love for people (*philanthropia*, Titus 3:4).

His interest in little children was more than His apostles could understand. When they rebuked mothers for bringing their little ones for Jesus to hold in His arms He became angry and rebuked the apostles (Mark 10:14). On a different plane, but emanating from a love for people, the apostles were shocked that He would even speak to a Samaritan woman. How shocked they would have been had they known that that particular woman had had five husbands and was "living-in" with a sixth (John 4:18).

Some people were so depraved the loving Savior had to describe them as dogs and hogs (Matt. 7:6). But His love for mankind was so deep He always looked for any redeeming quality. He would not break a "bruised reed," nor would He quench a "dimly burning wick" (Isa. 42:3; Matt. 12:19).

What would cause one carrying a cross, seeing weeping women sympathizing, to stop and say, "Weep not for me, but for yourselves?" (Luke 23:28). Truly He thought of others before He thought of Himself. How should one react when He, who came to save "his own" people, heard them taunt him from a cross. Only a sincere heart dedicated to man's welfare could then pray, "Father, forgive them for they know not what they do" (Luke 23:34).

The same spirit of philanthropy that motivated the Lord was in His apostle who gladly spent his own resources and himself that other people might be blessed (2 Cor. 12:15). Like Jesus, Paul poured out his life as a drink-offering to help other people to get to heaven (Phil. 2:17). And every gospel preacher who is worthy of the name follows Paul, as Paul followed his Lord in devoting time and talent to make the world better.

Hugo McCord attended Freed-Hardeman University, University of Illinois, University of Tulsa, Virginia Seminary, Southern Seminary, and New Orleans Seminary. A retired professor of Bible and Biblical Languages from Oklahoma Christian University of Science and Arts, he is the author of several books and has translated the New Testament.

The Man of God in the Old Testament

Stan Smith

Humans get weary when overworked and under encouraged.[1] The lies of Satan ring loudly in tired ears. This is an effort to say that what you are doing for God is not in vain (1 Cor. 15:58). The purpose of this chapter is to assume the role of Peter by reminding you of our brothers from long ago who both taught and inspired hope within men of God from every generation.[2]

"Man of God" is a descriptive term of the prophet in Scripture.[3] If preachers today were mentioned in the inspired text how might that description read? Would we, like the prophets, be men driven by a purpose and power greater than ourselves?

The prophets were realists. They felt. They cared. They believed. The man of God in the Old Testament is not one single individual but rather many men throughout Scripture. God used a wonderful variety of individuals to carry out His purpose. Get to know them. They will bless your study, your preaching and your walk with God. The man of God in the Old Testament appears in many shapes and sizes. Find one you can relate to. More if you can, but at least one. Let the prophets speak their timely message to you.

A personal story may help illustrate. Once I strolled through a Lakota Sioux museum in South Dakota in an effort to discover some family roots. One life-size exhibit of a figure in the traditional dress of a warrior caught my attention. Standing eye-to-eye with this figure, I realized we were the same size: shoulders, arm length, torso and knee height. Our clothes and culture were different but something of me was reflected in him. I was peering into part of my past.

Looking at the prophets I see similar reflections in these ancient preachers. The more I read of their lives the more I feel I am looking in a mirror and seeing related experiences of my ministry. They have become good friends and good therapy.

They are our ancestors in the family of faith. Their calling was undeniable even though some attempted to deny it and others tired of it.[4] They were all important and were fulfilling God's agenda. Yahweh used them to bring about his ends (Heb. 1:1-2). We tend to look at the wrong indicators for greatness. When God looks among humanity servanthood attracts his attention.[5] He likes servants. They remind him of his Son.

The Prophets

Several New Testament passages relating to the prophets are character observations of the prophets.

> Concerning which salvation the prophets sought and searched diligently, who prophesied of the grace that should come unto you: searching what time or what manner of time the Spirit of Christ which was in them did point unto, when it testified beforehand the sufferings of Christ, and the glories that should follow them. To whom it was revealed, that not unto themselves, but unto you, did they minister these things (1 Peter 1:10-12).

I find it fascinating that the prophets were our servants. Yours and mine. What is more, they realized it. It is one thing to serve a purpose unknowingly,[6] but something entirely different to realize and embrace the purpose.[7] Prophetic preaching served its generation and beyond. Focus on this concept in your ministry because your ministry is also to your generation and beyond. Lives you touch with the gospel today will continue bearing fruit until the Lord returns. Your ministry will outlive you. Your ministry can affect the course of human history.

Our hurdles have been encountered before. We are not the first to struggle and it remains unknown to us who the last generation of preachers shall be before the Lord returns (Mark 13:32). Our task is to carry the light of life giving sight to the blind.

The author of Hebrews writes of people characterized by great faith. Hebrews 12 informs us that we are to draw strength and courage from them. The prophets are tucked away neatly in the list, but they are there all the same (Heb. 11:32). The ancient author could have filled a scroll with their ministries alone. Their message is strong even for preachers today. Elijah could talk to us about burn-out, Jonah about running out, and Isaiah about holding out. When ready to quit meditate on the prophets before making your final decision.

The man of God in the Old Testament placed his hope and trust in God as opposed to man. I have lived long enough to see preachers prove themselves human. It has been a hard but valuable lesson. A long-time preacher said in a sermon, "The best of men are only men at best." I hope your faith is resting in God. If it is not, you will be disenchanted in the course of time.

If you are feeling the persecution, someone needs to rendezvous with you and strengthen your hand in God.[8] With whom shall you meet? For David, it was Jonathan. They met in the Ziph woods. You need someone that understands you (2 Cor. 1:3). Otherwise good intentions rarely find good expression. Jonathan could relate to David. Both had fought hand to hand with Philistines, commanded 1,000 troops, and were the recipients of King Saul's wrath.[9] They could relate. I am suggesting that the prophets can relate to you. They can revive your courage to proclaim God's message because they understand what it is like to face hardship. No one else in the congregation may understand but the prophets do. Perhaps a little soul-knitting of our own would help (1 Sam. 18:1). The knitting occurs as you see your ministry in the prophetic light. There is an obvious and immediate kinship.

It is normal to have highs and lows. Your mission can be confusing and, at times, very discouraging. Go sit with Elijah in the back of the cave on Mount Horeb and listen to him. He could lecture on discouragement. Elijah knew about trials. He was in the cave because he was on the run for his life. Has some person threatened your security? Have you found a suitable cave? This sounds rather desperate. It was to Elijah. God talked with Elijah and helped him. Walk out to the mouth of the cave and listen in on the conversation, "Go back to work, Elijah. Do what I have asked you to do.[10] Keep your focus and stop allowing the peripherals to blur your vision." There comes a time in a ministry when we all need this talk.

Hosea could write about pain. His pain came from within his family. Does anything hurt worse? The business of marriage is a delicate balance. Most men are wise enough to pray for a faithful wife but not everyone is fortunate to have a faithful spouse. What then? Watch Hosea. Was his marital situation reason enough to forfeit his calling? Not in God's eyes. We must be willing to minister through, in response to, and in spite of our pain (John 16:33). It is disturbing when shepherds of the flock end the ministries of men wearing Hosea's shoes. How many men of God have lost their mate and their preaching ministry in the same work-week? The ancient text delivers the message that God can use a man mired in pain to fulfill his will. The prophets are testimony to the fact that it will not be easy. Sacrifice demands a price.[11] You will not minister without hardship but you can minister through it. Remember that.

Jonah is a classic. He thinks he knows God so well. In fact, this is his defense for fleeing from God after his first call to preach to Nineveh.[12] His knowledge, as it turns out, is rather limited. He is selfish and has little love for the people he is serving (Jonah 4:1-5). You might ask yourself some pointed questions from time to time about your feelings for the saints you minister to. Be careful not to disdain them because they lack your background in rigorous study. Not everyone perks up when they hear a discussion over text families. They may not be interested in a critical analysis of the finds at Oxyrhynchus or Qumran. They may not share your joy over finding an infinitive absolute or multiple cognate accusatives in one verse. They may not smile and nod in affirmation when the Greek text is read aloud and correctly exegeted. They are still children of God through faith in Christ Jesus (Gal. 3:26). They remain your brethren. When you lose your love for the souls of men it is probably best to give yourself to another task. It was Paul who said our knowledge is worthless if we are void of love (1 Cor. 13:2).

I find it fascinating that Jonah faithfully delivered God's word to Nineveh. He told them what was right. But while done faithfully it was not done in faith. There is a subtle difference here but one worthy of consideration in your own ministry. Jonah did not believe in repentance for Nineveh. He did not want them to repent. He wanted to see them destroyed. That is different from Elisha, Isaiah and Paul. They wept over physical destruction and spiritual lostness.[13] And do not forget Jesus. Nearing Jerusalem to die for us he wept over the city due to their spiritual blindness (Luke 19:41-44).

Why are you going into your study and into the pulpit? To herald salvation and encourage repentance? Yes. Is there yet hope within you that the word of God shared faithfully can change men's lives?

I trust you still believe in the power of the Gospel to save (Rom. 1:16). We need to rejoice when sinners come home to our Father.[14] That is our purpose. Believe in the Word of God to change people and share that faith with your listeners.

When speaking of hell it should be with a note of sadness. It is disturbing to hear a herald speak of being lost eternally as if he is going to be pleased when it befalls certain ones. We would not wish that on anyone. God does not want that for people. That alone ought to mean something to the disciples. He wants all men to come to know the truth[15] and be saved (1 Tim. 2:3-4). Amazing! From Jonah to Jesus to today, God's wish for mankind has not changed. If that is God's wish, what should yours be as a preacher? Jesus' Thursday night prayer in Gethsemane is exactly the prayer we need to send up.[16] We need to want what God wants.

Jeremiah, a long-term minister, stayed with those he prophesied to and kept his ministry going even in the difficult years. They had not been too receptive to his message, but still he remained at his post. Much could be written about the average length of the relationship between a preacher and a congregation. I preach in a county with a man in his 37th year of ministry with the same congregation. He continues to have tremendous influence within the body he serves, throughout the county and the entire region. He has encouraged this writer on countless occasions. When you feel the urge to end a local work be sure to consider the good being done. Take a walk through babyland during the Bible class hour, stick your head in a teen class, show up for the meal after the ladies benevolent class, or go on a church retreat. You may find some reasons to stay with the people.

You may, on the other hand, find reasons to pack your gear. Sometimes there are reasons to leave.[17] Greater opportunities to serve, preservation of your own faith, and further education are just a few. But there are also reasons to stay. Endure hardship for the elect's sake. You have an opportunity Sunday after Sunday to make a difference in the lives of people. That is a privilege. Nineveh was better after Jonah's work there.[18] Dig through Assyrian history. The zenith of Nineveh's glory followed the work of Jonah. The same can be true for the congregations where you labor in God's work. Many of the prophets were not around to see the long-term fruits of their labors but they worked on anyway.[19] You must resolve to out last, out live, and out love your opponents.

The man of God in the Old Testament had an endearing quality about his message. So often in the oracle a message of hope was included. They were not always prophets of doom. Actually, they only condemned when necessary. Micah has this spirit in his work. The projected deliverance comes shining through. Consider the remnant passages in Isaiah's work. Grace, mercy and love of God are major themes in the writing of Isaiah. Interwoven among the woes was the wishful thinking we all need to relay. Be sure you remember to hold out hope to the hearer. Leave it intact whenever possible. Remind others of their responsibility and of Yahweh's *hesed*,[20] but offer reminders on both sides of the divine character. God keeps his promise of redemption also.

The good prophets were not for sale. Elisha is one man to watch here. He performed his ministry but made it clear that it was not a financial decision (2 Kings 5:15-16). Balaam is representative of the other extreme (2 Peter 2:15). He was instructed concerning this very thing by his beast and an angel. Preaching has never been about making money. It is about introducing the hopeful wanderer to a loving Father offering salvation to all. When gospel meetings and Saturday seminars are merely ways of making a few more dollars you have lost sight of the cross.[21]

The prophets were not swayed by the presence of men. I think of Samuel before King Saul and Nathan before King David (1 Sam. 15:10-23; 2 Sam. 12:1-15). Beware of watering down the Bible's message based on the assembled crowd. To have such a practice places one in dreadful company.[22] I am for salting our speech with kindness but not for editing God's plan (Col. 4:6).

The Gospel is for everyone regardless of earthly status. I have looked out into the eyes of a medical doctor, judge, mayor, school superintendent, dentist, bank president, country music star, college athlete, millionaire, pilot, law enforcement officer, state representative, military officer, nuclear physicist, rocket scientist and college professor. All were in need of salvation. Always be faithful in executing your mission. You are an evangelist regardless of who is in the assembly.

Conclusion

By way of conclusion I wish we had room for Malachi who reveals some failings after the remnant had returned.[23] We need to pray Elisha's prayer and ask for a double portion of the prophet's spirit (2 Kings 2:9). This remains a time to stand for God and good on all fronts. This generation need to go forth in the spirit and power of Elijah (Luke 1:17). Hosea expresses this idea as he reports that it is time to seek Jehovah (Hosea 10:12). The God who stood by the prophets will stand by you. You are not alone (Heb. 13:5-6). It is interesting that David and Paul realized the same fact (Acts 2:25; 2 Tim. 4:16-17). They were not alone either. No man of God ever is.

Isaiah saw the glory of God and it fueled his ministry for the remainder of his life (Isa. 6:1-10). We need to see the glory of God's mercy today and resolve to stay on the altar as a living sacrifice (Rom. 12:1-2). If we could only see what Simeon was able to see there would be cause to rejoice. Simeon was able to see Jesus as the Christ.[24] Paul tells Timothy in a long list of commands, "Remember Jesus Christ, risen from the dead, of the seed of David, according to my gospel" (2 Tim. 2:8).[25]

Remember to see Jesus as the one anointed to save and the prophets as men who answered an undeniable call. Remember to herald hope to your generation, that what you are doing matters, and to exhort someone along the journey home.

Endnotes

1. Heb. 3:12-14 shows that anyone can fall away from the living God. The biblical formula for preventing this is encouragement. It must be done daily to overcome the negative effects of Satan.

2. The apostle indicates his desire to remind the saints of certain aspects of the faith, 2 Peter 1:12-15.

3. Deut. 33:1; Judges 13:6; and 1 Sam. 2:27; 9:7,8,10, serve to illustrate the title.

4. Jonah tried to flee from the presence of Yahweh (Jonah 1:3). Elijah, under the juniper tree, tired of his calling (1 Kings 19:4-5).

5. Greatness reveals itself in how one treats the weak, dependent, position-lacking people (Luke 9:46-48). This is at the heart of servanthood.

6. Yahweh used Pharaoh without his awareness of Israel's God or purpose (Gen. 5:2, 6:1, 11:9).

7. In John 3:27-30, John the Baptist reveals inspired perception of his role in the Messiah event. The focus was not on John. The important thing then and now is that the people needing Jesus are joined to him. The wedding illustration is timeless.

8. This scene is related in 1 Sam. 23:15-18. Jonathan meets with David, as he is being hunted by King Saul, to give the outlaw son of Jesse some encouragement. Jonathan affirms his loyalty to David.

9. The texts for study give the event in the life of Jonathan fol-

lowed by the event in the life of David. The order given agrees with the order in the chapter (1 Sam. 14:14 and 1 Sam. 17:48-50; 1 Sam. 13:2 and 1 Sam. 18:13; 1 Sam. 14:43-46 and 1 Sam. 18:29; 19:1).

10. Yahweh tells His prophet to go anoint Hazael as king of Syria, Jehu as king of Israel, and Elisha as the successive prophet (1 Kings 19:15-16).

11. When David was told to go sacrifice to Yahweh at the threshing floor of Araunah, he sought to purchase the place from Araunah upon his arrival. Araunah offers it as a gift and David replies, "Nay, but I will verily buy it of thee at a price; neither will I offer burnt-offerings unto Jehovah my God which cost me nothing" (2 Sam. 24:18-25).

12. Jonah 4:1-2 records Jonah's reasoning for his attempted flight from the presence of Yahweh. His comments display a knowledge of the Torah (Ex. 34:6-7; Num. 14:18) and the Psalms (86:5,15). Jonah is not the only prophet that had this knowledge (Joel 2:13; Micah 7:18).

13. 2 Kings 8:10, reveals Elisha's distress over the coming persecution of God's people at the hand of Hazael. Isa. 22:4 reveals Isaiah's compassion for Jerusalem. Rom. 9:1-5 reveals Paul's longing for Israel to embrace Christ.

14. In Luke 15:11:32 God is portrayed by the father. The character of the older brother is a chance for us to gauge our own reaction to the idea of our brethren returning home after a trip into the world.

15. The truth is seen in John 3:16-17. God loves humans. He died for us all.

16. Jesus at 12 in the temple (Luke 2:49) and after he was 30 in Samaria (John 4:34) was about the same thing and living this prayer recorded in Luke 22:42, "not my will, but thine, be done."

17. In 1 Kings 17:3 the prophet Elijah is commanded of Yahweh to change his location.

18. The city of Nineveh became the capital of the Assyrian empire during the reign of Sennacherib, 700-612 B.C.

19. The prophets serve all believers (1 Peter 1:10-12).

20. This Hebrew word is translated in various ways: "kindness," "lovingkindness," "mercy," "love," and "steadfast love" are examples. The parallelism of Prov. 19:22 offers a clear definition. In the proverb, *hesed* is the opposite of lying. To display *hesed* is to keep your word. You are true to your promises, regardless of their nature

or the resultant consequences. The idea of being loyal to a covenant is within the bounds of this word.

21. Luke 9:23 instructs us to deny self and take up our cross daily, following Jesus. The cross for Jesus was His purpose for being in the flesh. It gave tangible insight into the mission of redemption. Our purpose is to share the Gospel with the lost and to exhort the saved to faithful living. This is our mission, our cross.

22. The false prophets fit this category (Luke 6:26). They were not men of God.

23. Mal. 3:7-12 reveals the problem the people had with their giving. They were holding back on God. Mal. 4:4-6 reveals the need for family relationships to be strengthened.

24. A lovely scene as the old prophet holds the young Messiah (Luke 2:25-35). His blessing indicates his awareness that this was much more than a mere baby. The salvation of God was before him.

25. There are 32 occurrences of the second person singular imperative verb in 2 Timothy.

Stan Smith attended David Lipscomb University, earning B.A. and M.A. degrees. He and his wife, Leanne, and two daughters, Jordan and Shelby, live in Centerville, Tennessee, where he has served as preacher for the Fairfield Church of Christ since 1992.

The Man of God in the New Testament

Terry Whee

The concept of the man of God is not unique to the New Testament. One sees the phrase repeatedly in the first covenant describing Moses, Samuel, David, Elijah, Elisha and a host of unnamed prophets. It speaks of a man devoted to God, to His holiness, and to His service. This man knows God and burns to make God known to the people around him.

The phrase is also found in the New Testament, but not often. We may deduce from this rarity of use that either very few measured up to the designation in this covenant, or that it is so much the way of men now that the phrase is simply a concept universally seen and fully understood.

Timothy As a Man of God

Actually, only one man in the New Covenant is specifically called a man of God — Timothy. The apostle Paul addresses Timothy this way only twice, once in each of his letters to him (1 Tim. 6:11; 2 Tim. 3:17). But the phrase is used in such a way as to imply not uniqueness but familiarity. Timothy joins the ranks of the great saints of old simply because he is a faithful Christian and a gospel preacher.

Timothy therefore stands before us as the New Testament definition of the man of God in this age. Since our Lord is no respecter of persons (Acts 10:34), it must be that He leaves the way open for any other so disposed to be called God's man. Let us consider this high honor, taking to heart the fact that such a calling is also possible for you and me in Christ.

As a sidenote, perhaps I need to emphasize that leadership in the Lord's church is always a male's responsibility (1 Tim. 2:11-15), though women may certainly influence and bless. We can justly conclude that there were and are women of God (Heb. 11:11, 31, 35). To whatever extent the picture of the man of God would apply to women of the church, all concerned should take such to heart.

Timothy is first seen as a replacement of sorts for John Mark "who went not" with Paul "to the work" (Acts 15:37-16:2). He had high recommendation from the home brethren; and Paul indicates that prophecy was involved in his induction to the place of "helper of the apostle" (1 Tim. 1:18; 4:14).

Timothy gives the appearance of a young, mild and gentle man. He comes from a godly family, at least as far as mother and grand-mother are concerned (2 Tim. 1:3-5). He is very obedient to Paul's commands. At the beginning, he allows Paul to circumcise him for the sake of ministering to the Jews (Acts 16:1-3); and at the end of Paul's first Roman imprisonment he brags about Timothy to the Philippians as he does on no other:

> But I trust in the Lord Jesus to send Timothy to you shortly, that I also may be encouraged when I know your state. For I have no one like-minded,who will sincerely care for your state. For all seek their own, not the things which are of Christ Jesus. But you know his proven character, that as a son with his father he served with me in the gospel. Therefore I hope to send him at once, as soon as I see how it goes with me (Phil. 2:19-23).

Timothy is a man totally concerned with the ministry. He has totally surrendered to the authority, doctrine and example of his apostolic mentor. He is totally lost in the welfare of the brethren. Paul can count on him to put the needs of others ahead of himself. He can trust him to inculcate among the brethren in the churches Paul's pattern of worship, organization, Christian living and teaching. Timothy is devoted to the Lord. He is a man of God:

> For this reason I have sent Timothy to you, who is my beloved and faithful son in the Lord, who will remind you of my ways in Christ, as I teach everywhere in every church (1 Cor. 4:17).

The Man of God Pictured in 2 Corinthians

One of the best pictures of such a faithful Christian ministry can be found, not just in the letters to Timothy, but in the letter of 2 Corinthians. Paul here describes his ministry among the Corinthians, which he shared with Titus and Silas as well as Timothy. A detailed study of this description gives us the general framework of what Paul truly means by "man of God." Timothy shines as an outstanding example in this context.

First, Paul stresses the unchangeable and positive nature of the message preached. It is "Yes" and "Amen" to all of God's promises in Christ. Everything depends on the faithful communication of these "exceedingly great and precious promises" to the audience. They must hear it, trust it and positively respond to it. All else in ministry relates to the central emphasis of the Gospel: What God has done for us through Jesus Christ His Son.

Second, Paul makes it clear that such a ministry comes from the sufficiency of God Himself. A preacher does not gain the ability to fulfill his task through self-help thinking. It is by recognizing God to be the power, the wisdom and the glory of the ministry that he succeeds.

Third, the minister works with the church to ensure that God's property, His inheritance, is ready for God to claim at the proper time. The man of God must recognize the value of his relationship with the church. They work together with God for the benefit of the saints, to bring them to repentance, to shine God's glory on them that they might be transformed into the same image of glory, full of grace and truth, according to Jesus Christ (John 1:14). This is "the new man," the one "created according to God, in righteousness and true holiness" (Eph. 4:24). This is what it means to partake of the divine nature (2 Peter 1:4). This is the essence of ministry in the Gospel. The church is God's special possession, God's treasure. The minister works to ensure that God's property, His inheritance, is ready for God to claim at the proper time.

The motivation of the man of God is seen in his faith in the Gospel. He may even appear insane to some, giving his life totally to an unseen dream; but he knows what it means since Jesus died for us all. It means all are dead to God, lost in sin, doomed to eternal exile from God in hell. If Jesus died for all, then all are dead in sin. And those who come to Christ out of sin come, not to live for themselves but for Him who died for them and rose again.

The minister lives to persuade these lost sinners and to bring them to repentance. He lives to see them changed into Christ's glory. He is a slave to their needs and struggles to be the very best example possible of what he wishes for them. He directs their focus constantly to the Christ, not to himself.

Which brings us to the fourth and final point: The weaknesses of the preacher makes manifest the great overruling power of the One whose Name is above every name. Paul and Timothy write this letter to the Corinthian Christians because many among them are listening to false teachers who seek to undermine Paul's authority as an apostle. These impostors make a big deal of Paul taking no money for his efforts, his weakness of style in the pulpit, his apparent waffling in his plans to visit Corinth, and his continual run-ins with authorities and mobs. There appears to be nothing impressive about Paul's work from an earthly or worldly standpoint. And these workers of Satan seek to make the most of it.

They, in contrast to Paul, are brazen with the church, demand respect and money, and make sure that things are as smooth as can be with the community. In fact, they are so adaptable to the world that fornication, uncleanness and lasciviousness are all hallmarks of their ministry. Yet, they maintain an air of respectability and righteousness with the church.

In this climate and context, Paul stresses the qualities of a true evangelist in terms of care and suffering for his brethren. He goes without eating, without sleeping, letting his own needs suffer that the brethren may be aptly cared for. He risks persecution, danger and slander that the truth of the gospel might be spread, upheld and defended. He is daily crucified with Christ that the resurrection of Christ may be obvious in his mortal flesh.

He speaks as he believes. He talks of joy in the presence of pain. He proclaims peace in the midst of riot. He spreads riches in the grip of poverty. He preaches the resurrection in the face of death. He willingly bows to sorrow as a tool of his ministry. In so doing, he demonstrates a power beyond human endurance, a peace that passes all understanding, and the fact that his Savior truly lives for all who believe (2 Cor. 4:16-18).

The true minister of God holds no stock in the world's standards; therefore, fleshly distinctions are not valid to him. Distinctions of race, monetary gain or loss, regional origin of a person, educational attainments, social prominence, none of these things move the man of God. This man sees as God sees; he looks and glories in the evidence of the heart. His standard is spiritual. The fruit he seeks is the fruit of Christ being formed in each individual Christian. The New

Testament, the Law of Christ, is his eyes, his wisdom, his standard, his concern, his authority, his sword, his defense, his plan, his will. It is his devotion to God's Word and nothing else that makes him God's man.

Are You a Man of God?

Now where do you fit into this picture? Do you feel that Timothy's shoes are too big for you? Do you feel yourself shrinking more and more, your adequacy and confidence vanishing before your very eyes? It would be easy to think so. Your timidity is very normal and a pretty good sign. It is like Timothy.

It is easy to see these principles as totally foreign to the kind of life we normally live, or foreign to the church's expectations, or out of the purview of society's understanding. To some extent they are exactly that. We are called to call people out of this world and its value system. As examples of a different Way and citizens of a different Kingdom, we will manifest what is to come a radically different lifestyle. The man of God will even startle and dismay some of his own brethren.

But we must be careful that our vision of this ministry is balanced. Keep in mind that Paul did receive money from other churches when he was at Corinth (2 Cor. 11:8; 12:13). Also keep in mind that style and delivery do matter (1 Cor. 9:22), and that we must always do our best in presenting the Gospel. Nor did any of these early preachers go out of their way to make others angry. They were not the ones stirring up the rabble. On the contrary, Paul is the epitome of the peacemaker (Acts 24:15-16; 1 Cor. 4:11-13).

These principles should not be interpreted as an indictment of a formal education. We need to learn as much as we possibly can about the Word and the society in which we serve so that we can be accurate in relating the Good News to others. Remember Timothy was told to be diligent in handling the word of God correctly, and to give attention to reading (1 Tim. 4:13; 2:15).

There is nothing especially righteous about poverty or wealth; the man of God can serve the Lord in either circumstance (Phil. 4:11-13). The church should properly take care of both you and your family (Gal. 6:6). But these things are no standard of faithfulness or authority. A pulpit does not define a ministry, nor a church salary the man of God.

The sick man is not necessarily more spiritual than the healthy. Therefore be mindful of your health as you serve God (1 Tim. 4:8;

5:23). Keep in mind that, if you marry, your wife and children should receive the primary benefits of your ministry (Eph. 5:25). Your work is God's alone to control, but your family should receive the greater blessing of your dedication, devotion and zeal for your Master.

You may question your place as Timothy's "successor." But in terms of work it is exactly the same (2 Tim. 3:14-4:5). The only difference is that Timothy had both the beloved apostle's presence and his letters. We, however, have God's written Word. This Message, the revelation of God, is complete in our hands now — something Timothy did not have except possibly in his later years. And He who worked effectively in Paul's ministry, Paul wrote to say, worked in Timothy as well. He is the same Master, Lord, Friend and Counselor who will work with us, if we truly belong to Him (Phil. 4:9; 2 Tim. 2:1-2).

Conclusion

As was said earlier, Timothy appears as a timid man, unsure of himself in the confident station the beloved apostolic mentor placed him. When Paul wrote those two letters to the young preacher, he was speaking to encourage this young man who had faced such obstacles and problems as the dynamic apostle himself faced. He had stomach problems. He had to be prodded to defend the gospel and the apostolic pattern. Especially in 2 Timothy, we see a young man who seems apprehensive, who perhaps has seen the inside of a prison once too many times. Paul the prisoner needs him immediately. Timothy has to be stirred up to come to Paul before it is too late. In this atmosphere of gentle admonition, Paul calls Timothy a man of God.

Please keep these thoughts in your heart when you remind yourself of your own failings. Remember that our sufficiency for this ministry is from God, not ourselves, nor even our beloved brethren. Forgiveness is available to the man of God as well as all others.

The power for the ministry is the Word, your confidence in it, and your zeal for it. It is the model, goal and subject matter of all true preaching. It is the Old Testament studied through faith in Christ Jesus. It is the New Testament of the Lord Jesus, as was written and put forth by the apostles and prophets of the Lord.

The sad fact is that the man of God is the rarest of all workers in this world. Yet the more you attempt to copy the evangelists of those Bible years, the less novel you will seek to be; the more faithful to your own work you will become and the brighter your efforts will shine.

Terry Wheeler began preaching when he was 19 years old and earned a B.A. in Bible from Freed-Hardeman University. He has worked with congregations in Scotts Hill, Tennessee, Spartanburg, South Carolina, Duncan, South Carolina, and Ann Arbor, Michigan. He hosts a live radio broadcast and helps coordinate campus ministry for the University of Michigan.

MAN *of* GOD

Part 2 — His Life

The Whole Man

J. J. Turner

In the early days of ministry I pillowed my head many nights feeling guilty, frustrated and inadequate. I was never able to get everything done. There was always another visit to be made. I needed to spend more time with my wife and daughter. I needed more research time for Bible class lessons and sermons. There was always something left undone. I was continually wondering why I was not accomplishing more for the Lord.

One day I was sharing my frustration with an older minister. In four words he said it all: "God wants you balanced." He proceeded to tell me I would never get it all done. There would always be another visit, phone call, lesson to prepare, sermon to preach and emergency to respond to. He told me to plan balance into my day. That was a tough assignment; one I have struggled with through the years.

The older preacher told me I had a responsibility to my family. "How sad," he said, "to save the world and lose your own family. It would be tragic to ruin your health while trying to encourage the health of others."

Billy came home after his first juggling lesson. He ran into the kitchen and grabbed two of his mother's cups and began to demonstrate his new skills. Things were going so well that he added a third cup. As he attempted to juggle the fourth cup he dropped them all.

Most preachers are a lot like Billy. We can juggle a few balls okay but as we add more balls we drop something. That something is often our health, family or effectiveness in ministry. Burnout has taken the energy, desire and commitment out of many preachers. It has never been easy, in a biblical sense, to do the work of a preacher. The preaching servant of God is challenged by a multitude of things in and out of the church. The apostle Paul wrote: "Beside those things that are without, that which cometh upon me daily, the care of all the churches" (2 Cor. 11:28). The preacher has never faced more demands than he faces today. He must be able to minister to the young, middle aged and senior citizens in his congregation.

When the preacher's life is out of balance it is difficult for him to function in a manner pleasing to God. Most of us feel like the preacher who posted this sign on his office door: "If you have troubles, come in and tell me about them. If not, by all means come in and tell me how you avoid them." We need to learn how to take care of our whole being.

The Whole Man

The preacher, as a whole man, consists of the mind, heart and soul as the center of his divine task of preaching. Paul had the whole person in mind when he wrote these words:

And the very God of peace sanctify you wholly; and I pray God your whole spirit and soul and body be preserved blameless unto the coming of our Lord Jesus Christ (1 Thess. 5:23).

Preaching is more than what you do. It is what you are. Thus, the preacher is the same on Monday as he is on Sunday. He is God's spokesman. Preaching flows from the heart to the lips. Jeremiah spoke of the whole man being consumed with passion to speak God's word, "But if I say, 'I will not mention him or speak any more his name,' his word is in my heart like a burning fire, shut up in bones. I am weary of holding it in" (Jer. 20:9).

Jesus is never called "a preacher" or "the preacher" in the gospels. Preaching, however, is what He did — it's what He was. On one occasion He said: "Let's go into the next towns, that I may preach there also: for therefore came I forth" (Mark 1:38).

The Physical Side of Preaching

Preaching takes physical strength to preach with power, zeal and conviction. A healthy soul and healthy body go together. John told Gaius, "I wish above all things that thou mayest prosper and be in health, even as thy soul prospereth" (3 John 2).

Many preachers take Monday as a day off because they are exhausted from Sunday's activities. Most preachers preach two sermons, teach one Bible class, and spend the rest of the day visiting the sick. Sunday is a real work day for the preacher.

It has been suggested that one hour of preaching is the equivalent of eight hours of physical labor in terms of the expenditure of nervous energy. Arthur S. Phelps has stated, "I have found a half-hour address equals to a day's work in the fields." I once spoke 30 times in six days. It took me almost a month to recuperate from that energy and emotional outlay.

Since preaching makes such a demand on the preacher's physical strength, it's imperative for him to keep his body in good physical condition. The body is the temple of the Holy Spirit (1 Cor. 6:19-20). Just as smoking, drinking and gluttony can harm the body, a lack of physical exercise and fitness is also harmful.

Some days I come home exhausted. I know, however, from years of past experience, that if I can get on my running gear and hit the streets the fatigue will be gone after a few miles of jogging. After a shower and a good meal I am ready to go again. It still amazes me after all these years of running and exercise, how many benefits come from sweating.

I have had people kid me about my running and exercise program. A popular remark is, "Do you think you'll live longer because you exercise?" I usually reply, "I hope so, but it really doesn't matter. I'm doing it for benefits I get from it today. Today it makes me feel great. That's all that matters."

Along with his physical fitness program the preacher should watch his diet. Good eating habits are a must for good health. Some basic guidelines for proper eating include: be sure to eat a balanced diet, try to eat your food as close to nature as possible, take plenty of time to eat your meals, and drink a lot of water each day.

The preacher must also get enough rest and sleep. Note these interesting words by the psalmist: "It is vain for you to rise up early, to retire late, to eat the bread of painful labors; for he gives his beloved even his sleep." Jesus told his disciples to take some special time to rest (Mark 6:30-32). You need to take some special time.

The Preacher's Image

He was wearing overalls, chewing tobacco and carrying about one hundred pounds over his normal weight. Was he a farmer? No, this man was a preacher. When I asked him about his appearance, he said he was trying to blend in with the folk in his community and congregation, even though it was not a farming community. He quoted Paul's "becoming all things to all men" statement as authority for his approach.

The preacher has an image assigned to him by his brethren, society, himself, and the Scriptures. Self image is how a person sees himself; image is what you convey to others through your dress, actions, grooming, and attitudes. Everyone who knows you as a preacher will see the image you convey.

Many preachers balk at this type of discussion. They feel that being concerned with what others think is insincere; that placing an emphasis on the preacher's image is a display of phoniness bordering on show business.

I do not think it is wrong for a preacher to be concerned with what others think about him and how they see him. He is communicating an image so why not convey a dynamic one? Men do look on outward appearances (1 Sam. 16:7). It is a demonstration of part of the whole person.

The media has made a major contribution in distorting and changing the image of the preacher; especially in character and integrity. Thus, the man of God who preaches the Word must move in a world that makes fun of him. I once saw a cartoon which depicted an awkward looking character dressed in a clergyman's frock. He was fat and had his collar turned backward. The caption read: "I used-ta-not be able to spell preacher, now I are one."

Preachers, as a general rule, are all lumped into the same basket. If one is proven to be a hypocrite, they are all hypocrites. If one is a charlatan, all are charlatans. If one dresses funny, all dress funny. This is wrong but it still occurs. This is why the preacher must guard his image; this is why he must strive to be God's man in life and actions. The preacher must go the second-mile in establishing his integrity and image.

The preacher's appearance preaches a message long before he opens his mouth. Dress and grooming are powerful tools of communication. One may argue that dress, grooming, and appearance are minor matters, and that people should not judge by them. That will not change the truth. You portray an image and are judged according to it.

Fashions and styles change as often as the weather. Culture and subcultures play a vital role in what constitutes proper dress. The preacher must be conscious of where he is, as well as aware of clothing norms among the people he is ministering to.

The nature of the minister's work automatically places him in the role of being a leader, an out-front person, one to whom people look for direction. This means that people expect more from you. They expect you to be an example and role model.

While training preachers at the School of Biblical Studies, I saw numerous attitudes toward dress, grooming and appearance. Without exception, the men who took pride and care in their dress and grooming were always better received by congregations than those who dressed inappropriately. One leader in a congregation told me, "Don't send us anymore student preachers who dress like bums." When I told this to the student who had fostered the remark, he became angry and began to lecture on how unbiblical such an attitude was. Right or wrong, the student had gotten a taste of what some churches expect from preachers. Image does matter.

The preacher must ask himself several questions relative to image, dress and grooming. What do I want to communicate by my clothing and appearance? Why are these clothes appropriate for communicating the image I want to communicate? What image am I communicating?

Enthusiasm and Passion in Preaching

Another quality that goes into making the whole man is enthusiasm in preaching. There is a scarcity of passionate and enthusiastic preaching in our day. The preacher is rare who preaches with enthusiasm and conviction. In our day the "casual talk," "fireside chat," and brief homily have become the norms for many preachers. Excitement, passion and fire are out. An aged saint recently asked, "Where have all the preachers gone who used to have fire and a heart in their preaching?" Dewitt Matthews, in *Capers of the Clergy: The Human Side of the Ministry*, wrote this graphic description of the boredom induced by bored preaching:

> The preacher's voice may be unappealing, with every word spoken at the same rate and pitch. Further, he may stand practically motionless, looking almost like a paralyzed body speaking. Still further, he may 'hide' so completely behind a large pulpit stand that his head and shoulders are all that ever 'get into the act.' Even when using illustrations he may be lifeless and unconvincing. His humorous side may rarely show when speaking and his emotions may be carefully hidden.

Consequently, as the 'chanting' continues, is it any wonder that drowsiness descends upon the congregation?

Whatever else a preacher ought to be when preaching, he should be alive, moving his face, body, and gesture, and giving off 'electricity' in speech and person, or his effort may indeed become something like a 'sermonic Sominex.'

I conducted a survey asking people to list the five top qualities they liked in a speaker. Ninety percent of the respondents placed enthusiasm first. Second was knowledge of subject; third was sincerity; fourth was openness; and fifth was good gestures.

Charles H. Spurgeon, in his book *Lectures to My Students*, wrote,

A blacksmith can do nothing when his fire is out, and in this respect he is a type of a minister. If all the lights in the outside world are quenched, the lamp which burns in the sanctuary ought still to remain undimmed; or that fire no curfew must ever be rung. We must regard the people as the wood and the sacrifice well witted a second and third time by the cares of the week, upon which, like the prophet, we must pray down the fire from heaven. A dull minister creates a dull audience. You cannot expect the office-bearers and the members of the church to travel by steam if their chosen pastor still drives the old broad wheeled wagon.

Since God has chosen the Gospel as the means to save the world, those of us who preach this Gospel dare not approach it half-heartily or simply as a job.

Conduct and Personality

Another part of the whole man is his personality. The importance of personality must not be overlooked when discussing the preacher and his work. The attitude which expresses that all the preacher needs in order to preach is Bible knowledge, is wrong. On this point Henry Gerber said, "Our possibilities of success are much more limited to personality traits than by our intellect."

The Bible is the world's best self-improvement book. Therefore, it has a lot to say about the personality of man. Let's note a few of these examples and how they apply to preachers.

Daniel was selected above the "presidents and princes" (Dan. 6:2). Why would a young man, some think no older than 18 or 19, be chosen instead of the older and supposedly wiser men? The answer is in these words, "Daniel was preferred above the presidents and princes, because an excellent spirit was in him" (Dan. 6:3). Thus, one reason Daniel was chosen above the others was because of his pleasing personality. Men are still being chosen for the same reason in our day. We influence others by our personalities.

Jesus must have had a pleasing personality. In Luke's gospel we read, "And Jesus increased in wisdom and stature, and in favor with God and man" (Luke 2:52). It is interesting to note that the charges brought against Jesus did not say that he was rude, antagonistic, unkind, belligerent or vehement in his dealing with people. In every situation, even when He had to teach and say things that were not popular, He conducted himself properly. That is why we must follow His example in attitude and action.

When the apostle Paul told Timothy to "be thou an example of the believers, in word, in conversation, in charity, in spirit, in faith, in purity" (1 Tim. 4:12), he was encouraging the young preacher in the areas of personality and relationships with others.

The biblical emphasis upon personality is not based upon looks, a diploma from a charm school, wit, winning a popularity contest, fashions, or some other rare quality. The Bible emphasizes godliness and Christ-likeness as the basis of one's personality. These qualities come from within the heart of man. Commitment to these qualities produce such conduct traits as: love (John 13:34); forbearance (Eph. 6:2); kindness (Eph. 4:32); consideration of others (Heb. 10:24); meekness (Matt. 5:1-12); forgiveness (Luke 17:1-5); patience (James 1:1-7); and other qualities which make up the whole being of the preacher.

Conclusion

The whole man, including body, soul and spirit must stay in contact with God and his Word. Two verses provide the key: "Love the Lord thy God with all thy heart, and with all thy soul, and with all thy strength, and with all thy mind; and thy neighbor as thyself" (Luke 10:27); and "Let us hear the conclusion of the whole matter: Fear God, and keep his commandments: for this is the whole duty of man" (Eccl. 12:13).

J. J. Turner attended Sunset School of Preaching, Florida Beacon College (B.A., M.A.), Southern Christian University (M.R.E.) and Luther Rice Seminary (D.Min.). He is presently writing his Ph.D. dissertation in biblical counseling at California Graduate School of Theology. In addition to local ministry, he has taught through television and radio. He is the author and speaker on four video series and numerous books. He served as editor of *Christian Family Magazine* and has been editor of *Christian Bible Teacher* since 1988.

The Spiritual Life of the Preacher

F. Furman

To attain a goal one must clearly identify and visualize the goal. To become spiritual the preacher must understand what is true, genuine spirituality. Perhaps the easiest way to visualize a spiritual person is to get a clear picture of the great spiritual role models God has described in His Word.

The only perfect spiritual example is Jesus Christ. To be spiritual a preacher must become Christlike. The preacher must read, study and meditate on the life of Jesus. He must visualize His sinless, moral and spiritual character and conduct. The preacher must imitate Jesus, for He left an example that we should follow in His foot steps (1 Peter 2:21-25).

The preacher must envision the love, character and spirituality of Christ until he grows into His likeness. Paul's goal for the Galatian Christians was, "Until Christ be formed in you" (Gal. 4:19). Paul said that God had set all things in the church,

> ... for the perfecting of the saints, unto the work of ministering, unto the building up of the body of Christ" till we all attain unto the unity of the faith, and of the knowledge of the Son of God, unto a fullgrown man, unto the measure of the stature of the fullness of Christ (Eph. 4:12-13).

Christ came to show us the Father (John 1:18). To be godly is to be Christlike. To be Christlike is to be spiritual.

God's Word provides many other examples of spiritual people for us to emulate. Example is easier to follow than abstract precept. The apostle Paul, though he acknowledges imperfections, is a great example of a spiritual man of God.

Genuine Spirituality

True spirituality begins by recognizing, accepting and stressing the reality of the spiritual world. We live in and emphasize the physical and material so much that we tend to ignore and doubt the reality of the spiritual world.

To be spiritual, the preacher must first have faith in God, recognizing that God is Spirit. Second, preachers must fully accept that we are spirit and our spirits are made in the image of God (John 4:24; 1 Thess. 5:23; Gen. 1:26; 2:7).

To become spiritual, God's men must clearly understand that the real eternal existence is in the spiritual realm. The physical body and existence are only temporary. Preachers must, with Paul, say:

Wherefore we faint not; but though our outward man is decaying, yet our inward man is renewed day by day. For our light affliction, which is for the moment, works for us more and more exceedingly an eternal weight of glory; while we look not at the things which are seen, but at the things which are not seen: for the things which are seen are temporal; but the things which are not seen are eternal (2 Cor. 4:16-18).

To be spiritual we must clearly distinguish and set bounds between the spiritual (*pneumatikos*) and the fleshly (*sarkikos*). The spiritual is that which pertains to the spirit and seeks the things of God. Having interest in and pursuing those things of God, Christ and the Holy Spirit will make us spiritual. It also involves recognizing, fleeing and fighting against the devil and his angels, who are evil forces in the spiritual world.

The fleshly aspect of our nature emphasizes our physical, sinful and lustful appetites. Paul said to the Corinthians, who were guilty of many sins:

And I, brethren, could not speak unto you as unto spiritual, but as unto carnal, as unto babes in Christ. I fed you with milk, not with meat; for you were not yet able to bear it; nay, not even now are you able for you are yet carnal: for whereas there is among you jealousy and strife, are you not carnal, and do you not walk after the manner of men? (1 Cor. 3:1-3).

Peter warns us to "abstain from fleshly lusts" (1 Peter 2:11). The lust of the flesh, the lust of the eyes, and the vain glory of life emphasize the sensual things of the world that lead us away from God (1 John 2:15-17).

To be spiritual ministers we must draw near to God, Christ and the Holy Spirit, communicate with them, and seek the things above (Col. 3:1-17). We must put to death the sinful nature. We must put on the characteristics of holiness, purity, godliness, morality, compassion and all of the virtues set forth in God's Word.

In *The Minister's Spiritual Life*, E. W. McMillan defines spirituality in these words:

> Spirituality is not some strange magic or something unreal; it is not an imaginary abstraction. It is the total character qualities of Jesus Christ, gradually learned from the Bible, and constantly transferred by the Christian to himself, or herself, so the Christian's life represents well the character which was so wonderfully portrayed in the Christ himself. This character is not obtained by a miracle or abruptly in any sense. It is fed, developed, and matured through three channels — a constantly growing love for God and all men; a growing trust in God and seeking for a closer walk with him; and an increasing awareness of one's own inadequacy and unworthiness accompanied by an equal need to make us as we should be. This three-fold development is the Christian's spiritual life. Each Christian should pray for God to develop these qualities in him.

Becoming Spiritual

Becoming spiritual is a matter of growth (James 4:7-10). It does not happen suddenly, miraculously or by some overwhelming change of being possessed by the Spirit or experiencing Spirit baptism. The inspired apostle Peter commands, "But grow in the grace and knowledge of our Lord and Savior Jesus Christ" (2 Peter 3:18).

Spiritual growth is not achieved by one process, then another and another in sequence. Rather it is achieved by an intermingling of several factors simultaneously.

First, to grow spiritually one must have a desire to be spiritual. Jesus said, "If any man wills to do his [God's] will, he shall know of the teaching, whether it is of God, or whether I speak from myself" (John 7:17).

One must have a strong desire to achieve a goal before he will put forth the necessary effort to do so. One must draw close to the eternal Spirit to become spiritual. A spiritual being separated from God but constantly attached to the flesh will languish and die. A spiritual being constantly drawing near to God, Christ and the Holy Spirit can receive spiritual nourishment and grow.

Second, a strong, deep and obedient faith is essential to become spiritual. Without faith it is impossible to please God (Heb. 11:6). But Paul teaches that faith comes by hearing the word (Rom. 10:17). Abraham became spiritual because he believed God, and it was reckoned to him for righteousness. Paul became spiritual because he believed, trusted and obeyed God.

Third, the preacher must study the Bible extensively, systematically and thoroughly in order to become spiritual. The Bible is the source of our faith. Through revelation we know God, Christ and the Holy Spirit.

Study must be done in many settings. Preachers must study privately and personally. They must know God's will, memorize it, lay it up in the heart, meditate upon it and apply it in life. Ezra set the proper example for preachers. He set his heart to know the law of the Lord, to apply it in life, and to teach God's will to others (Ezra 7:10).

Fourth, ministers can grow more spiritual by thinking, reflecting and meditating on spiritual things. Paul exhorts,

> Finally, brethren, whatsoever things are true, whatsoever things are honorable, whatsoever things are just, whatsoever things are pure, whatsoever things are lovely, whatsoever things are of good report; if there be any virtue and if there be any praise, think on these things (Phil. 4:8).

Fifth, as one must protect the physical body against disease to grow strong, one must protect his own spirit against sinful things. Preachers must stress ethereal things not physical; eternal things not temporal; godly things not devilish; spiritual things not carnal or fleshly. Many preachers spend too much time in the sinful world with sinful worldly activities and people. They spend too little time with spiritual people and in spiritual activities. If a minister would be spiritual, he must read spiritual books, attend spiritual activities, and look up to spiritual people.

Sixth, to become spiritual preachers must communicate with God through prayer. The truly spiritual preacher will pray often, fervently and with faith. To do this effectively requires much study of prayer.

Paul urges us to pray that we might become spiritual:

For this cause I bow my knees unto the Father, from whom every family in heaven and on earth is named, that he would grant you, according to the riches of his glory, that you may be strengthened with power through his Spirit in the inward man; that Christ may dwell in your hearts through faith; to the end that you being rooted and grounded in love, may be strong to apprehend with all the saints what is the breadth and length and height and depth, and to know the love of Christ which passes knowledge, that you may be filled unto all the fullness of God (Eph. 3:14-19).

Spiritual people in the Bible were people who prayed. David's prayers are numerous in the book of Psalms. Nearly every one of Paul's epistles reflect that he was praying for all of the members of all of the churches to whom he wrote. The man of God who goes often to his knees in prayer can ascend to mountains of excellence in the pulpit afterwards.

Seventh, the fruit of the Spirit not only gives evidence of spiritual growth and development but also as practiced become sources of even greater and stronger spirituality. Paul lists this fruit in opposition to the works of the flesh in Galatians 5:16-25. The fruit of the Spirit is love, joy, peace, longsuffering, kindness, goodness, faithfulness, meekness and self-control. Such is the result of listening to and obeying the Spirit. However, as preachers bear this fruit and exhibit it, they become more spiritual and stronger spiritually, thus being more able to overcome the flesh.

True Spirituality Demands Service

A false concept associates spirituality with personal, private pietism. The most spiritual being to ever walk this earth was Jesus. At times He went apart into a desert place to commune with God. He refreshed himself spiritually by private times for communication with God. So should ministers.

However, the main thrust of Christ's life was to live and work among people. He came not to be ministered unto but to minister and to give His life a ransom for all (Matt. 20:20-28).

The spiritual preacher must constantly be in contact with God, Christ and the Holy Spirit to obtain spiritual strength. However, he must also be in contact with his fellow human beings to minister to them. For he who would the greatest must be a servant.

The spiritual life of God's man is not a monastic life, not the life of a hermit or an ascetic. The spiritual preacher will spend appropriate time in the cathedral but also appropriate time in the convalescent home. He does not simply move from the study to the pulpit but also moves into the pathways of life, going out into the highways and byways to seek and save the lost. The spiritual man of God is mindful of and tuned into the heavenly spirits but is also living daily in service to people in the church and in the community. The spiritual preacher brings himself, his family, his congregation and his community closer to God.

F. Furman Kearley attended Alabama Christian College (B.A.), Harding University (M.A.), Auburn University (M.Ed.), Harding Graduate School of Religion (M.R.E., Th.M.), and Hebrew Union College (Ph.D.). He serves as editor of the *Gospel Advocate* magazine and is a noted writer. He has served as Professor of Bible and in administrative positions at Abilene Christian University, Lubbock Christian University, Alabama Christian School of Religion, and presently at Magnolia Bible College in Kosciusko, Mississippi.

The Christian Minister As a Family Man

Howard N

While browsing in a bookstore in Houston, Texas, a number of years ago I discovered Gerald Kennedy's *The Seven Worlds of a Minister*. Kennedy, a Methodist bishop now deceased, affirmed during his lifetime that a minister is a general practitioner and not a specialist. He identified and defined seven "worlds" in which the minister needs a high degree of competency as generalist.

The discovery of Kennedy's book came at a time when I was experiencing great difficulty in understanding my responsibilities as a minister of the Word. His work helped me see that a minister is indeed a general practitioner rather than a specialist. The minister's work will require him to have expertise in seven worlds, designated by Kennedy as that of preacher, administrator, pastor (caring for the saved), prophet, theologian, evangelist and teacher.

As I reflected on those seven worlds of the minister, I was disturbed by the fact that Kennedy did not say more about the minister's role as a family man. Some think that the minister's family is no more related to church work than a physician's family is related to medicine. According to this view the minister's church work is in one compartment of his life and the home is in another. Churches and ministers know, however, that the compartmentalized view of the family does not work for the man of God. A physician may be able to separate his family from the practice of medicine, but the preacher cannot separate his family from the practice of ministry.

The minister must make every effort to be a good family man. The man of God cannot be faithful to the God he proclaims unless he seeks with all his heart to provide happiness and security for his own family here on earth and makes every attempt to prepare them for eternal life in heaven.

The man of God seeks to be a good family man because his family determines to a great extent the effectiveness or ineffectiveness of his ministry. The congregation and the community perceive the preacher's family to be an indicator of the real character and personality of this church leader. This perception is not always valid, but it is present. Not to take care of one's own family — spiritually, socially, emotionally, and financially — is to court disaster in the ministry.

Special Challenges of the Minister's Family

Since the preacher's work is closely tied to the state of his family, this presents him and his loved ones with several special challenges.

First, the minister and his family are public figures. Like the school superintendent or the mayor in a small town, the minister and those in his immediate family live in a glass house. They are topics of interest and conversation. People watch, evaluate, cheer and criticize them. Certain members may wonder how the preacher and his wife can buy a new car, send their children to a certain university, or take such expensive vacations on the salary they make. Being in the public eye can be both a reward and a burden for the minister and his family.

Second, the congregation and the community often have a certain expected standard of the preacher and his family that is not expected of other church members. People want these public figures to be friendly and warm. They also want them to be much more circumspect in word and deed than other folk. People tolerate childhood behavior in church members' families that is absolutely condemned when the preacher's children behave the same way. The other side of the coin, according to one preacher's child, is that when the minister's children behave at a higher level than their classmates, their peers consider them to be nerds. The minister must help his family cope with this part of their reality.

Third, some people can be hard on the preacher's wife. Wanting her to fit a certain mold that an "ideal" preacher's wife in the past carefully crafted. Perhaps they expect her to be the leader of the women, the organizer of social events, or the life of every party. When the present minister's wife chooses not to play this role, members are disappointed and the wife feels guilty, angry or both.

The good news is churches seem much more willing to let a minister and his wife be themselves than they did in years past. I believe that it is important for the minister to protect his wife when people want to place more demands on her than she is able to bear. I once pointed out to an eldership that the person they were paying to serve as their preacher was me, not my wife. Generally speaking, if the preacher and his wife will be humble, honest and up-front about their strengths and weaknesses, congregations will accept them as they are and love them for it. What will not work is for a family to get in trouble internally because it is trying to meet someone else's arbitrary demands.

Fourth, ministers and their wives often feel a sense of isolation. Sometimes this isolation happens because the preacher and his spouse are better educated than those whom they serve. Sometimes their loneliness springs from the fact that they do not have anyone with whom they feel free to share their thoughts and feelings. Bottled up emotions quickly degenerate into frustration, anger and depression. I have never agreed with the idea that the preacher and his family cannot have good friends in the local church. True, they cannot spend all of their time with one or two families and they cannot be a part of groups that exclude others, but they can have best friends in the church they are serving.

My wife and I have nearly always been blessed with good friends in the congregations we served. We have also kept close ties with friends in other places. There may be situations in which the minister and his wife need to talk about certain subjects they do not feel comfortable discussing with people in the local congregation. At those times meeting with good friends from another town for lunch or taking time off to be with them can be therapeutic. The minister must make sure that each family member has opportunities for friendship and discussion so that feelings of isolation are quickly banished.

Fifth, inadequate financial support is a burden that many men of God and their families bear year after year. It is true that preachers' salaries have improved greatly from what they were in times past. Some churches even make sure that their ministers have a retirement plan and hospitalization insurance. In spite of the improved salaries and fringe benefits provided by some congregations the fact remains that many preachers and their families can hardly survive on what they receive from the local church. This situation can create anxiety, frustration, anger, resentment and depression. Even in those churches that provide excellent salaries, God's man cannot usually look forward to the kind of economic progress that people connected to other professions can expect.

Unless a minister and his wife can make peace with those special challenges they face and then convey that sense of contentment to their children, they should probably give up on the idea of a full-time ministry. A root of bitterness in the ministerial family can lead to serious marital problems and to spiritual infidelity in the couple's offspring.

God's Family Expectations for Ministers

One of the earliest descriptions of what God expects from male religious leaders appears as He thinks out loud about whether to tell Abraham the divine plan to destroy Sodom and Gomorrah:

> Shall I hide from Abraham what I am about to do? Abraham will surely become a great and powerful nation, and all nations on earth will be blessed through him. For I have chosen him, so that he will direct his children and his household after him to keep the way of the Lord by doing what is right and just, so that the Lord will bring about for Abraham what he has promised him. (Gen. 18:17-19)

God expected Abraham to teach his offspring and everyone in his house to obey God by doing what was right. If he expected that of Abraham does he expect anything less of his men today?

The Bible is clear concerning the fact that males in general, and ministers in particular, are to be good family men. For the minister to be a good family man in the broadest sense of the term he will need to wear a number of hats.

First, God expects preachers to be good husbands. The apostle says,

> Husbands, love your wives, just as Christ loved the church and gave himself up for her ... husbands ought to love their wives as their own bodies ... After all, no one ever hated his own body, but he feeds and cares for it, just as Christ does the church. (Eph. 5:25-29)

A preacher who does not love his wife has no business preaching the Gospel because his lack of love indicates the absence of Christlikeness and basic spirituality. Furthermore, a minister who fails to love his wife provides a negative example of family life for the people to whom he ministers.

Second, God expects ministers to be good sons. Jesus, our example, in the grip of death while on the cross, provided for the welfare of his mother (John 19:25-27). To be a good son implies that the preacher sees to the needs of his parents. In the process of caring for his father and mother, he also sets in motion the probability that his life will be long and go well (Eph. 6:1-3). For people who read the Bible and observe life over the years, it should come as no surprise that the commandment to honor father and mother "is the first commandment with a promise." I have known of ministers who demonstrated open hostility toward their parents. Claiming to honor God while dishonoring one's own parents is an inconsistency that disqualifies a man from the ministry of the Word. God's man is supposed to be a good son.

Third, God expects his servants to be good fathers. The Holy Spirit says through the apostle Paul, "Fathers, do not exasperate your children; instead, bring them up in the training and instruction of the Lord" (Eph. 6:4). This passage is for all men; therefore, ministers must obey its teaching.

Being a good father is not an easy task. Louis Sullivan, former U.S. Secretary of Health and Human Services, wrote an article during his tenure in office in which he quoted nineteenth century German poet Wilhelm Busch as saying, "Becoming a father is easy enough, but being one can be rough." Sullivan then added, "Too many American fathers have decided it is too rough for them to handle. So literally millions of our nation's children — rich and poor alike — live with the anger, loneliness and insecurity produced by absentee fathers" (*USA Today*; June 14, 1991).

I wish we could exempt ministers from the term "absentee fathers," but we cannot. Although Sullivan was speaking about geographical absenteeism we can safely say that many preachers are guilty of emotional absenteeism. They eat and sleep in the same house with their children and provide them financial support but are absent from the center of their offsprings' deepest needs. Although these preachers claim to be spiritual servants, they do a better job of ministering to other people's children than to their own. God never intended family life to end up this way for any man, much less a minister of His divine Word.

Fourth, the preacher has responsibilities to his extended family. Most countries in the world think of family in bigger terms than

Americans do. For many people in America the nuclear family that
consists of father, mother, brother and sister is almost the sum total
of significant family ties. Even the nuclear concept of family is
shrinking in the United States. Moore and more families are becoming one-parent homes in which the parent who is away has little or
no daily influence on the offspring.

The minister, must seek to fulfill his multiple roles in the extended family. He is likely to have many roles at once: father, son, grandson, brother, cousin, nephew, uncle, son-in-law, father-in-law,
grandfather, and so forth.

Principles by Which to Live

The Christian minister has serious responsibilities as a family
man. The following principles can help God's man as he strives to
fulfill them.

First, the preacher must not view himself exempt from God's
teachings about the family. People involved in great causes can easily fall prey to certain myths. They reason, for example, that since
they are doing God's work He will see to it that everything turns out
well. I have known of ministers who get into serious financial trouble because they believed that somehow God would handle their
financial mistakes in a different way from those of ordinary men.
They did not need to worry about balancing their checkbook, paying
bills or preparing for retirement because they thought God was
watching out for them. Common sense shows the folly of such reasoning and the eventual disillusionment that will overtake any person who lives his life this way.

Sadly, some ministers apply this same kind of reasoning to their
own family. They know what God teaches about the role of the
father. They preach sermons to other people based on these teachings. Somehow, though, they believe they are exempt from these
requirements because they are ministers. They evidently suppose
that God will suspend his laws on their behalf and make it all turn
out right. Just as surely as God will not suspend the laws of nature
when a man steps in front of a speeding truck, he will not change his
laws governing the family on the basis that the father of that family
is a preacher or a missionary. Wise and faithful preachers will face
this fact and act accordingly.

Second, God's man will understand that his call to preach and his
family responsibilities are not in competition. If there was ever a
time when leaders members expected the minister to neglect his

family in order to perform his duties in the local church this is not the way it is today. I have been preaching for more than 40 years and I have never served in a congregation that expected me to neglect my family in order to carry out my work as God's man.

How is it, then, that so many active ministers have the reputation of neglecting their families? Preachers too often look on family as a distraction from their church work. Frankly, they would rather work than be with their family.

If this is not so, explain why some ministers never take a day off. How do we explain their decision never to take a family vacation? If family is not a distraction, why is it that some ministers never have time to attend their children's sports events, plays or recitals? Why is it that they are too busy to listen to their children's stories or their wives' conversations? If family life is not a distraction to the ministers' work why is it so easy for him to program everybody and everything into his calendar except family?

Preachers, like men in any other area of life, can be workaholics. When ministers suffer from this compulsion, they need to avoid blaming the church for their problem, accept full responsibility for their addiction, and seek help to overcome it.

Third, the minister will acknowledge that being a good family man takes time and effort. Good family men are in short supply in the United States. One of the reasons is that so few are willing to invest their personal resources of time and energy to lead and manage their families. They would rather invest themselves in jobs, hobbies, civic work, sports or church than do the much more demanding job of shepherding their families.

I once read a story about Theodore Roosevelt's rebellious daughter. Reporters saw her sitting on the roof of the White House smoking a cigarette at a time when such behavior on the part of a woman was unthinkable. When asked what he planned to do about the incident Roosevelt said something like this: "Look, I can either be President of the United States or control my daughter but I cannot do both." Chances are that the popular President made the statement with tongue in cheek to get reporters off his back, but it illustrates that it takes diligence and perseverance to be a good family man and also a good minister. The minister is wrong who thinks he must neglect his family because of his duties at church. Other people can be found to help carry out the work of the church, but no one can take the place of a family's husband and father. This is the way God instituted the home.

Fourth, the preacher will understand that his role within the family is that of a major care provider. Paul says, "If anyone does not provide for his relatives, and especially for his immediate family, he has denied the faith and is worse than an unbeliever" (1 Tim. 5:8). Before a minister does anything else he must provide food, clothing, shelter and other basic needs for those under his care. As the context of this passage indicates, this responsibility extends beyond the nuclear family and includes members of his extended family who may have unmet, basic needs.

God's men are idealistic by their very nature if they are sincere in what they are doing. They carry a burden for people who have never heard the Gospel, for people who have abandoned the faith, and for people who are struggling with the normal problems of life. Ministers have a strong sense of calling, a belief that the ministry is the most important work in the world, and that it is this work that God wants them to do. Good ministers have made peace with the frustrations that come from knowing that they will never be rich, famous or powerful. Their joy comes from leading the lost to Christ and feeling that they are living their lives within God's will for them.

In light of their idealism, preachers are confident that God and the brethren will provide necessary funding for them to carry out their ministries and provide for their families' needs. Unfortunately, we live in a real world that does not always work out the way our idealism thinks it should. When God's man realizes that he cannot provide for his family with the amount of money the church can afford to pay, he must do something about it. If his wife and children can feel good about helping supplement his income through their work in order for him to give his full time to the church well and good. What a minister must not do, however, is abandon his responsibility to provide for his family and excuse such conduct on the basis that he is a servant called by God to work with the church. The minister's first task is to provide for the basic needs of his family.

The minister needs to remember that generally the only people in the church who give any significant thought to his financial needs are he and his wife. True, the elders thought about his salary when they asked him to come work with them. They may even be a quick conversation once each year when determining the new budget. Yet, in the average church it is unlikely that anyone but the minister and his wife spend 10 minutes a year reflecting on what the minister needs financially in order to keep his family functioning.

Not understanding this phenomenon in church work, and fearing that any mention of money will indicate a materialistic, non-spiritual attitude to the church leaders, God's man waits year after year for a raise that never comes. He becomes embarrassed in front of the family that needs to respect him, his wife becomes bitter, and his children lose faith in the church and its leaders. He decides to move to find a better salary and his wife and children pay the consequences by being uprooted from familiar surroundings and old friends.

What is the solution? Preachers must talk openly with leaders about their families' financial needs. Most elders who underpay God's men do not act this way because they are mean and stingy. They underpay because they have not thought about the preachers' salary circumstances in a long time. Many moves and great frustrations in the minister's family could be avoided if preachers would learn to speak lovingly, but courageously, about what they need in order to provide for their loved ones. Ministers can, and must, address the issue if they want effective ministries and happy families.

Money is not the only need the minister must take care of in his family. He also has the responsibility to provide emotional strength for his wife and children. When anyone in his family suffers harsh and unseemly criticism, he must be the protector. When people attempt to load up his wife with church duties just because she is the preacher's wife, he is the one who must come to her rescue. Church bullies can be found almost everywhere. Some wear skirts and some wear pants. Preachers have to deal with church bullies the same way children deal with them on the playground. They must stand up to them and make it clear that they are unwilling to be intimidated by them or to permit their loved ones to suffer abuse.

I am not suggesting that the preacher and his family become bullies. What a tragedy when this happens! I am saying that a minister must stand up for himself and his family in some circumstances. Learning to be assertive without being aggressive and hateful is a vital step in the life of the man of God and his family. Cowardice in the name of spirituality is unbecoming of the man of God.

Summary

Being a good family man is a part of every Christian man's service to God. Ministers, especially, must work at the task of being good husbands and fathers since the effectiveness of their homes is so closely tied to the work they do year after year.

We all need to remember, however, that in the wisdom of God every individual has the freedom to espouse or reject the spiritual training he or she receives in the home and church. While the preacher should make every effort to create and maintain a home that prepares his family for heaven, he must realize that eventually each member in that home will make a personal decision concerning his or her own destiny.

If the minister can look back through the years and realize that he did the best he knew how to do as the leader of his family when he had his children at home, he can still fulfill his ministry as he preaches the wonderful story of love.

Finally, brothers, "let us not become weary in doing good, for at the proper time we will reap a harvest if we do not give up" (Gal. 6:9).

Howard Norton has been preaching the gospel since 1952. He served as dean of the College of Biblical Studies at Oklahoma Christian University of Science and Arts and as publisher of *The Christian Chronicle*. He earned a B.A. at Abilene Christian University, a M.A. at the University of Houston, and Doctor of Human Sciences degree at the University of Sao Paulo. He served as a missionary from 1961 to 1977 in Sao Paulo, Brazil, and has written extensively.

The Humanity of the Man of God

Jim Bill Mc

It would seem a settled conviction that you, preacher, are a "man of God." In contrast to this holy relationship and your work you are still a human being. God's servants get tired, sick, frustrated and know disappointments. God promises no immunity but He does promise his presence and love. He will not remove the flesh, however, until the other side.

You are a male. Seeking to honor God will not remove the hormones. Temptations come. The devil wants you to fall. You sin and need forgiveness in all matters. Yet your unique work puts you in a confidential position. Secrets are shared with you as no other. Souls will be bared and you must constantly protect the confidentiality and trust placed in you. Your maleness must not maul you.

You either are or were young. With youth we associate vigor, strength, energy, optimism. You have chosen the most glorious path a man can walk — preaching the Gospel. The devil does not want this powerful continuity and will earnestly try to disrupt it. Any particular glitches he can throw to sidetrack you he will. A few surprises will come to you even though you think you are well prepared. Someone said, "Sic' em," and you took on the world only to find it was not ready for your attack nor was it overly responsive. Do not be discouraged. Few men convert hoards of people.

As one saint said, "The Lord does not demand of you success — he does demand faithfulness."

Humanity is a term you will deal with a lot. Daily tasks will be yours and you will sometimes wonder, "How do I have time even for a haircut?" You will get blue, you will know fatigue, you will feel two hundred pounds of pressure, and you'll wonder at times, "Is it really worth it?" You will doubt your own worth. You will be embarrassed about accomplishing so little and you will feel the ascendancy of the flesh above the spirit. Just remember you are mortal. To His own Jesus said, "Come you apart and rest awhile." This you must do. Privacy must be yours. Even the Lord, Mark tells us, went into a city and did not want anybody to know he was there (Mark 7:24). At times elders will not understand your need for a battery recharge. Man of God, know the extent of your abilities and frame. It is evident that God wants every part of you in his work. Please keep the temple of your soul clean.

It seems advisable to state a word of caution about relationships. If you are married none is more important than your wife. She holds in her power the making or breaking of you. Love her dearly and respect her endlessly. There are a few matters, born of confidentiality of your work, that of course you cannot discuss with her. This restriction calls for understanding of a most delicate nature. Contrary to this, all that you can discuss, share with her. Her good mind and sympathetic spirit will help not only you but the folk with whom you work. You will find it is the quality of a woman to be most perceptive. She will see some dangers and pitfalls before you do. Her rich wisdom must not be denied you. After all, you made her a holy promise — to "love her as Jesus loved the church." That means at the sacrifice of self you place her in the ascendancy. If *agape*, reverence, honor, and submission is shown her she will follow as quietly as dawn the dark.

Do Not Neglect Personal Attention

Preachers have a tendency to think in terms of the group and they neglect the personal attention they need for themselves. It is not what "they think," what "she said," or parroting what "he wrote." The acid test is "what do you feel." Self examination comes every Lord's day for every Christian at the Lord's Supper, but for the preacher it should come with greater frequency. Ask yourself why you are preaching. Are the positions held born of pressure, popularity, or power?

While "bodily exercise profiteth little" (1 Tim. 4:8) the implication is that something does profit. This is not the scripture to authorize you to be a "couch potato." There is a "toning" that helps every Christian and it is vital to the man of God.

Day by day without fail the man of God should feed on the word of the Lord. Yet, one can become so involved making preparation for his next assignment — sermon, class, paper, radio lesson — that he takes no time for his personal devotion as he drinks eternal truth. To the Word and the study of it he is faithful. In his own life he is loyal to the profession of faith. Preaching is not a job, it is a burning desire to accurately tell others of Jesus Christ and His salvation. From Christ and his teaching there is no variance.

The man of God must have a good conscience. The feeling for what is right or wrong comes from the guidance the word gives. Be true to yourself. The moral policeman within you must be true to his "beat." It's from the precinct of heaven that you get your orders.

Prayer and supplication (night and day) are so much a part of the man of God's make-up that he employs it to the upbuilding of his soul. Regularity in prayer moves men closer to the court of heaven.

You will find that prayers for elders are a blessing to you. It will also temper you when the decisions they made did not coincide with that which you wished to be enacted. Your carrying the name of others to heaven's court will increase your affection for those you are remembering. Grow in all these acts of graciousness.

Finally, be assured that God did not call you to weakness but to strength. Take a personal inventory. Are you stronger now than a year ago? Knowing that Jesus abides in you, do you draw on the strength He provides? Grace is God's way; the obedience of faith is your response to it. You are declaring one beyond comparison who, out of the goodness of His heart, makes salvation possible. His power is limitless. Since you preach one "with whom all things are possible," go forth in His strength and faithfully declare the unsearchable riches of Christ. This is your work which of necessity includes your humanity. Go, O man of God, to the highest task on earth. Preach Jesus and Him crucified.

Jim Bill McInteer attended David Lipscomb and Harding universities. The author of numerous articles, books and tracts, he also serves as president and publisher of *21st Century Christian* and *Power for Today*. He began preaching in 1939 and served as minister of the West End Church of Christ in Nashville, Tennessee, for 30 years.

Expectations of the Man of God

Larry D. Mathis

Men of God are expected to perform well in areas which bear little or no resemblance to the role revealed by God. Most preachers would admit the presence of tension generated by their knowledge of what God expects of them as opposed to demands imposed by well-meaning brethren.

The result is stress and conflict within the preacher. The problem is so great many good men leave the ministry while those who do remain often struggle with frustration, disenchantment and disorientation. God's man would like to change the system, but it is awkward for him. He often feels that no one understands his dilemma. He knows most members of the church will never come to realize the high stress level ministers work under.

Modern Expectations

First, God's man is expected to be positive and motivational. The modern preacher is expected to preach positive sermonettes which keep constituents happy, calm and contented. God's man is expected to be a dynamic performer.

In some places his task is to be visionary and to dream up new ideas and then push every work to fruition. Designated leaders of his congregation do not always shoulder their responsibility; consequently when a program flounders all eyes turn to the preacher.

A second expectation is that God's man should possess administrative skills comparable to top executives in the secular world. In some cases God's man is loaded down with administrative responsibilities which are demanding and time consuming. These considerations often deter him from his real calling, thus interfering with his God-given duties.

He may have the responsibility of regulating the work of a staff. Part of his work may consist of making sure the assistant ministers, secretary, and janitor all put in a day's work for a day's wages. He is their supervisor.

It is not uncommon for the local minister to be responsible for organizing everything from the nursery to advertising for the annual gospel meeting. He may be expected to collect news tidbits for the church bulletin, change the marquee message, and monitor the committees in the congregation. He is often expected to be on every committee in the church, work with all the special interest groups within the congregation, and in some places he draws up the proposal for the annual budget.

He is also frequently expected to: counsel, perform weddings, baptisms, sit with the dying, conduct funerals, hold seminars, write for local papers, act as purchasing agent, host a radio or television program, work with the youth, visit the sick, shut-ins, hospitals and nursing homes. The preacher is expected to teach or conduct day Bible camp, oversee vacation Bible school, and be actively involved in community organizations and functions. All this is to be done while still producing highly motivational sermons every Sunday.

The preacher is a much-sought-after man. Members and leaders expect their preacher to be popular and to have a high profile. He is also expected, in some instances, to keep strict office hours.

Third, modern-day preachers are often expected to be errand boys for their congregation. His automobile becomes public property. Ministers are given jobs others could and should do. They are given jobs that other members do not want. The rationale, the preacher is told, is, "we have to work." Thus, the message conveyed to God's man is that he does not work. Nothing undermines a hard-working man of God more than to witness this attitude being reflected among the people to whom he ministers.

Church members have been known to tell their minister that "preaching is not work" or "you get paid plenty for giving two talks." Hard-working preachers tire of such remarks. Men of God often find themselves the object of stale jokes about trimming their salary each time church finances are mentioned in business meetings (1 Cor. 9:14). Preachers and their families are further humiliated when the church budget is flashed on the screen in the auditorium showing the preacher's annual salary. No one else would like such treatment. It is not the business of unbelievers and visitors, who may be in the audience, to know all about the local preacher's income.

Often God's man is given a multitude of odd jobs unrelated to his real calling. In some places he has as many "bosses" as he has members. He is told, "order this," "do that," "keep the bulletin board neat and current," "be here," "be there," or "did you list the names of nursery attendants on the bulletin board?" It is not the work of an evangelist to be a gopher for the members and leaders of his congregation (2 Tim. 4:1-2, 5). It is not his job to do all the footwork. It is not his responsibility to carry out the garbage, be concerned with the maintenance of the plant and grounds, control the thermostat, or do all the visiting for the entire flock. Can you imagine John the Baptist, Jesus, Paul, Apollos or any other New Testament man of God having such concerns?

God's Expectations

First, the preacher is to be God's man. He must view himself in this light. He is not the property of the church. Nor is his family. He is not responsible to jump at their beck and call. God expects allegiance from His man. The preacher must not be bought or manipulated for he belongs to God. He is God's man even if he stands alone. The minister must view himself in this light.

Although all Christians are referred to as "priests" and "the people of God" the preacher is called "man of God" (1 Peter 2:9-10; 1 Tim. 6:11). Spain wrote:

Timothy is a man of God whose ministry is that of teaching, reproving, correcting, and training the people of God. ... The reference to Timothy as a man of God calls to mind the frequent use of this appellation in reference to the prophets who spoke for God in the Old Testament (e.g. 1 Kings 17:24; 2 Kings 7:17; 8:2) and Peter's reference to the holy "men of God" who spoke from God (2 Peter 1:21).[1]

Preachers are "men of God," serving as counterparts to the "servants of God" or "men of God" in Old Testament times.[2]

This is not to suggest a clergy-laity arrangement or caste system among us. Nor is this to advocate placing the preacher on a pedestal.

However, this is to suggest that the preacher is uniquely God's man. He serves the Lord differently than others. He and his family should be highly esteemed for the work's sake. Do modern-day preachers view themselves as "men of God" in the place where they live, work, and preach? Do they act accordingly? What would happen if every minister among us immediately approached his ministry believing, "I am the man of God in this place"? If he believed he was representing God as he moved among men? I think it would likely revolutionize the ministry, churches and communities.

How many Christians view their preacher as God's man? I think such a concept might usher in a new day of respect among God's people with better treatment and appreciation for God's man and his precious family.

While God's man may never be famous, accomplish great feats, preach to the masses, reach great prominence, have vast influence, nor have a large church, the man of God can take heart. He should derive encouragement from the fact that even the obscure and unknown can be a man of God.[3]

Second, the preacher is to proclaim God's Word. A preacher is to preach. If he does not preach why call him a preacher? Man of God, no matter what else you may or may not be doing, God expects you to preach the Word (2 Tim. 4:2). This is your major concern.

It is not pleasing for God's preachers to forsake the Word of God and serve tables (Acts 6:2).[4] Others in the congregation must be appointed over this business (Acts 6:3). Men of God should devote themselves to prayer and to the ministry of the Word (Acts 6:4).[5]

God's man is an evangelist, a messenger of good tidings, and a preacher of the glorious gospel of Christ (2 Tim. 4:5). The preacher is to be a laborer and a toiler. It is specifically his work to handle the Word of God correctly (2 Tim. 2:15; 4:5). He is to give close attention to his teaching and be absorbed in this work (1 Tim. 4:16).

God's man is to be true to God in proclamation of the Gospel. He must not be a mercenary hireling. God solemnly charges every herald to preach the Word in view of judgment day and eternity (2 Tim. 4:1-2).

Every preacher has the task of preaching the whole counsel of God without fear or favor of men, without dodging vital themes his audience needs to hear (Acts 20:27). He is dealing with spiritual life and death. Any man who refuses to preach the truth is a hindrance to the cause and is not fit for this ministry. He may be popular and friendly but he is a miserable failure as a preacher.

God expects his preacher to keep focused. This world is lost without Jesus. Man of God, it is your business to preach "the truth in love" (Eph. 4:15). It is your assignment to stand for the ancient faith reproving, rebuking and exhorting with great patience and instruction (Jude 3; 2 Tim. 4:2). God commands you to speak, exhort and reprove with all authority (Titus 2:15). As the man of God unsheaths the sword of the Spirit (i.e., the Word of God), he will cut some clear to the heart while others in the same audience may be comforted by that same message (Eph. 6:17; Acts 2:37; 1 Thess. 4:18).

Far too many have abandoned real gospel preaching. Everything but the Gospel is preached. What is being said may be true and said sincerely, but it is not the Word of the Lord. I am suggesting that what really matters is that the message proclaimed be true and that it is indeed the Gospel. The crucial factor is not that the preacher has the ability to swoon the people with his polished words, but whether or not he preaches truth.[6]

Finally, God expects his man to be impartial and unprejudiced as he fulfills the Great Commission. The Great Commission includes every creature in every nation (Mark 16:15-16). God's man is to preach to sinners and saints. Since "the field is the world," God's man has a universal field of labor (Matt. 13:37-38). In carrying out the Great Commission the preacher will hopefully convert sinners and strengthen saints.

The length of time an evangelist remains in one area or with one local congregation is not specified by God. Obviously, God's man will attempt to preach long enough in one locality to produce a group of Christians. Once a church is established it will need to be edified. Paul remained with a local congregation long enough, teaching Christians, until men were properly trained and qualified to become elders (cf. Acts 20:17, 28, 31). How long this takes is dependent upon the circumstances at hand.

Man of God, God expects you to preach the Word.

Endnotes

1. Carl Spain, *The Letter of Paul to Timothy and Titus* (Austin: R.B. Sweet Co., Inc., 1970) 99-100.

2. In Deut. 33:1 Moses is called, "Man of God."

3. Ronald A. Ward, *Commentary of 1 & 2 Timothy*, 11th ed. (Waco: Word Books, 1983) 103-104.

4. Joseph Henry Thayer, *Thayer's Greek-English Lexicon of the New Testament*, 12th ed. (Grand Rapids: Baker, 1986) 72.

5. That this originally applied to the apostles of Christ is freely admitted. But compare Paul's apostolic charge to evangelist Timothy to, "Take heed unto the doctrine" (1 Tim. 4:16). Timothy was to be "absorbed" in the work of an evangelist (1 Tim. 4:15 NASB).

6. Shawn D. Mathis, "Real Challenges in the Twentieth Century," 1990.

Larry D. Mathis is a graduate of Freed-Hardeman University (A.A., B.S.), Southern Christian University (M.A., M.Div.), and David Lipscomb University (M.A.R.). He is presently serving as the minister of the Southside Church of Christ in Dresden, Tennessee.

MAN *of* GOD

Part 3 — His Ministry

Day-to-Day Ministry

Cecil May

What do you do when you go to work each morning?

The answer to that question will vary from preacher to preacher. Some go straight to their desks to work on a specific project or lesson. Some start with a visit with friends or prospects at the mail box or coffee shop. Some may have an early morning radio or television program. Some may just loaf around aimlessly, waiting for something to react to.

Some of us may be like Richard Armour,

> I've dusted my desk and I've wound up my watch.
> I've tightened (then loosened) my belt by a notch.
> I've polished my glasses, removed a small speck.
> I've looked on my check stubs to check on a check.
> I've searched for my tweezers and pulled out a hair.
> I've opened a window to let in some air.
> I've straightened a picture. I've swatted a fly.
> I've shifted the tie clip that clips down my tie.
> I've sharpened each pencil till sharp as a dirk …
> I've run out of reasons for not starting work.

A little girl on Art Linkletter's "Kids Say the Darndest Things" show insisted, "My daddy doesn't work. He's a preacher."

I suspected at the time that her problem was one of semantics. When she asked her daddy where he was going in the morning, he probably answered, "I'm going to the office." My children never told anybody I did not work, because I always said when I left home, "I'm going to work."

There are those who facetiously say, "What a cushy job! Just one hour a week to work!" Preaching, however, is not just a Sunday job. Of the early preachers for the Jerusalem church it is said, "And daily in the temple, and in every house, they ceased not to teach and preach Jesus Christ" (Acts 5:42). Paul, looking back on his time preaching at Ephesus, said to the elders there, "Watch and remember, that by the space of three years I ceased not to warn everyone night and day with tears" (Acts 20:31). Much more than an hour a week in public proclamation was involved in the work they set themselves to do.

It is asking to be misunderstood if, in a community where everyone is expected to be at the factory by 7:00 or the office by 8:00, the preacher arrives at the church building about 9:30 or 10:00. Certainly, if he has been up half the night counseling with a potential suicide, or at the hospital with the family of a dying father, he may be late coming in. But the preacher must be careful not to develop the habit of watching late television every night and getting up late every morning.

> Laziness steals time and opportunity.
> A little slip, a little slumber,
> a little folding of the hands to rest,
> and poverty will come upon you like a robber,
> and want like an armed man (Prov. 6:10-11).

Most preachers are hard working and dedicated, but some are lazy. I have a problem with lazy preachers, and face a temptation to direct a major portion of this chapter to them. A preacher who comes into the office late every morning, chats with the same friends for several hours, rarely decides what he is going to preach Sunday until late in the week, and golfs or hunts or fishes several days a week, is not doing his job, no matter how busy he feels. Laziness manifests itself not so much in doing nothing as in finding other things to do than the things that need doing. Unfortunately, lazy preachers will likely not read this book.

Study

Study must be a primary element in the preacher's daily ministry. "Be diligent to show yourself a workman approved of God, who needs not to be ashamed, rightly handling the work of truth" (2 Tim.

2:15). Most of my days begin in the study. I am sympathetic to the view that modern-day church problems began when preachers stopped having studies and started having offices.

It takes time and effort to handle the Word correctly, as a proclaimer of the Word must do. The preacher must be "diligent" (ASV), "study" (KJV), "try hard" (NEB), "concentrate" (Phillips), and "do your best" (NIV). Each of these translations catches the spirit of the original word, which implies a special effort given to a task. The task under consideration involves proper use of the Word of God.

Paul said in 2 Timothy 4:13, "When you come, bring the cloak that I left at Troas with Carpus, and the books and, especially, the parchments." It is easy to understand why Paul would want his cloak; Roman dungeons were not known for winter warmth. But he also wanted "the books and, especially, the parchments."

Most books were on papyri, a forerunner of our paper. That was the least expensive way to produce a book. Parchment was much more expensive, but also more lasting. Likely, the parchments refer to scrolls containing Scripture. Paul continued to study until the very end of his life.

Hearers of the Word in Berea were commended for searching the Scriptures daily (Acts 17:11). Surely those who proclaim the Word should be noted for no less.

"The tyranny of preaching," observed Batsell Barrett Baxter, "is that Sunday comes every seventh day." Add Sunday night sermons, Sunday morning classes, Wednesday night classes, week-day ladies' or senior citizens' classes, bulletin articles, newspaper articles, and radio sermons, and time is at a premium. But we must fill our reservoirs in order to have something helpful within to overflow into those hearing.

We must grow in knowledge, both of the Word of God we preach and of the world to which we preach.

A hundred people listening for thirty minutes involves fifty hours. We must not take that lightly. We must not let Sunday approach and, having nothing to preach, out of necessity preach it.

Study Book-by-Book

A good way to study the Bible is to master a book at a time. Choose your book of study. Read it, all at one sitting, several times. Get a pencil and paper, or computer and monitor, and outline it.

For example, when studying an epistle, see what it is about. Answer questions like: What is its basic thesis? What idea does the writer use to advance the thesis? What was going on that caused it to be written?

Learn what the book says so well that you can reproduce it, not word for word by rote, but idea by idea. Then do the same with another book.

Topical Study

Also study the Bible by topic. Choose a subject. Use your concordance, Bible dictionary, a topical Bible and your knowledge that comes from having studied book by book. Choose the passages that are relevant. Gather them together and consider what the truth is about that topic.

"The sum of your word is truth" (Psalm 119:160). The totality of what God has said on a given subject is the truth about that subject. You can put the whole together studying the Bible topic by topic.

Some consider this method flawed, but it is only flawed to the extent that passages are misused or taken out of context. It is a good method if Scripture is "rightly handled." Good topical study consists of a series of brief expository treatments of Scriptures relevant to that topic.

Study Other Sources

In addition to your study of the Bible — never as a substitute for it — read good religious books.

Read for variety. One way to become stale and unbalanced is to read only one kind of material. Some preachers read only church growth books. Others only current brotherhood issues, and then only from writers with whom they already agree. Some almost never read anything but popular denominational preachers; others read virtually nothing but brotherhood standards.

We need to read that which will establish us in the things of which we are already convinced, but we also need to read things with which we do not agree. The latter will challenge our thinking, sharpen our reasoning powers, and may even have something to teach us. It is foolish to believe that, because a person is wrong about one thing, he has nothing to say about anything that might be beneficial.

In addition to reading the Bible and other religious books, preachers also need to do some reading that will help them keep up with the times. Read a newspaper, and not just the comics or the sports pages. Read editorials and columnists. Read a news magazine.

It is a tall order to do that much reading. Unsaid is the fact that some study must be directly related to particular lessons. But the other reading fills the reservoir; so that, as one sermon is finished, something else is ready in mind to do next.

Contact With People

A second important component of the time spent in the work of God is personal contact with people.

It is popular in certain circles to negate the idea that preachers ought to visit: Get in your study, learn the Word of God, and get out and preach it in the pulpit. One lecturer made fun of what he called pastoral work. He ridiculed giving any time and attention to members of the church in their everyday ills and difficulties, or being out in the community with people who are sick, hurt or dying. He felt preachers wasted their time doing that sort of thing when they ought to be studying to more effectively preach the Word.

The basic flaw with that reasoning is not that preachers do not need time for study. The mistake is in thinking that preaching is confined to what is done from the pulpit. That belies the very first description of the preacher's work: And daily in the temple, and in every house, they ceased not to teach and preach Jesus Christ" (Acts 5:42)

The task of the preacher involves more than public proclamation. And the public proclamation is better done when it is done by someone who knows and is known by those to whom he preaches.

There is, of course, a limit to how many people one person can adequately serve, and in every situation more people than just the preacher need to be visiting. But the pulpit preacher, even in larger churches, must be careful not to isolate himself from those to whom he preaches. Visiting is not wasted time. It is some of the most valuable time spent.

Visit Church Members

Visit the church to know their needs and be better able to apply the Word of God to their needs. Work to know by name those who attend regularly, their children's names, where they work, what they do as they are about their work, where they live, and the kind of circumstances in which they live. You will not learn that just by standing in front of the church building, shaking hands as they go out the door. It is necessary to be in their homes or work places.

See them when they hurt. Those who are sick need to be visited. If that is not considered to be part of the work of a preacher, consider it part of being a Christian, and recognize that preachers need to be Christians, too.

When there is a funeral, when someone in the family has died, when there is a divorce, when a child has been caught with drugs or shoplifting; these are times when those of us who preach the Word need to show that we love and care for the people to whom we regularly preach. As has been often said, people do not really care how much you know, until they know how much you care.

Visit the leaders and potential leaders. If appropriate, eat lunch with them. Talk about the work of the church. Talk about their ministries as Christians. A major part of the preacher's work is to "equip the saints for the work of ministry" (Eph. 4:12).

There is no limit to the work that can be done in a congregation, if the preacher is not concerned about who gets the credit. If we will give others all the credit for everything done in the church, the work will go well and the preacher will end up with the credit for it anyway.

Visit in the Community

Visit to know and be known by the people in the community. It is possible to move to a church, stay busy every day visiting the sick, having contact with members, studying for sermons, officiating at funerals and weddings, and live in a place several years knowing hardly anyone in the community.

A specific effort must be made to keep this from happening. What is done will vary, depending on individual interests; Little League baseball, Boy Scouts, PTA or civic organizations.

Remember, the purpose of day-to-day ministry activities is reconciliation. God "has reconciled us to himself in Jesus Christ, and has given us the ministry of reconciliation" (2 Cor. 5:19).

It is not our purpose just to get acquainted. We will not convert everyone we get to know, but we are not likely to convert anybody that we do not know.

> We visit a lot of people we do not get,
>> And we get a lot of people we do not visit.
> But we wouldn't get the people we do not visit,
>> If we didn't visit the people we do not get.

Can It Be Done?

How in the world can one man do all of that?

No realistic schedule will cover all of those bases. Any one of several things suggested could be a full-time job by itself. Some of it will go undone. At the end of the day, when you have done all you can do, you will still know there are other things that need to be done.

Schedule carefully, with prayer and thought to priorities. The urgent may have to be done immediately, but do not let what merely seems urgent root out the truly important. Make time for family and save some time for self. Recognize that regardless of how carefully you schedule, you will not be able to follow it exactly. People do not die, get arrested or suffer heart attacks according to the preacher's schedule.

How Much Time?

How much time should a preacher spend in the work of the church overall? Here is a rule of thumb. Most church members employed at a full-time salary spend at least 40 hours a week on their job — professional people usually more than that. In addition, they are expected to attend all services, participate in visitation and other congregational activities.

The preacher may think about his weekly schedule as he feels the most dedicated among his members should think about their schedules: Spend about 40 hours a week at work, plus time attending services and doing other church work. Obviously, there needs to be time for family and for recreation. But if he works five days a week (including Sunday), works from 8 a.m. to 5 p.m. on weekdays, and has two full days off, the preacher is not even doing what he expects the other members of the church to do. That type of situation will make a difference in his attitude toward himself, his work and in the influence he will have on others.

A few years ago I gave a questionnaire to a congregation where I was preaching. It showed the actual time involved in pulpit and classroom, and then had blanks for the members to fill in the amount of time they thought the preacher ought to use for study, visitation, cultivation of prospects, managing the office, answering the phone, fellowship, time with young people, class parties, weddings, writing articles for papers, correspondence and the other things preachers typically do with the work time.

I went down the list with members of one of the classes and asked them to fill in the blanks, as I talked about each component of the work. The totals the class came up with were interesting. The smallest was 61 hours; the largest was about 180. There are only 168 hours per week. Preachers have to learn to live with the reality that there is always more to do than there is time to do it.

Albert Schweitzer was a man of great learning and reverence for life. He gave up distinguished careers in music and theology to study medicine and go to Africa to treat human misery and sickness. Lines of the sick and dying were at his clinic daily. At the end of many days, more were still waiting than he had been able to see. Facing reality, he said, "A man can only do what he can do. But if he does that each day, he can sleep at night and do it again tomorrow, even if he is flinging himself at a continent."

Whistle While You Work

Jeremiah was discouraged with the people to whom he preached and, almost it seems, with God. He decided to quit.

I will not make mention of him, or speak any more in his name. But his word was in my heart like a burning fire shut up in my bones; I was weary with holding it back, and I could not (Jer. 20:9).

Who has not felt as Moses felt?

Why have you afflicted your servant? And why have I not found favor in your sight, that you have laid the burden of all these people on me? Did I conceive all these people? Did I father them, that you should say to me, "Carry them in your bosom as a nurse carries a suckling child"? ... I am not able to bear all these people alone, because the burden is too heavy for me" (Num. 11:11-14).

However, when the Lord showed his anger against the people, Moses' love for them prevailed, and he interceded on their behalf.

There is no job, profession or calling on earth that does not have its unpleasant tasks. The most exciting and glamorous job imaginable has its moments of boring drudgery. That is as true of ministry as it is of other callings. Which part is drudgery varies from preacher to preacher. Some love the personal contact, some the private study, and some enjoy administrative tasks. Putting out a bulletin, may be one preacher's idea of fruitful fun; for another it is a boring waste of time. While there is no way to escape all unpleasantness, and it is ultimately undesirable to do so, there are ways to maximize the joy and minimize dull routine.

Often there are volunteers in small churches, or in larger congregations perhaps staff members, who are pleased to handle some of the things you find not enjoyable. Sometimes it helps to do the unpleasant things that need doing first and then enjoy the rest.

Duke Ellington, great jazz musician, is reported to have said, "Retire? What could I retire to? What else am I going to play with?" He had music in his bones, and could not hold it in.

Like Jeremiah, we find our joy in the essence of our work. I preach because I love to preach and minister to people because I love people. It is an amazing blessing of life that there are those who will pay me to do that, but if there were not, I would earn my living another way and pay for the opportunity to preach and minister.

The day-to-day tasks of the preacher are rarely the same day to day; rarely exactly what was planned. But if the purpose is kept in view, the tasks stay challenging and important.

God is faithful. He calls us to be faithful stewards of the Word of God which he has committed to us (1 Cor. 4:1-2). If we will be faithful in the little things, day by day, God will bless us with greater opportunities (Matt. 25:21, 23). If we will be faithful workers together with Him, He will make us fruitful (1 Cor. 3:5-9).

Cecil May Jr., president of Magnolia Bible College, graduated magna cum laude in Biblical Languages from Harding University (B.A.) and Harding Graduate School of Religion (M.A., M.Th.). He served as instructor at Columbia Christian College and dean of International Bible College. He is an elder and a gospel preacher.

The Preacher As a Planner and Dreamer

Willard Collins

Daily Bible study and prayer should be in every preacher's plan for spiritual growth. Decisive planning and enthusiastic execution of the plan should be the preacher's motto for successful living. The following examples will encourage the preacher to plan and dream.

Great Planners and Dreamers

In my many years of preaching, M. Norvel Young and Ira North stand out in my mind as great planners and dreamers. It has been my privilege to work closely with these two men in gospel meetings, Christian education and social activities.

Norvel was the local preacher for the great Broadway congregation in Lubbock, Texas. One can see evidences today of the dreams he had, the plans he made, and the enthusiastic execution of these plans.

There is a children's home in Lubbock that he helped plan and build. As a local preacher, Norvel encouraged the new Broadway building. Lubbock Christian University was also a part of his dream. He worked with faithful friends in helping get this school started. Because Texas Tech was located in the town, Norvel pushed for a Bible chair and student center for young people.

It was Norvel who helped plan the first city-wide meeting of our generation. He called it "Campaign for Christ." It was held in the Lubbock Civic Center with Batsell Barrett

Baxter as the preacher. Thousands attended, and it began a tradition of successful city-wide meetings.

Ira was a master in working with a congregation and an eldership. Ira bred enthusiasm. He said that enthusiasm was "as catching as the measles" and that no project could be carried out in church work without enthusiasm.

I remember preaching in a meeting at Madison in 1960. I mentioned to Ira that of all the places I had visited, it seemed to me that Madison was the location with the best potential for building a congregation as large as that first congregation on the day of Pentecost, 3,000 in number. Ira talked to the elders, who met that very same weekend. The announcement was made the next Sunday that the elders were accepting the challenge. Sunday night I announced that I would come back 10 years later and preach in the new 3,000 seat auditorium that was being talked about. It was my privilege to go back in 1968. They beat the original plan by two years. Ira was the man with the fan who kept the flames of enthusiasm going.

Ira could see a need and find the money to fulfill that need. A camp was built by Ira, his wife, Avon, and the people at Madison. The Golden Age Village for the elderly and a home for orphans were constructed. They began to have women volunteer for Meals-on-Wheels, providing disabled people one warm meal a day. Ira began the Family Life Center to help people train their children. He started a furniture shed so retired people could mend and polish furniture for those in need. Later a refuge for battered wives was started, and these activities are still going on at Madison.

Ira had big Sunday School goals. He set goals for thousands to come, knowing that many would keep coming back. C.J. Garner had taught Ira that as a Sunday School goes, so goes the congregation.

Ira and Avon began a monthly weekend workshop to train elders and members who would come from congregations outside the city of Nashville to find out about Madison. He was a great teacher and pulpit motivator. I have never met another with such abilities to dream, plan and carry out the plans with such enthusiasm.

This type of growth and action can still happen if we dream, plan and execute our plans for God. The Great Commission challenges us to be planners, dreamers and doers for the Lord.

He said to them, "Go into all the world and preach the good news to all creation. Whoever believes and is baptized will be saved, but whoever does not believe will be condemned" (Mark 16:15-16).

The Pulpit Planner

A primary work of the preacher is to share the gospel of Jesus Christ from the pulpit. Sermon planning is so important. John Banister, minister of the Skillman Avenue Church in Dallas, showed me how he planned his sermon subjects one year ahead. In December of each year, he was able to announce the sermons he would be preaching the next 12 months.

John Vaughan, pulpit minister for the Graymere congregation in Columbia, Tennessee, says, "Planning ahead allows one to take things in bite size pieces rather than being overwhelmed by all of the duties that fall upon you." Here are some suggestions that John sent to me in preparation for writing this chapter on planning and dreaming.

Each year Graymere has a men's meeting from which many good ideas and plans evolve. Often at the beginning of a year, Vaughan and the other two preachers at Graymere will get together and make plans for the coming year. They discuss the Annual Summer Series, Vacation Bible School and other special events. Graymere tries to plan one special event each quarter. These special events cover topics like Parenting, The Christian and His Finances, or Grief and Suffering. There is also the need to plan for evangelistic work. Graymere usually schedules several mission trips by ministers and members of the congregation each year. The young people make an evangelistic trip to the Bahamas each year while a group of adults, including several doctors in the congregation, plan a medical mission trip to Central America.

John states that elders' meetings with the ministers are also planned on a yearly basis. He quotes Charles E. Jefferson, who says in *The Building of the Church*, "A church likes to feel itself in the grip of a man who knows where he is going. Nothing is so discouraging to Christian people as to feel that their leader is not leading. The outlook is indeed dark if the minister does not know what he and the church ought to bring to pass." To fail to plan is to plan to fail.

God's Unfolding Plan

Every gospel preacher should make a determined effort to find out what God's plan is for his own individual life and then work with God to fulfill this plan. The late Batsell Barrett Baxter discussed this important theme in the first chapter of his autobiography, *Every Life a Plan of God*: "In a very real sense, every person created by God has a place in his ultimate plan and each of us, as a creature possessing freedom of will, either facilitates or frustrates God's plan for his life."

Batsell stated that B.C. Goodpasture spoke of a sermon by one of America's best known 19th century preachers. The sermon was titled, "Every Man's Life a Plan of God." Batsell cites the case of Saul of Tarsus in Acts 9:10-16: "God had a four-part plan for Saul: One, to preach the gospel to the Gentiles; two, to preach the gospel to kings; three, to preach the gospel to the children of Israel; and four, to suffer many things for the Lord's sake." In the main body of his book, Batsell goes back to this point and says:

> I believe I have seen the plan of God unfolding in the lives of many people. I saw it in the lives of my own parents: a father who came from a humble background to be a leader in Christian Education, an effective preacher of the gospel, and an influence for good wherever he lived and worked; and a mother who was a quiet figure in the home, with love that influenced people on a very wide scale.

Gospel preachers have the privilege of dreaming about building the church, the greatest institution in the world. What a great blessing and responsibility to be part of God's plan.

Think How Much Good Has Been Done

Successful plans make it possible for good to be done in the name of Jesus. In 1888, James A. Harding came to Nashville for the purpose of preaching in a meeting at the South College Street congregation. David Lipscomb was an elder of this church, and during this particular meeting a great plan was outlined.

The Civil War had laid the South in ruins. Families were sad, and the people had lost heart. At this time in Nashville, many congregations had been divided. Lipscomb talked to Harding about what could be done in rebuilding the South and the community and what could be done in helping to unite the people.

After days of talk and prayer, Lipscomb and Harding decided to begin a school where the Bible would be a daily text. Other branches of learning would be added as needed to promote good citizenship among men.

Lipscomb, editor of the *Gospel Advocate,* had been writing about such a school because he had been to the school in Nashville that was started by Tolbert Fanning. Harding had been to Bethany College, where he had felt the influence of Alexander Campbell. These two men believed in the power of Christian education and proposed that a Christian school be started in Nashville.

Lipscomb was ready to begin announcing a date for beginning classes. However, Harding said that it would be about three years before he could get through with the meetings he had promised and get to Nashville. Lipscomb was willing to wait because Harding was perhaps the foremost evangelist of the period. Those who knew Harding told of his eloquence as a speaker and talked about this man who believed so strongly in the providence of God.

As a result of the dreams and plans of these two Christian men, the Nashville Bible School was started in October 1891. Only nine students came that first day, but Harding did not walk out in disgust to say, "It is no use, we do not have enough students." He and Lipscomb worked with these students and several more were enrolled during the first year. They rented a building near what is now Nashville General Hospital. In this rented building, with this handful of students, the Nashville Bible School was begun.

Harding was an eloquent preacher. It has been said that he could get up in chapel and make those students believe they could do just nearly anything. He had the power to persuade and to uplift. Dreams and plans are essential.

The Nashville Bible School is now David Lipscomb University, with more than 36,000 living alumni. Without the plans of Lipscomb and Harding there would not be a David Lipscomb University. Lipscomb and Harding were able to influence Nashville, the state of Tennessee, the South and the nation.

It is a wonderful privilege to preach the Word of God. What a joy it is to work for God in dreaming, planning and carrying out the dreams and plans in the name of His Son, Jesus Christ.

Every life is a plan of God. Our dreams and plans must include the fact that each person is a living soul and that each person can become a child of God. The God who can take an acorn and produce a giant oak can produce great Christians who can help build the church and change this earth. What a privilege it is to dream and plan with God.

Willard Collins started preaching in 1934 while a freshman at David Lipscomb College. He is a distinguished educator, having served as president, chancellor and president-emeritus at David Lipscomb University. He has published four books, written a weekly newspaper column, and serves as back page columnist for the *Gospel Advocate* magazine.

The Man of Compassion

Jeffrey Dill

A father brought his demon-possessed son to Jesus saying, "If you can do anything, have compassion on us and
help us" (Mark 9:14-29). This man addressed the very heart
of Christ — His compassion. If we are to be men of God,
compassion must be our heart also. We must have compassion for people that stems from our passion for Christ.
Compassion makes the man of God effective for it is his
very being, the internal fire of his bones. We cannot minister for God without portraying the Christ of compassion. We
might preach good sermons, minister daily in our congregations, conduct campaigns and address the controversial
issues, yet lack compassion for people. The man of God
who is deficient in compassion deprives humanity of the
heart of Christianity.

Compassion is action toward men, whereas pity and sympathy are feelings. Compassion extends beyond emotion
and tries to eliminate or alleviate the dilemma. As Jesus
rebuked the demon in the boy, He put into action the feelings of sympathy and pity that He had for the father and son.

The most common New Testament term for compassion
is the verb *splanchnizomai* (to have compassion). It occurs
only in the Synoptics. Kittel says, "the term reflects the
totality of the divine mercy to which human compassion is
a proper response."[1]

Our Lord was a compassionate man. When describing Jesus to Cornelius, Peter said Jesus went about doing good and healing all that were oppressed of the devil (Acts 10:38). Not only did He teach the 5,000, but when He saw their hunger He fed them. Jesus healed people of their diseases. It was compassion for a lost and dying world that moved Him to the cross. It was compassion for the lost city that moved Jesus to say:

> O Jerusalem, Jerusalem, you who kill the prophets and stone those sent to you, how often I have longed to gather your children together as a hen gathers her chicks under her wings, but you were not willing (Matt. 23:37).

Jesus criticized the Scribes and Pharisees for their hypocrisy. They kept the letter of the law to the absurd. They would even tithe garden herbs. Yet they neglected the more important matters of the law: judgment, mercy and faith (Matt. 23:23). The Scribes and Pharisees forgot that people matter most and that God is compassionate. Heavy burdens were placed on the people by these religious leaders (Matt. 23:4). They cared more about the donkey and the ox in the pit on the Sabbath than the man who was suffering.

Without compassion, we become modern-day Pharisees. The minister without compassion is not a man of God.

When telling the disciples how the world would view them, Jesus said people will recognize real disciples by their love for each other (John 13:35). When defining the word love used in 1 Corinthians 13 and John 13, I discovered the relationship between love and compassion. Love (*agape*) is that which does not desire, but gives. When fully implementing *agape* one puts others above self. Thus Jesus says, "Love your neighbor as yourself" (Matt. 22:39). The relationship between compassion and love is so interwoven that one must have the other to be complete. It is only by understanding the compassion/love relationship that one can understand in detail the parables now discussed.

First, Jesus describes judgment day by speaking of separating the sheep from the goats (Matt. 25:31-46). Mankind will be divided into two groups, those going to heaven and those going to eternal punishment. That which separates the two groups is compassion. Those on the right displayed compassion when He was thirsty, hungry, naked, sick and in prison, but they did not even remember ever doing those actions for Jesus. Jesus replied, "As much as you have done it unto one of the least of these my brethren, you have done it unto me." Compassion will be one factor that determines our destination.

"Compassion calls for Christian action. Apparently, a major difference between the righteous and the unrighteous is action. Compassionate Christians do something, not just anything, but appropriate actions that meet the needs of others.[2]

Second, observe the parable of a man owing a great sum of money (Matt. 18:23-35). The king beckons this debtor, demanding him to repay the money. The man falls down at the feet of the king and pleads for time. Through the generosity of the king, the man is made debt free. This debtor, forgiven of his great debt, finds another servant who owes him a relatively small sum of money. The forgiven man demands repayment, but the servant cannot pay. The man then has his fellow servant thrown into prison until he can repay the money. When the king finds out how the forgiven man reacted, he calls the man into his presence. The words of the king are harsh, but teach a lesson on compassion. The king remarked, "You wicked servant. I cancelled your debt because you begged me. Shouldn't you also have had mercy on your fellow servant as I had on you?"

Compassion is taken to new heights by this parable. No longer is compassion just meeting a need of someone less fortunate, but Jesus says compassion is meeting the needs of someone by forgiving them. No one has hurt us like we have hurt our heavenly Father. He has forgiven our debt we could not repay. We need to learn to forgive others. A man of great compassion said, "Once, I was preaching and a gentleman, I'll call him a gentleman, for he thought he was, came into the pulpit and hit me with a pair of brass knuckles. I love him today. I thought then, it may be the greatest thing that ever happened to me. If I could keep hate out and love in and love him, it would be the greatest thing that could happen. He staggered me when he hit me, but I never stopped preaching. At the invitation, seven men came to obey the Gospel."[3] Until we become compassionate toward those who wrong us we cannot represent Christ to modern man. The compassionate preacher knows the need for mankind is not simply food, shelter or clothing, but forgiveness.

Third, Luke tells about a man who had been beaten, robbed and left for dead (Luke 10:25-37). The mountainous terrain had left him at the mercy of those who might follow. Two religious men who should have had compassion on the man walked away. A Samaritan came along who had compassion on him. He bandaged up his wounds, put the stranger on his donkey, took him to an inn, paid for his medical expenses, and promised more later if needed. When Jesus asked the lawyer which of the three was the neighbor he answered, "the one who showed mercy." Jesus encouraged him to go and do likewise.

Our world has been beaten, robbed and left to die spiritually. The world is filled with spiritual dropouts. We can traverse the streets of America and see the drunk lying in the gutter, the prostitute on the corner, the drug addict in the back alley, and the patient in the hospital. We can walk by on the other side or we can have compassion. Risk accompanies compassion. The Samaritan did not know if he was walking into an ambush or if the man was really hurt. When we go to the world with the Gospel we go with risk of being laughed at, humiliated and rejected. The world needs the Great Physician. Only Jesus can bind the broken hearted or make the sinner a saint. McGavran, a leading author in church growth, says that the way to build a strong church is to "find the hurt in the community and heal it."[4] It is true that people don't care how much you know, until they know how much you care.

Fourth, Luke 15:11-32 is one of the most famous compassion narratives. The rebellious son took his money and went to the far land where he squandered his riches on riotous living. Then, when his money was gone a famine overtook the land. The young boy was forced to feed hogs. While he looked upon the husks as food for himself, he realized his father's home was not such a bad place. He swallowed his pride and prepared to ask his father for a job as a servant:

> So he got up and went to his father, but while he was still a long way off, his father saw him and was filled with compassion for him, he ran to his son, threw his arms around him and kissed him (Luke 15:20).

The father did not wait until the son walked up the path. The father did not wait until the son apologized. The father had compassion upon the son and ran to meet him. The implications of running are enormous. It was not proper back then for a man of stature to run, but this man ran to meet his boy. Facing the possibilities of ridicule he was moved with compassion.

When the wayward sinner is coming home to God, compassion does not wait until he or she walks down the aisle and sits on the front pew. Compassion goes to them on their long journey home and welcomes them. Compassion draws them. Compassion ought to take Christians out of the church building looking for those who have fallen and are still a great way off. Many times people realize the hurt they have caused and want to rid themselves of the guilt, but they cannot quite force themselves to go back into the church building and face people they have wronged. Preachers need to go to people's homes and let them know they are always welcome. When they do come we need to make them feel at home again, not excusing the unforgiven sin but giving compassion to the sinner.

Preachers need to be men of compassion, forgiving others as God has forgiven them. We need compassion to see the dying world lost without the mercy of God. We need compassion to meet the fallen saint who is returning home. The man of God must be compassionate.

President Bush told the story of a man who walked along the beach with his grandson. The boy picked up each starfish they passed and threw it back into the ocean. "If I left them here," he said, "they would dry up and die. I'm saving their lives."

"But, son," objected his grandfather, "the beach goes on for miles, and there are millions of starfish. What you are doing won't make any difference." The boy looked at the starfish in his hand, gently threw it in the ocean, and said, "It makes a difference to this one."[5]

There are many in the world who are hurting. One man cannot help them all, but he can help those he meets. He can show them compassion of a man of God.

Endnotes

1. Bromiley, Geoffrey W. *Theological Dictionary of the New Testament*. Eds. Gerhard Kittel and Gerhard Friedrich. Bromiley, comp. (Grand Rapids: William B. Eerdmans Publishing Company, 1985) 1068

2. Prentice A. Meador Jr., "The Gospel According to Compassion," *Gospel Advocate*. Jan. 1991, 8

3. Willie Cato, *His Hand His Heart* (Nashville, TN: J.C. Choate Publications, 1990) 24.

4. Flavil Yeakley, *Why Churches Grow* (Nashville, TN: Christian Communication, 1986) 105.

5. Joe R. Barnett, "The 'Issue' Is ...," *Gospel Advocate* Jan. 1991: 19.

Jeffrey Dillinger has preached for congregations in Georgia, Tennessee and Wisconsin. He earned a B.A. in Bible from Freed-Hardeman University.

The Preacher As a Teacher

Avon Malo

Paul's instruction to Timothy and Titus laid upon them the responsibility of teaching and instructing. The pastoral epistles picture the evangelist's work as "preparing God's people for works of service, so that the body of Christ may be built up" (Eph. 4:12). Without the edification of the church there will be little evangelization of the world. Therefore, one work of the evangelist is to edify and that means the preacher must be a teacher. His preaching must be "with great patience and careful instruction" (2 Tim. 4:2). Teaching, instructing and imparting knowledge is an integral part of preaching itself. The preacher is a teacher as he fulfills the New Testament ideal.

The preacher's public ministry has been succinctly summarized: "Until I come, devote yourself to public reading, to exhortation, and to teaching" (1 Tim. 4:13). The word *anaginosko*, translated here "reading," means to read aloud. This word is used when Philip heard the eunuch reading from Isaiah (Acts 8:28-32; cf. Acts 13:15; 2 Cor. 3:14-15).

What are the essential elements of authentic biblical preaching? First there is Scripture. There can be no biblical preaching without the Bible. The Scripture lies at the heart of real preaching. Public reading of Scripture then is central in Paul's definition of preaching. The worshiper must be confronted with the inspired Word.

In addition to Scripture there is to be exhortation and teaching. Without exhortation preaching will lack persuasiveness, practicality and motivating power. Exhortation clearly has its place (Acts 2:40; 4:36). However, when preaching consists only of exhortation, assemblies of worship may become little more than one pep rally after another. Preaching of this kind lacks substance and can result in spiritual anemia on the part of the hearers.

Preaching is the communication of saving truth through the teaching of "God-breathed" Scripture (2 Tim. 3:15-17). Paul's letters to Timothy make it clear that preaching consists of teaching and instructing the hearer.

While serving as evangelist in Ephesus, Timothy was to work at teacher training (1 Tim. 1:3; 2 Tim. 2:2). Methods are not the concern here. Timothy did not lecture on how to have meaningful discussion or how to have a great "buzz session." He taught a body of truth to able men so that they could teach others also.

Titus was exhorted to speak sound doctrine (Titus 2:1). The preacher is to communicate a body of instruction, "sound doctrine," by means of teaching. The cumulative force of Paul's instructions in the pastoral epistles makes it apparent that much of the work of preaching is teaching. Timothy then, and the preacher today, must teach. Preaching, by the definition given in Paul's letters to preachers, involves didactic discipline. The pulpit is a place for providing instruction.

This is so because Christianity is a taught religion. Jesus said, "they shall be taught of God" (John 8:45). Jesus is frequently referred to as a teacher (Matt. 8:19). *Didasko*, a form of the verb "teach," is often used to refer to His work. Only infrequently in Scripture does the word "preach" refer to the ministry of Jesus. The word "disciple" (a learner, follower or student) appears in the Gospels and Acts. The school concept with its emphasis on teaching pervades the inspired Word.

The fact that Christianity is a taught religion becomes apparent when it is remembered that it is a revealed religion. It is a redemptive system that rests squarely upon God's revelation of Himself and His will. Paul makes this clear: "For who among men knows the things of a man save the spirit of the man, which is in him? Even so the things of God none knoweth; save the Spirit of God" (1 Cor. 2:11).

Paul affirms "that the things of God no man knoweth." That being true, man must have a revelation from God to know God and His will. God's existence, power and divinity can be seen in "the things made" (Rom. 1:20), but His will for man can be understood only through His revelation. One could gaze at the mute but majestic mountains all his life and not know God's redemptive will. One might feel a deep sense of awe as, night after night he or she scans "the heavens" that declare "the glory of God," but that alone would never make God's will apparent for one's life. Human wisdom, philosophy and man's unaided intuitive abilities could never grope their way to the divine will for man. We must have a revelation from God — and we do. In Jesus, the incarnate Word, and in Scripture, the inspired written Word, God has revealed His will for man.

Paul spoke of the revelation that he and other inspired men received:

> But we received, not the spirit of the world, but the spirit which is from God; that we may know the things that were freely given us of God. Which things also we speak, not in words which man's wisdom teacheth, but which the Spirit teacheth; combining spiritual things with words (1 Cor. 2:12-13).

Inspired men, apostles and prophets, received by revelation truth that man, alone and unaided, could not know. They, in turn, communicated the very words of the Spirit (cf. 1 Cor. 2:6-13; Eph. 3:3-5).

In light of this it is clear why God's Word must be taught and why teaching is such an integral part of preaching. Christianity, a revealed religion, is of necessity a taught religion. One will never find Christians among people who have had no contact with God's inspired revelation. The message must be taught to all-every nation, every creature (Matt. 28:18-20; Mark 16:15-16).

Therefore, every Christian is to teach. We must teach the lost and the saved. The lost must be taught in order to be saved, and the saved must be taught in order to remain saved. The edification and spiritual education of the Christian demands that he be taught "all things" that Jesus commanded (Matt. 28:19). No wonder Paul defines the work of the preacher as a teaching ministry (1 Tim. 4:11, 13, 16; 2 Tim. 2:2; 4:12).

This makes it mandatory for the preacher to be equipped to present the message "with all longsuffering and teaching." That means he must be a prepared man. To be a teacher of the Word he must be a student of the Word. If he does not intend to be such a student then public ministry of the Word is not for him. The first law of teaching is that the teacher must know the material to be taught. Someone has said, "You can no more teach what you do not know than you can come back from where you have not been." The one who would fulfill this ministry (2 Tim. 4:5) is one who will spend much of his life with the Word. L.R. Wilson was once told, "Brother Wilson, I would give half my life to know the Bible as you do." Brother Wilson simply responded, "That's exactly what it cost me."

We who teach and preach need to count the cost and pay the price. With the Lord's help we must become diligent, disciplined workmen who "handle aright the word of truth" (2 Tim. 2:15). Paul used an expression here which could describe the plowing of a straight furrow or the cutting of a straight line. It is an expressive way of saying that the Word is to be handled accurately.

How can the principles discussed here be implemented practically? The preacher can make his preaching full of Scripture, exhortation and teaching. He can do more expository preaching. After laboring and praying over a text, he can then "expose" that passage to show exactly what it teaches. This exposition of the text, perhaps a paragraph or chapter or even an entire book, will ensure that teaching will take place. This will satisfy the definition and the demands of 1 Timothy 4:13, and, with motivated listeners, will result in changes of concept and conduct. Such preaching will be possessed of substance and strength that is lacking in much contemporary preaching.

The preacher should go into the classroom of the local church prepared to really teach God's Word. Unfortunately, much of the "discussion" so desired in classes is little more than the pooling of collective ignorance. Sometimes neither teacher nor class have made serious preparation for the study of God's Word. Preachers who teach and who take heed to themselves and the teaching (1 Tim. 4:16) can begin to change that condition. Godly elders, able to teach and holding fast the faithful Word, can make an immense contribution to improvement in this area.

Preacher, there are many people who are hoping and hungering for some solid spiritual food. Do not betray them or your God. Give attention to Scripture, to exhortation and to teaching (1 Tim. 4:13).

Avon Malone has a special commitment to training preachers. He has taught on the Bible faculty of Bear Valley and Preston Road schools of preaching, Harding University and Oklahoma Christian University of Science and Arts. He attended Abilene Christian University (B.A., M.A.).

Soul Winning

There is a crisis in the kingdom of God. Preachers have lost their passion for the lost. Men of God, you have a charge to keep.

The task of Jesus is our task. His purpose is our purpose. Seeking the lost begins with the evangelist. He must conceptualize a new vision for his role in the world and his work in the local church (2 Tim. 4:2, 5). One preacher prayed, "Bring this church revival. Let this revival begin with me." God's spokesmen are to publicly and privately present the good news of forgiveness.

Men of God are also to honor the second half of the Great Commission by "teaching them to observe all that I commanded you" (Matt. 28:20). Ministers of reconciliation are not only to convert, but to nourish, encourage and strengthen those whom they brought to the cross (Acts 14:21-23).

Paul portrays the evangelist not only as one who convicts men of sin, but one who equips saints for service in the body. He is to be a people enricher, enabler and enhancer. While elders have the special responsibility to oversee, feed and nurture the flock, evangelists are portrayed as co-ministers to the saints.

A Word of Caution

Churches and their evangelists must not confuse the task of the church with the mission of the church. The task of the church is to evangelize and equip. The mission is to glorify God by making men like God. Confusion will bog us down in methods, programs and the numbers game, causing us to miss our real mission: The indwelling of God in men (Col. 1:27).

Mobilize to Evangelize

First, give the church a clear reason for its existence. Often preachers lose their reason for existence. Christians have substituted so many human purposes and trite traditions that their function has been blurred. Arthur Harrington declared, "The majority just continue to exist, listlessly plodding along an aimless course which is bound for nowhere."[1] Any church which has an ill-defined sense of purpose will be susceptible not only to stagnation, but conflict. A church that does not turn out with purpose may turn in with a vengeance.

A comprehensive reason for being could be scripted as follows: The local church exists to glorify God by making men like God through the dual task of evangelism and edification.

Second, convince the church that men are lost. The first century church believed that the world was lying in the power of the evil one (1 John 5:19). No wonder they went everywhere preaching the Word (Acts 8:4).

Third, be a role-model for outreach. Live a life worthy of imitation. Paul was supremely aware of his example among the churches. God's preacher leads soldiers of Christ into the war zone. An evangelist cannot lead where he has not been. Let him turn theology into biography (1 Thess. 1:6-8).

Proclaimers who never look into the faces of the lost during the week cannot preach with convicting power on Sunday. If heralds retreat to their studies and offices all week they will lose touch with the man on the street. A pulpiteer may know Peter, James and John, but he may not know Tom, Dick and Harry. Spokesmen for God can lose their speaking acquaintance with the times because they seldom know the problems, feel the pain or cry over the human predicament.

There is no way to properly measure the far-reaching effects of a local preacher who is not only dynamic in the pulpit, but a fisher of men throughout the week. He must demonstrate successful fishing before others will wet their lines. There is power in demonstration.

In the birth and history of every great church is an evangelist who was consumed with compassion for the lost, believed in the worth-whileness of his endeavors, and was confident that the Gospel is the answer for every man.

Fourth, put the church on a wartime basis. The early church understood the race with catastrophe. They were no peacetime army. They never signed an armistice with the enemy. They were out to win the ultimate battle for the undying souls of men (Eph. 6:10-12; 2 Tim. 2:3).

William Banowsky observed, "The recruiting power of any institution is directly dependent upon the relevance and vitality of its cause. There was no shortage of Marine recruits when the Japanese bombed Pearl Harbor. The stakes were high. The risk was great But the purpose was clear."[2] During the Great War, American citizens did without sugar, gas, autos and nylons. Americans bought war bonds, worked in defense plants and sat through blackouts. Our nation was willing to make any sacrifice because our battle was for survival.

Soldiers of Christ cannot simply show up on Sunday for dress review. Local meeting houses must be viewed as the armory where the troops are in training. The forces must land on the beaches of spiritual tyranny as they vow, "Satan, we will bury you."

Fifth, impress the church that she is under orders. Outreach is not optional. Soul winning must be her passion. There is no other viable choice.

Sixth, encourage evangelism as a lifestyle. The early church lived as "exiles and strangers' in a hostile environment (1 Peter 2:11-12). As a minority group their beliefs and lives clashed with the pagan culture. In *The Church in Exile*, James Thompson wrote, "During the first four centuries Christians met in small house-churches surrounded by neighbors and family members who scorned their belief and their morality."[3]

The Christian community was able to have such an impact because its evangelism took two forms: The saints had both an evangelistic proclamation and an evangelistic presence. The church in Jerusalem was "having favor with all the people" (Acts 2:4-7). The testimony of their lives led Luke to declare that the populace "were marveling, and began to recognize them as having been with Jesus" (Acts 4:13). There was eloquent power in their non-verbal demonstration (1 Thess. 1:9; Rom. 1:8). They employed the daily events of their lives to enhance the beauty of their message.

The church is under fire. There is a war going on. An anti-Christian spirit has arisen in our land. Believers are not paranoid — there really are people out to destroy the church. They are not out to merely scandalize the people of God and preempt Christian ethics. The unbelieving forces are angry, militant and intolerant.

Seventh, empower others to win. God gave evangelists to the church for the purpose of equipping it (Eph. 4:11-12). Training soul winners is a priority matter. It is often imprudent to offer training sessions on busy Sunday afternoons or on inopportune nights of the week. Such courses of study could be offered as a vital part of the Sunday morning or Wednesday evening curriculum, or at other times that meet with the needs of the congregation.

Eighth, recruit every Christian to be involved in evangelism at some level. All evangelists are Christians; but not all Christians are evangelists. To capture the spirit and the work of the first century church, Christians must be soul winners.

If our aim is the total penetration of the whole world, we must aim at nothing less than the mobilization of the whole church. Tragically, we are limiting our efforts. For too long we have limited the place of evangelism to our buildings. Our strategy has been the cafeteria style when it should have been a catering service. We must take the bread of life right to the doors of lost men.

We have also, in some quarters, limited our evangelism by leaving it to specialists. We hire preachers, personal workers, associates and missionaries to do the major portion of teaching the lost. The early church repudiated the trend of today. Without buildings, staffs, preachers, secretaries, speaker systems, radio or television, the body of Christ effectively registered its protest against Satan and won a world (Col. 1:23). They did it by every member evangelizing. Faithful members were aflame with the love of Jesus' name — and told others so. A church that bottlenecks its outreach by depending on specialists to do its soul winning has missed the power of the New Testament pattern.

Evangelism is to be a daily activity. It must be lifted into the daily lives of mothers, factory workers, clerks, soldiers, farmers and students. Every vocation must become a means of service and every location a place of teaching and winning.

Ninth, focus on the harvest. Jesus said that the harvest is plentiful, but the workers are few. Prospects for conversion are all around us: mates of members; visitors at services; children on the Bible school roll; Vacation Bible school Contacts; senior citizens in the community; newcomers to town; benevolence contacts; radio and television contacts; prospects from a religious census of the community; those at the local jail; the youth taught at summer camp; those contacted through hospitals and nursing homes; and those who attend our gospel meetings.

There are many wonderful services we can render to the community. We can care for men's physical, emotional and spiritual needs with such efforts as: a home for needy children and the aged; serving the deaf and the blind of the community; offering daycare services to children of working mothers; offering recovery programs for alcoholics, the divorced, drug addicts and homosexuals; assisting those who have suffered personal disasters with food, clothing and shelter; maintaining a "We Care Center" where used furniture is repaired and distributed; setting up a distribution center in a ghetto or downtown to provide food, clothing, transportation and medical services for the poor; offering a "Dial a Devotional" program that the community might receive encouraging and instructive messages from God's Word; offering marital counseling services to abuse victims; providing a "Meals On Wheels" service to the elderly and handicapped; and mailing encouraging letters and tracts to people or the community when there has been a death, marriage or other major event; and thousands of other forms of service.

Preaching can create a universal awareness by: teaching courses on missions in our Bible classes; taking mission trips; recruiting members to adopt a missionary; attending mission forums to hear men fresh from the field; bringing missionaries home for a time to live among the congregation; challenging members to keep an exchange student in their home; encouraging members to see videos of other nations; listening to tapes from missionaries; giving to missionaries, through money or even just notes; having a special Day of Prayer for missions in the congregation; inspiring Christians to become vocational missionaries; holding up our missionaries as heroes and role models for our youth; and sending evangelistic journals into church homes.

Conclusion

What you hear ticking is a potential spiritual explosion. The need has never been greater and the multitudes have never been more accessible. It is a poor time for God's evangelists to develop evangelistic laryngitis.

It is time we get on with the Great Commission. Evangelists must view the whole world as needing Christ. We must start at home and then reach out to all the nations of men. God's people must not fail the Lord who sends them, nor the world who needs them.

Endnotes

1. Arthur Harrington, *What the Bible Says About Leadership* (Joplin, MO: College Press Publishing Company, 1985) 66.

2. Bill Banowsky, *The New Generation* (Austin, TX: Sweet Publishing Company, 1969) 57.

3. James Thompson, *The Church in Exile* (Abilene, TX: ACU Press, 1990) 4.

Harold G. Taylor attended David Lipscomb University (B.A.). He conducts seminars in church growth/leadership, evangelism, spiritual enrichment and family enrichment. He has served as an instructor at the Sunset School of Preaching and editor of *Christian Family Magazine*.

Working with an Eldership

Neale T. Pr

The preacher-elder relationship is one of the most important factors in ministry because the effectiveness of both depends on their relationship. In fact, this relationship will be either "a source of strength or a source of constant frustration."[1] Even more than that, the growth and stability of the church depend on their relationship. Harold G. Taylor writes, "No one can defeat a church where the elders and the preacher stand together."[2]

There is an old adage that states, "The preacher is doing the elders' work, the elders are doing the deacons' work, and the deacons have nothing to do." When roles are poorly understood, preachers and elders often get in each other's way, not knowing what is expected of one another. In order for preachers and elders to work together, all must know their particular responsibilities and expectations. This chapter will furnish an overview of the distinctive roles of preacher and elder, offering practical suggestions for developing and maintaining good relationships.

The Role of the Elder

Most of the prayers for elders are to help them "make good decisions." Therefore, it seems they often are looked upon as a board of directors who set the policies to be carried out by the preacher and other members. But the principal role of the elder in the New Testament is caring for and tending to the needs of the members. This role can be seen in the three Greek words that are commonly used to describe them in the New Testament.

The first is *presbuteros*. The *presbuteros* is an "older man." It refers to older men in general, as in 1 Timothy 5:1 where Paul instructs Timothy not to rebuke an older man, but to exhort him as a father. Paul then proceeds to show Timothy how to treat younger men, older women and younger women.

Presbuteros is also the word that is used for the elders of the Jews (Matt. 16:21). The church followed, to a large degree, the same type of government the synagogues had, by having elders to oversee the congregation. The word *presbuteros* indicates an older man with more wisdom and experience than his younger brethren.

The second word for elder is *episcopos*. The word literally means "overseer." He is an on-looker who moves among the flock to determine and meet the various needs. In the King James Version, *episcopos* is usually translated "bishop." It is translated "overseer" in Acts 20:28: "Take heed therefore unto yourselves, and to all the flock, over the which the Holy Ghost hath made you overseers." The *episcopos* is a supervisor. He has authority. It is his responsibility to see that the work goes well.

The third word is *poimen*, the common word for shepherd. In many groups the preacher is the pastor or the elder. But the biblical distinction between elder and preacher must be observed. Elders look after the flock as a shepherd cares for his sheep. In Ephesians 4:11 elders are called shepherds (*poimen*), translated "pastor" in the King James Version: "And he gave some, apostles; and some prophets; and some evangelists; and some, pastors and teachers."

All three Greek words are used to describe elders in Acts 20. Paul called for the elders [*presbuteros*] of the church in verse 17. In verse 28, Paul told them they were overseers [*episcopous*] and encouraged them to shepherd (a verb form from *poimen*) the church of God.

All three words also appear in some form in 1 Peter 5. Peter calls himself a fellow elder (v. 1). He exhorts the elders to shepherd the flock (v. 2). Christ is never called an elder in the Scriptures, but in 1 Peter 2:25 he is called "the Shepherd (*poimena*) and Guardian (*episcopon*)" of our souls. Therefore, the elders are following the example of Christ in caring for the souls of men as shepherds and overseers.

The elder is a man of wisdom and maturity, one who has good judgment. He also has authority as a shepherd to feed, care for and tend to the flock. As a bishop he is to oversee or supervise the flock.

The role of elders is to watch over the souls of the congregation "as those who shall give an account" (Heb. 13:17).

The Role of the Preacher

There are two Greek terms for preacher: *kerux* and *euangelistes*. The *kerux* is the proclaimer. This is a word used for the town crier who comes to the city and announces the news. Another translation would be "herald." Paul uses *kerux* in 1 Timothy 2:7 and 2 Timothy 1:11, where he says that he was appointed a "preacher." *Kerux* is also found in 2 Peter 2:5, where Noah is called a "preacher of righteousness."

The word *euangelistes* literally means "a bearer of good news." It is a combination of *eu* (good) and *angelos* (messenger). Our word "evangelist" comes from this work. Philip was called an evangelist in Acts 21:8. Evangelists were among those appointed in the church in Ephesians 4:11. Paul encouraged Timothy "to do the work of an evangelist" (2 Tim. 4:5). The primary duty of the preacher is to proclaim the gospel.

Based on these definitions, it is clear that in many instances the work of the preacher and elder overlap. In Titus 1:9 the elder is commanded to exhort in sound doctrine and convict the gainsayer. This is very similar to the work of the preacher. On the other hand, the preacher will find much of his time taken up in visiting, counseling and doing other things that elders normally do.

In the early church it was not uncommon for preachers to serve as elders. Peter called himself a fellow elder (1 Peter 5:1). Paul said that elders who labor in the Word and in teaching are to be counted worthy of double honor (1 Tim. 5:17).

Charles Hodge uses an analogy to illustrate our relationship in the church. In the United States there are three branches of government: executive, judicial and legislative. These three branches are separate, and yet they must work together. So the elders, the preacher and the members may have separate roles, but they must work together and support each other for the common good.[3]

Keys to Good Preacher-Elder Relationships

There are many practical ways that we can work towards maintaining good preacher-elder relationships.

The first year of a preacher's ministry with a congregation is crucial. It is during this time that the foundation for his ministry is set. Good personal relationships must be formed. One author notes, "No time can be invested more wisely during the first year ... (when, as a matter of fact, much else cannot be done, anyway) than the time he spends developing and cultivating a close relationship to his elders."[4]

It is tempting for a new preacher to want to do too much too soon. He may have great plans and goals for the church, but he is certain to fail if he does not first cultivate meaningful relationships with the members and elders, securing their confidence and support. Sam Stone, author of *The Christian Minister*, warns, "Many ministries have been weakened, shortened or ruined because the preacher attempted to make rapid changes before he knew the people or had their confidence."[5] It is usually wise for a preacher to wait at least a year before attempting any significant changes.

For the young preacher, an age gap between himself and the elders can be a problem. The preacher may regard the elders as uninformed, out-of-date and a general hindrance to many of his plans. On the other hand, the elders may regard the young preacher as one with little background and experience, having little confidence in him.

The elders usually know the congregation better than the preacher does. Many of these elders have lived in that community all their lives. They were there when the preacher came. They will be there when he is gone. Those who have served as elders for a good while have seen many preachers come and go, and they have seen what works with the congregation and does not. The preacher would do well to listen to them. After all, Stone concludes, "These men have lived in the community and worked with that congregation for some time. What may seem to be arbitrary or provincial on their part may well be the wisdom of experience."[6]

There are many ways a preacher can build good relationships with the elders. One excellent idea is to have a special day for the preacher and elders to be together, spending time sharing, praying or just getting to know each other better. The preacher can share with them good books, articles and devotional materials. He should also invite the elders to go with him on visits and Bible studies. It would be good for the preacher to have the elders in his home on a fairly regular basis so the families can get to know each other better.

A preacher may come back from a lectureship or a workshop excited about things that the church needs to do. Yet often the elders don't share in his excitement because they did not attend the workshop. It would be valuable for the preacher to invite the elders to go with him to attend these programs.

Preachers and elders should realize that more can be accomplished by being patient with each other, building personal relationships, and helping one another to be more effective. Many elders would like to be more successful in their ministry but do not know how. According to one writer: "The training that most elders lack is discipleship, or on-the-job training. They need to be taught by example."[7]

As a preacher continues to work with elders, he will grow to love and appreciate them even more. He will see the reason why they were chosen as elders — their manner of life, their love for the Lord, and their wisdom — which it would pay the preacher to heed. "But, we request of you, brethren, that you appreciate those who diligently labor among you, and have charge over you in the Lord and give you instruction, and that you esteem them very highly in love because of their work" (2 Thess. 5:12-13 NASB). Certainly one of the most important things a new preacher can do is spend the time and the effort to build good relationships with the men who work with him.

Keep the Lines of Communication Open

The key to successful cooperation between the preacher and elders is communication. When the preacher is hired, all contractual agreements between the preacher and elders should be written down. That includes vacation time, salary, leave time for meetings, moving expenses, housing arrangements and the renewal of contracts. It is true that "we all are brethren," but brethren tend to forget. There should be a clear agreement on all such matters. The preacher and the elders both should have a written copy on file.

A preacher cannot succeed if he fails to communicate with his elders about plans and program. A good rule to follow is "no surprises." The preacher should avoid public announcements that have not first been cleared by the elders. Neither should the elders surprise the preacher with announcements of a change of policy — or a change of preachers.

Michael Weed admonished preachers to eliminate surprise situations: "It is embarrassing for both you and the elders when situations arise and elders are not aware of certain plans, programs, etc. Keep the elders up to date on your activities, plans, etc."[8]

On the other hand, the main spokesman to the church is the preacher. Any program the elders would like to advance should be promoted by the preacher. One of the quickest and most effective ways of getting the cooperation of the entire congregation is for the elders to let the preacher know exactly what they are wanting to do and have him sold on the idea.

Of course, the preacher should not attend elders' meetings unless he is invited. But a wise eldership will invite the preacher to their meetings frequently. A preacher may not have a vote in the elders' meetings, but he should have a voice. The preacher can increase his effectiveness greatly by attending the elders' meetings as he is invited, and in the right manner giving his wisdom on the issues discussed. Elders need to know what their preacher is thinking.

The preacher needs to communicate his concerns to the elders. There are very few conflicts that cannot be resolved by good communication. The preacher does the elders a disservice by not letting them know of problems he is having, or of his concerns for the church. The Greek work for "boldness" is *parresia*. It means "the freedom to speak one's mind." Elders and preachers must have this boldness with each other, even on unpleasant subjects. This is especially true in regard to the preacher's family. Too many preachers have been embittered by the way their family was treated. Most elders would be more mindful of them if the preacher boldly and kindly let them know their needs. A happy preacher's wife and family will pay great dividends in the effectiveness of the preacher's work. Stone writes, "The elders should take particular concern for the well being of the minister and his family. The minister and his family are the only members of the church who do not have a minister."[9]

The preacher should let the elders know that he needs their support, publicly as well as privately. One preacher summarizes this need: "How many times have I secretly longed for elders to mount the pulpit behind me and speak for all of the elders with a firm endorsement of the unpopular, but totally true message I had just preached."[10]

Simply Love Them

"I am convinced that many young ministers would have longer and more powerful ministries if they would invest the time to communicate to elders that they love them."[11] With these words, Denny Boultinghouse located the crucial element in preacher-elder relationships. Right actions and relationships stem from the right attitude — genuine love for one another. The preacher must never badmouth the elders, or use one against the other, nor should he allow others to criticize the elders in his presence.

In the King James Version, 1 Corinthians 13:7 says, "Love beareth all things." The New International Version reading is "always protects." This word bear can also mean "cover." Applied to the preacher-elder relationship, it means that the elders protect the preacher and the preacher protects the elders. It is good to know that others will stand up in our defense and protect us when we cannot protect ourselves. The preacher can do a great deal to help the congregation to have confidence in the elders and to follow their leadership. Preachers should give attention to opportunities to commend the elders publicly and privately. They should let the congregation know when their elders are serving in an admirable way.

When preachers and elders have lived together, worked together, prayed together and hurt together, they are brought closer to each other. One of the most beautiful illustrations of preacher-elder relationships is seen in Acts 20, where Paul gives his farewell address to the Ephesian elders. In his exhortation to them, Paul reflects on their work together during his three years at Ephesus.

But it is after he concludes his address that the relationship between Paul and the elders is especially highlighted.

> And when he had said these things, he knelt down and prayed with them all, and they began to weep aloud and embraced Paul and repeatedly kissed him, grieving especially over the word which he had spoken, that they should see his face no more. And they were accompanying him to the ship. (Acts 20:36-38)

Would to God we could love each other like this! The way to treat an elder is to love him, simply and sincerely.

Endnotes

1. Michael Weed, Ed., *The Minister and His Work* (Austin, TX: Sweet Publishing Company, 1970) 55.

2. Harold G. Taylor, *Holy Spirit Elders* (Chino Hills, CA: Penman Productions, 1972) 99.

3. Charles Hodge, *Your Preacher* (Ft. Worth: Star Bible Publications, 1972) 73.

4. Jay E. Adams, *Shepherding God's Flock* (Phillipsburg, NJ: Presbyterian and Reformed Publishing Company, 1980) 361.

5. Sam E. Stone, *The Christian Minister* (Cincinnati: The Christian Standard Publishing Company, 1980) 116.

6. Ibid., 113.

7. Adams, 362.

8. Weed, 56.

9. Stone, 115.

10. Dub McLish, "Elder-Preacher Relations," *The Christian Worker* (December, 1982, Volume 68), 12:2.

11. Denny Boultinghouse, "Preachers and Elders," *Image* (July 1, 1991) 4.

Neale T. Pryor attended Harding University (B.A.), Harding Graduate School of Religion (M.A., Th.M.) and New Orleans Baptist Theological Seminary (Th.D.). He is professor of Bible and a vice president at Harding. He has also served as a minister and elder for the College Church of Christ in Searcy, Arkansas.

Long-Term Ministry

Paul Watson

Alan Bryan used to say that if he wanted to get rich he would go into the moving business, and just move preachers. For many years it seemed that preachers and elders felt that there should be a change in the pulpit every two to four years. Consequently, there was no long-term continuity between the preacher and the pew. The congregation came to look upon the preacher as only a temporary member. The preacher looked upon the congregation as only a short relationship in his long-term ministry for Christ. Because of this the preacher did not feel like investing himself fully in the work of the church and the members did not respect and cooperate fully with the preacher as otherwise they might.

Hindrances to a Long-Term Ministry

It is not always profitable or practical for a long-term ministry to develop. Sometimes the preacher and the congregation just do not bond together.

Too often there are critics in the church who make it difficult or impossible for the preacher to work effectively. This is especially true when elders begin to listen to the criticism and begin to be critics themselves. The preacher's spirit may become so frustrated and hurt that he must move for his own peace of mind and self-esteem.

Some time ago a friend of mine told me about visiting a church to consider moving there. The elders of this particular congregation thought that only a certain version of the Bible should be used, but the preacher liked a different version. It was obvious that it would not be good for him to move there.

T.B. Larimore did not want to locate with one church because he thought he could do more good in evangelistic meetings in which he could preach many times per week. Strong churches at different places made very lucrative propositions to locate him as their preacher, but he declined all overtures of that kind and kept steadily to the idea that "the wide, wide world is my field." He wrote from a country meeting:

> I am way out here in the country, among good people, where I see but one paper and hear little of what is going on in the world — preaching twice every day and three times every Sunday, and hunting "scaly-bark hickory nuts" between sermons. I hope to be able to keep up till Christmas and be in good condition for work next year. I am getting old now, but I may have reserve force enough to enable me to rally for a few more campaigns for Christ before I "go hence." I have several liberal propositions and strong appeals to locate in easy places with good churches. I would willingly go to any good church to preach twice every day and three times every Sunday as long as I can do more good there than anywhere else, if they would consent for me to go anywhere else at any time and stay as long as I thought I could do more good. I might compromise on a proposition to preach one time — at night — every day in the week, except Saturday, and twice every Sunday, making seven sermons every week, or an average of one sermon every day.[1]

We should also note that it is impossible to please everyone, and we should not even try. Our task is to "Preach the word! Be ready in season and out of season. Convince, rebuke, exhort, with all longsuffering and teaching" (2 Tim. 4:2). Marshall Keeble used to say that "in season and out of season" means when they like it and when they don't. We strive to please our God and when we have done that, that is enough (Gal. 1:10).

Another problem is in the area of finances. Preachers do not work for money, but the "laborer is worthy of his hire" and they that "preach the gospel should live of the gospel." Today's bills probably can not be paid by last year's salary. The elders that I have worked with these many years have provided a raise every year for 28 years.

They try to keep up with the rate of inflation. However, it was not always this way in other churches. Years ago I preached for a church that paid me $40 per week. When I left to go to school, the next preacher got $80 per week. The next church I was with did a similar thing. I wold my wife, "Sometime I want to be the next preacher." If elders really want the preacher to stay they should be aware of his financial needs and make it possible for him to stay without being burdened with financial worries.

As Paul Rogers wrote: "It is not always possible to 'move to stay,' but if you find a place where you fit like a pocket on a shirt, where people share your dreams and hold up your hands, by all means go and stay."

The Advantages of a Long-Term Ministry

A long-term ministry will promote the growth of that church as the people and the minister work together to become a great soul-winning team. In the 10 churches with the largest Bible schools, the average length of the minister's tenure is 22 years and one month.[2] The largest church in our fellowship benefited from the long-term ministry of Ira North. It would seem difficult for a preacher to really contribute greatly to the growth of the church in only three or four years.

Long-term ministry provides an opportunity for the preacher to really know the members and the members to know and love their minister. Cleon Lyles once was invited to move to another church, but the elders where he was serving objected: "You have married us, been present at the birth of our children, baptized our children, and buried our dead. They could not possibly know you and love you like we do." This is one of the greatest benefits of staying at one place a long time. You get to marry a young couple, watch them mature in the Lord, be present when their children are born, and perhaps even marry their children. You do your best to sympathize with and comfort those whose loved ones die. Through the years you are involved in the lives of people you love and who in turn love you. These ties make it very difficult to even think about moving to a new town and a different congregation.

Working with a congregation for a long period of time enables the elders and the preacher to work together in long-range planning. For example, we have been able to build a new building and are now planning to expand our present facilities. We have also been involved in a Capital Stewardship program to raise money to build a church building in a nearby town so we could help start another congregation. New programs have begun, associate ministers have been employed, and we have been blessed with a strong youth program.

Requirements of a Long-Term Ministry

I believe that the first necessity for a long-term ministry is an eldership that does not have the idea that the preacher must move every few years, or whenever there is a set back in the work.

Of course, the elders and the minister must be compatible. They must love and respect one another and work in peace and harmony. The congregation needs to know that the elders back the preacher and the preacher respects and appreciates the elders. There is no place in the elder-preacher relationship for back-biting, criticism or feelings of superiority.

In connection with this, the preacher should be invited to elders' meetings so they can discuss the work together and plan together. The preacher is something like the quarterback on the football team, he must know the plans and plays of the team. So it is that the preacher must know the plans and goals of the elders if he is to have a part in promoting them.

The elders should treat the preacher with consideration and respect. One Sunday morning a friend of mine was told by one of his elders, "We are going to play a sermon on tape from one of our missionaries, so you will not be preaching today." Needless to say, that preacher did not stay at that congregation long. To have a long-term relationship, the elders and preacher must work as a team, with mutual concern and respect.

The preacher needs to decide to stay at one place as long as the congregation works well with him and the elders want him to stay. He should not be searching for a larger church with more pay or prestige.

I do not think it is good for the elders to demand an accounting of the preacher's time as though he was punching a time clock. This seems to me to indicate a lack of trust on the part of the elders and can create resentment on the part of the preacher. The preacher should be the kind of person that the elders can have enough confidence in to believe that he will be at work and available as needed. Most preachers work more than 40 hours per week, but their time is not like that of a worker who puts in eight hours and goes home. He may work six hours one day and 12 the next. His hours must of necessity be flexible.

Certainly, the preacher needs to take time to study. A man once remarked, "Preachers do not buy books after the age of 50." This should not be true. The preacher needs to spend time in studying the Word and also in reading inspirational books, study helps and books that will keep him abreast of the ideas of his time.

Times change, ideas change and people change. To keep up, the preacher must study. God's Word does not change, but methods may. Sermons need to be new and fresh. Preaching needs to be varied, using topical and exegetical styles. He must search for new and helpful illustrations. He needs to preach on the life and teachings of Jesus, on the work and role of the church, and on the letters that tell us how to worship and live as Christians.

The preacher also needs to set the example in evangelism. Try to conduct two or three Bible studies per week outside of congregational assemblies. This is one of the best ways to win souls and to help the church grow. It also sets the example for the congregation to follow in soul winning.

Insights from Long-Term Ministers and Elders

Ray Frizzell, an elder of the Crieve Hall church in Nashville, wrote:

> Ministers of the gospel are servants of God and serve him whole heartedly and are totally committed to him ... however their commitment to the areas of (1) evangelism, (2) ministry, and (3) administration are critical to an effective work. Elders and ministers must be of the same mind and heart, they must be totally committed to the Father, the Son and the Holy Spirit and must maintain a servant attitude. Equally important is their sense of cooperation, trust and team work together toward a common goal. Their cooperative spirit should be the same as the commitment shown in the early church by their 'singleness of heart' (Acts 1:41; Col. 4:22; Eph. 6:5). ... In order for the elder-minister team to function effectively in their common goals of serving God, they must regularly communicate and share new and updated information in their daily and weekly activities. Continued communication and sharing of information are keys to a working relationship of mutual trust and respect. ... The minister is evangelistic, both in and out of the pulpit. He encourages members to be evangelistic. ... In the area of ministering, the long-term minister endears himself to the flock by his concern and dedication to them during times of joy and sorrow. He

maintains a vigil, keeps involved with the members and actively
reaches out to them. ... Administratively the minister is important to the overall flow of current information to the membership,
the office staff and the elders-deacons team. He is an effective
communicator and is the hub on which most information evolves.
In summary, the long-term minister is a trusted and valuable servant of God and one that is loved and respected by the members
and leaders. He enjoys a special relationship with all who know
him personally and professionally. His relationship with the
elders is unique, in that they work in many areas as peers, however in the overall scheme of responsibilities, the minister
respects the position and leadership role of the elder and strives
to fully assist them to accomplish their God given responsibilities
as the shepherds of the Lord's church. [3]

James Thomas, an elder in the congregation where I preach, provided some additional insights:

Elders should attempt to understand better the preacher's
personality. By doing this, personality conflicts between elders
and preachers can minimized.

There should be more association between the eldership and
the preacher. The association at business meetings alone is not
sufficient. Frequent social contacts would facilitate an increased
understanding and a greater mutual appreciation.

Elders should be diligent in according the preacher the respect
which is rightfully his. After all, usually no one devotes more
time to church work, or has a better knowledge of it, than the
preacher. He generally possesses training and experience. Thus
his counsel should be sought and respected by the eldership. This
does not mean that his views are infallible and must always pre-
vail. But in truth they should always receive the most careful consideration.

The eldership should periodically give the preacher a public
vote of confidence. This would show the membership that there
is splendid accord between them and the preacher. It would serve
as public evidence that the preacher's work is approved and
appreciated by the elders. The need of this would be especially
important when the preacher courageously denounces sin.

There should be a greater exercise of insight by elders relative
to the preacher's personal needs. For instance it would be helpful
if elders could see that the preacher needed an increase in salary
without the preacher having to call it to their attention. Doubtless

more eldership perception in various ways would prove invaluable. It would simply serve as a source of strength and encouragement to the preacher.

The eldership should not attempt to delegate to the preacher responsibilities and problems which are uniquely theirs. As an illustration, if a member needs admonition or discipline from the elders, they should not simply send the preacher thinking that thereby they have discharged their obligation. In no way should the eldership slip into the habit of using the preachers as a congregational "trouble-shooter." [4]

Obviously, a long-term stay for the minister depends as much on the elders and their attitudes as it does the preacher.

The practical aspects of the minister's life and practice are also important if he desires to develop a long-term ministry with a congregation. Charles Chumley, who served the Granny White church in Nashville as minister for many years, shared with me the following:

A preacher cannot move into a new work with a congregation and try to make drastic changes right away but must build a foundation of mutual respect and love. Move slowly.

The preacher must preach to please God and not man. Men are not consistent and change their attitudes, so you cannot please every one. However, we must stay close to the Word and to our convictions. Do not compromise convictions of God's Word.

We must also respect every individual and see in each member the image of God. Show no partiality in care, concern and service.

Be an example of Christian conduct and character and so maintain a relationship of compatibility, a mutual respect. In these relationships to sure to keep a confidence. Many times it is helpful for the preacher's wife to be able to say, "I do not know," when asked about a problem. [5]

Paul M. Tucker, who has been with the Crieve Hall church in Nashville for more than 30 years, has some more good advice:

The preacher must make the church and his work for the Lord the first thing in his life and his wife and family must recognize this. They must be living demonstrations of the teaching of God's Word. He must know the Book or his well will run dry.

He must have a genuine love for people and be available at all times, day or night. Availability and approachability are very vital, encouraging people to feel free and welcome to very significant amounts of his time and interest.

There must be an ability to take criticism and suggestions from the elders and others gracefully, even though they may seem to be unwise to the preacher.

There must be a fair amount of circulation among the members, in their homes, hospitals and nursing homes. When calls come for consultation, counseling, home visits, opportunities for Bible study, when death or other crises arise make that visit as soon as possible. It may be more urgent than we imagine and that is the time of peak interest. [6]

Jim Bill McInteer served the West End congregation in Nashville for many years. He shared these thoughts:

People should know that you are serving the Lord and love him and people. The preacher should do much visiting among the members, in their homes and in the hospitals. He should know the needs of the members and relate them to the elders.

He should not play politics among the elders or play to their strengths or weaknesses. It is good to present an agenda before an elders' meeting to each elder for their consideration. Each elder would get the same list. If the preacher's ideas are not accepted, he should not take it personally and think about moving. Accept this gracefully and do not brood over it. Go on, do your work, be dependable, loving and caring and doing your best to meet the needs of the members. [7]

Conclusion

As we look through thoughts of various preachers and elders we can see common threads running through them. The preacher should plan to enjoy a long-term relationship with the congregation and the elders should have the attitude that they will work with a preacher to help him want to stay, understanding him and meeting his needs. The preacher must spend much time in planning his sermons and Bible study. He needs to keep up with the current trends, but not be moved about with every new idea and change promoted. He should keep up with current events, so as to be able to apply the Bible to current situations.

It is good to plan sermons in advance and yet be flexible enough to change the sermon if there is a special need. The preacher should spend much time in expository preaching, but vary it with topical studies and appropriate illustrations. The preacher should concentrate on the life and teachings of Jesus, but not neglect the value and identity of the church. People need to hear about marriage and the family. The preacher should preach where the people are in their thinking, preaching God's Word without compromise but with genuine love for people and the truth.

Preachers need to grow in their own knowledge. Attending lectures, classes and seminars will help keep their thinking and approach fresh and new. Since people are liable to judge a preacher by his preaching, he needs to do his best. Even more importantly, salvation depends upon preaching: "It pleased God by the foolishness of preaching to save those that believe."

Preachers should never become bitter, fault finding or critical. They need to spend time expressing praise and appreciation. Ira North used to say, "Give a dog a name and he will live up to it." Give all the legitimate praise that you can and help others to be better.

An excellent way to keep in touch with the members is simply to use the telephone and the post office. When members miss the services, telephone them to tell them they were missed. This is not done with an attitude of condemnation, but rather of care and concern. Nothing encourages those facing illness like a visit, note or phone call. When a member is honored, promoted or has a special occasion of joy, send them a letter of congratulation. Genuine expressions of interest will pay rich dividends in your relationships.

Preachers also need to spend much time in prayer. Prayer for the members, elders, deacons, teachers and all who work with you. When there are problems and heartaches, take the names of these people to God's throne of grace. We need to pray for ourselves, for our attitudes, for a stronger faith and for spiritual growth. Let people know we are praying for them and ask their prayers for us. This will help greatly to bind us together.

Finally, stay in the Word of God. Let Jesus teach you how to get along with people, how to be compassionate and forgiving, and how to treat others as we would be treated. He has shown us the ultimate in long-term relationships — He sacrificed himself so that each of us could live with Him for eternity.

Endnotes

1. Paul Rogers, "The Secret of a Long Ministry," Middle Tennessee Midwinter Preacher's Forum, Centerville.

2. Rogers.

3. Ray Frizzell, letter to the author.

4. James Thomas, Michigan Christian College Lectureship, 1963.

5. Charles Chumley, telephone interview.

6. Paul Tucker, letter to the author.

7. Jim Bill McInteer, telephone interview.

Paul Watson began preaching in 1940 and received his academic training from Freed-Hardeman College, Eastern Michigan University, Pepperdine University, Bowling Green State University and Ashland Theological Seminary. He has served many years preaching for churches in Nazareth and Abilaboun, Israel. He continues to serve as preacher at Echo Meadows Church of Christ in Oregon, Ohio, and travels periodically to preach in Israel.

The Preaching Pen

Basil Overt

Every man of God needs to be convinced of the importance of the preaching pen. The written word has a unique power either to lead people to Christ or to mislead them, depending on what is written.

The Bible Is a Product of the Preaching Pen

God affirmed the tremendous power of the preaching pen by guiding the writers of the Bible.

One way sinners can come to salvation is through reading the Gospel message from God's Word. The pens of the writers of the New Testament were powerful indeed. They were preaching pens.

Methods of the Preacher's Pen

The Great Commission guides the church in each generation. One of the ways Christians can fulfill this work is through the written word.

The Gospel can be spread, for example, through books that contain lessons and sermons on the soul-saving message of Jesus Christ. Books of gospel messages can have a long-lasting influence. We need to support more men to write about salvation.

Tracts also can be effective in sharing the truth of God with many people. We need to produce more plain and simple tracts containing the plan of salvation. Christians need to distribute such tracts. Giving tracts to lost people is a good way of sowing the seed of the kingdom.

Another place for preachers to use their pens is in public newspapers. Newspapers are read by many people who will not read the Bible or a tract. Letters to the editor and editorial columns are two forums available to local preachers. Advertising space in newspapers can also be purchased for gospel messages.

Preachers should consider writing for gospel journals. These journals provide an opportunity to write on many topics and in many styles. In addition to writing, the preacher needs to read what others are writing.

Some Techniques of Good Writing

No one will applaud when a writer uses correct grammar, but poor writing skills damage a writer's credibility. An important message can be lost if it is presented in a poorly written manner.

Preachers should write so as to be understood without difficulty. The preacher's pen loses its effectiveness when statements are unclear. Many times attempting to be clever only makes the real message unclear. Writers should avoid using unnecessary words and overworked expressions. Grammar and punctuation can clarify, obscure or even change the meaning of what is written. A good writing handbook or style manual should be a part of every writer's library.

A writer should be sure he understands the meaning of the words he uses. When in doubt, do not hesitate to consult a dictionary. Effective writers are careful to select the correct word and to spell it right. One's credibility as a writer is decreased considerably by misspelled words.

Harry Shaw in *Spell It Right* stressed the importance of correct spelling (Barnes and Noble Books, New York, 1965). He says that one who is considered to be educated can get by with not being able to add, not remembering dates of historical events, or not knowing common facts of science and economics. However, he says if one cannot spell, he is in trouble!

It is very important to make sure that quotations are accurate and properly attributed. Many preachers misquote Bible verses, writing them from memory. Often the gist of the verse is captured, but the writer's credibility is damaged if the quote is not exact. Reckless statements and exaggerations also must be avoided. If something is put in quotation marks, the writer must be able to verify from an outside source that the statement is accurate.

Writing is almost always improved by editing. An editor needs to be objective. The editor's goal is to find ways to improve the clarity and impact of what is written. Writers should not be offended when an editor suggests changes. When self-editing, allowing some time to lapse between the first draft and the editing process will improve the writer's objectivity.

Writing About Sinners

A situation may arise where it is necessary for the preacher to write about the sins of an individual *whose name is given*. Much prayer needs to precede any writing of this type and what is written must be motivated by love for that individual and the others he or she might influence.

Such writing should not be allowed to become the focus of the preacher's pen. While there are a number of instances where the Holy Spirit directed the biblical writers to address sinful individuals and situations directly, these passages are surprisingly brief. Paul used only 12 Greek words (15 in the KJV) to describe Demas forsaking him (2 Tim. 4:10). The Greek text contains only 25 words describing the harm done to Paul by Alexander the coppersmith (vv. 4:14-15). The sin of Ananias and Sapphira occupy only 10 verses in Luke's account of the early church (Acts 5:1-10).

The inspired writers did not ignore situations of individual sin, but they also did not dwell on them. Writers today should remember this approach and focus their efforts on sharing the Gospel with the lost.

Sowing the Seed of the Kingdom

In the parable about the sower in Matthew 13, Jesus said fowls of the air devoured some of the seed the sower sowed. He explained that the birds represent the Wicked One's taking the seed, which is the Word of God, from the hearts of some.

One of the many lessons we learn from this parable is that we must keep sowing the seed, preaching the Gospel, although the birds devour some of our efforts. We should not spend all our time in preaching, whether from the pulpit or by the written word, in chasing birds. We also must keep sowing the good seed, sharing the Good News with the lost, and encouraging the church.

Basil Overton attended Freed-Hardeman University, Eastern Kentucky State University (B.A.), University of Kentucky (M.A.), and Morehead State University (D.Hum.). He is editor of *The World Evangelist*, author of many books and tracts, and frequent speaker in lectureships and gospel meetings.

Influence in the Pulpit

Don DeLuk

Many preachers have unbalanced views of their roles, which harms their effectiveness in the pulpit. This imbalance can be addressed by remembering three things: attitude, education and ability.

First, we must be aware of our attitude. The man may be an oratorical genius, dazzling people with his rhetoric and recall, but if he does not know an epistle from an apostle he will accomplish very little. If he is well dressed and charming in the pulpit but outside of the pulpit is rude and gives the impression he does not have time for people, he cannot reach full effectiveness. Those who trust their pulpit ability and educational accomplishments to cover obnoxious behavior are sadly mistaken.

Second, preachers must rise above the tendency to think their particular education is superior to others. Pride in educational accomplishments may foster downfall. Those with impressive resumes must never forget that education is a continual process, particularly in the reading and study of God's Word.

Third, men with kind personalities and educational credentials must remember to use their abilities in order to be effective in the pulpit. If one speaks in a monotone voice, utilizes poor gestures and body language, misplaces or fumbles with his notes, and uses humor and illustrations that do not match his point, the people may be kind and love him but they will not mature as they struggle to figure out the point of his lesson.

Many men with tremendous potential have hurt themselves with their audiences before they even enter the pulpit. Strangely some men cannot understand that poor performance in an adult Bible class where they hammer or intimidate members and get into emotionally charged confrontations hurts their pulpit influence. Some cannot understand that when they make themselves a pest in people's homes or act without discretion in hospital visitation that they hamper their audiences emotionally. This chapter will look at some practical guidelines for the totality of the minister's life that will grace his influence when he gets into the pulpit.

The Minister's Private Life

The private life of a minister is known to God. While the membership may know little about this aspect of a man's life, the private areas of life can have a telling effect on influence from the pulpit.

First, the man of God must be a man of prayer. Others do not know if or how much we pray, but God does. Many men receive blessings in their ministry and influence by praying for God to help and bless them (Psalm 34:15).

Second, we must read on a regular basis. What we read can cause us to enter the pulpit angry or invigorated. Can we feed on constant controversy and trivial material without being affected? Can we turn our backs on issues affecting our people? Balanced choices must be made so that the influence remains balanced (1 Tim. 4:13).

Third, we need to be conscious of telephone etiquette. Many sound gruff and threatening on the telephone. Set people at ease with a pleasant and courteous voice. Treat the caller with kindness and express appreciation for their call. Much good can be accomplished for the pulpit, when it is reinforced by timely and sincere calls to members (Eph. 4:1-3).

The Minister and Other Ministers

First, respect your co-workers. Realize individual personalities and the unique effectiveness of them. Treat co-workers with loving respect and as equals. Never undercut them and do not fall victim to jealousy when some prefer them. Work together as yoked men to get the job done; then your pulpit efforts will be praised by them and the church (Eph. 4:3).

Second, be humble, loving and cooperative toward visiting speakers. Showing true courtesy and make them feel welcome. Beware lest you envy them. Then when people observe your good treatment of these men and they compliment you to the congregation, your influence will be heightened (Titus 3:2).

Third, treat other local preachers as men of God. Do not needlessly criticize them. Making yourself look good at the expense of another man is wrong. His methods, modes and schedules are his; you must respect them. Pray for other churches and their ministers. Compliment them and their congregations as often as is possible and people will respect you more.

Fourth, men of God must be cautious of jealousy. Can we honestly appreciate the efforts of others? The brethren know whether or not we can. Do we dare envy a brother when God is blessing him? Are we so insecure that the good works of others annoy us? If we wait until a missionary leaves and then "run him down" to the church, will they not lose respect for us? If we are subjected to careless bigotry and we refuse to engage in it, we earn the respect and the listening ear of our audiences (1 Tim. 1:5).

The Minister's Style

First, the preacher must be punctual. When we say we will be somewhere we should be on time. Our word must be our bond. Call to apologize when you cannot keep an appointment. The reason that so many people think a minister does not have anything to do is often because of carelessness and thoughtlessness. This withers pulpit effectiveness (2 Tim. 4:13).

Second, be honest. Should the man of God tell his wife to tell people that he is not home when he is? What will this do to people when they discover this untruth? Do we preach on liberality and give only five or $10 ourselves? Do we get involved in marketing secular products so that people do not know if we're coming as a minister or a salesman? Honesty and ethics boost listeners attention; they know we practice what we preach (Rom. 12:17).

Third, be friendly. The man of God must be easy to approach. Many men bemoan that they are not liked or appreciated when they are the cause of scowls and insolence. Friendliness must not be a facade.

Fourth, the pulpit is not the place for revenge, and those who use the pulpit to get even with anyone will damage their influence. Overt or disguised barbs are actually a form of cowardice. Keep the preaching centered on Christ. Work out personal difficulties on the side and the influence in the speaker's stand will stay strong.

The Minister's Duties

First, set a daily schedule. Few things harm a man's influence more than not rising early in the morning. Establish a schedule and follow it. The best way to show people we work more than one day a week is to be seen moving among the people.

Second, be accessible. All people, including preachers, need privacy. Jesus had a habit of taking time to be alone. Some ministers are missing continually. They keep no regular schedule of any sort. During emergencies and death no one can find them, not even their wife. Unless prior arrangements are secured, be available to people when they need you and they will be available for you when you preach (2 Tim. 2:21).

Third, we can never please everyone or fill every request but we can do our best. Stay honest with self and the Lord. You will win the respect of the church.

Fourth, be alert to ministerial duties. Visit the sick in the hospital; check on them when they go home. The request to conduct a funeral should be viewed as an honor. Go immediately to the family when they suffer the loss of a loved one. Express heartfelt sorrow, maintain dignity, offer Scripture reading and prayer. Your presence will be deeply appreciated. These people will want to know what you have to say in the pulpit.

The Minister's Example

First, be an example before the congregation. Know that everything going on in a worship is vital and act accordingly. If people see us smirk or act silly, they take it a step further. We must maintain proper posture, attitude and facial expression since people are constantly observing our actions.

Second, be an example in public. We represent the congregation to the community. If we stay pleasant, bring honor to Christ and create a favorable image without sacrificing the truth, we endear ourselves to members and visitors alike. I have known men who threw fits at the public library, bawled out the grocery store clerk, and told the school board "a thing or two." Their influence was set back for years with such exhibitions (Titus 2:8).

Third, be an example in evangelism. Ministers frequently mention the importance of sharing the Gospel with others and yet we often get too busy to do it. Evangelism is the responsibility of every member, including the preacher. Preachers must lead, encourage, remind and demonstrate this task.

Fourth, a good working relationship with church leaders is essential. This is established by good communication. Have fellowship time with elders often to learn one another. This establishes good relations. When these leaders have positive experiences their endorsements help people hearken to our message.

Fifth, effective record keeping will allow a minister to see his overall direction and prevent unwanted repetition. The best of minds often fail to retain all that has been preached.

The Minister and the Pulpit

First, be aware of your appearance. The minister must show proper respect for the occasion by his dress. You say a great deal to others before you ever utter a word.

Second, be prepared. Some choose to use notes while others speak without them. A man holding his notes in a special folder conveys the idea that he is prepared and thinks enough of his material to protect it.

Third, consider your style. Every style is unique and can be very effective. Look at the audience. Modulate the voice according to the passion engendered by the subject. Use gestures markedly. Vary the rate of speech. Put proper emphasis where it belongs.

Fourth, perhaps the most important matter that influences an audience is sincerity. A sincere man who transfers that sincerity to his audience will have a far reaching influence. Even a hint of insincerity, doubt or lack of confidence in what is presented will provide negative results. Certainly we will deal in areas where we can tell the audience of differing opinions, but for those basic doctrinal matters we must be totally sold on Scripture as the answer.

Fifth, some men use themselves for examples too much. They disguise illustrations that are actually ways of bringing one's family and accomplishments to the listener's ear. Listeners are easily disgusted with displays of boasting rather than allowing the Word of God to display expertise.

I once left a convention early and stopped to worship with a small congregation. I noticed that the minister, whom I had seen at the convention, used the same illustration I had heard another use at the convention and apply it to himself. He probably never figured anyone would have been present that heard the original. The same problem occurs when men plagiarize sermons. Honesty is always the best policy.

Conclusion

Men of God, your influence is a most important aspect of your role as a preacher. Your influence in the pulpit has a direct relationship to the influence you earn outside the pulpit. Never do anything that will cause shame to be brought on your name. Strive to be the best you can be. You are a man of God.

Don DeLukie attended White's Ferry Road School of Biblical Studies (A.A.) and Alabama Christian School of Religion (B.A., M.A.). He has served as an instructor at both schools. His current ministry is with the Jackson Street Church of Christ in Monroe, Louisiana. His writing experience includes contributing editor in *Christian Family Magazine* and editor of *Far and Near*. His ministry includes extensive work in foreign missions.

Encouraging Men to Preach

Warren Wi

We need men who will devote their lives to full-time work in the kingdom. Many opportunities exist to spread the Gospel. If men do not rise to the call, the Word will not be given to the world within our lifetimes. Those who deny their call show they have misunderstood the main purpose of being God's workmanship, that is, to do good works (Eph. 2:10). There is a crying need for thousands more to spread the Word. There are many churches in the United States that do not have a full-time minister. Simply stated, we need more preachers.

Sources of Encouragement

Sources of encouragement which may result in men becoming preachers include parents, church leaders, wives, young ladies, schools and universities. More parents should plan for, prepare and encourage their sons to become preachers. With today's attitude of success based on the attainment of wealth and prestige, fewer parents have any real desire for their sons to enter a work force that has relatively low pay, few health or retirement benefits, questionable job security, and which might even take them to some distant land.

Church leaders have a responsibility to encourage others to preach. Large churches generally have the greater opportunity to do this due to numbers and funds. Church leaders sometimes fail to recognize the severe shortage of preachers world-wide and offer little encouragement to their members to consider preaching as a life-work.

Current ministers, one would think, would be more than zealous in making sure their own work in the kingdom would not be hindered in the next generation by lack of workers. Yet many ministers see such frustration, discouragement, pain and sorrow, they actually discourage hopeful young prospects from further consideration of the work by relating their own disappointments. Usually this is not done intentionally but in casual conversation over a period of time.

In many circumstances a faithful, loving, Christian wife may be the one who can best encourage her husband to preach. Many men are preaching today because of gentle persuasion from a devoted helper. In all circumstances the wife must be considered before a man makes a decision to preach. But when the wife is willing, and sees potential in her husband to do this great work for the Lord , that husband needs to seriously consider her encouraging observations.

Likewise, ladies, both young and old, need to be supportive of men becoming preachers. Single women have commented that they would never date a man who wanted to become a preacher because they would not want to be married to a preacher. This may reflect a particular home situation more than an understanding of what might be involved in being a preacher's wife. Parents of young ladies help determine their daughter's attitudes toward spiritual values in life and could cause such attitudes as those described. The fact is some men have not seriously considered ministry, or have given up preparing for it, because of such comments.

Sources of encouragement also include Christian colleges and universities, schools of preaching and similar places where men receive an education. By offering classes in the Bible and in practical aspects of ministry, men are better equipped to face the task of preaching.

Until more good men receive encouragement to enter the rather difficult but extremely rewarding work called ministry, the task Jesus left to be done on earth will not be accomplished.

Should we then encourage every man among us to become a full-time preacher of the gospel? Obviously not. God does not expect everyone to perform the same function (1 Cor. 12:14-30). This was not true relative to miraculous gifts; certainly it is not today as we see individuals with various God-given talents making up the body.

Some have suggested that everyone ought to be ministers because after her persecution the early church "went about preaching the word" (Acts 8:4). However, in this discussion, ministers refer to those who will be working with congregations in a full-time capacity. It is easy to see that everyone in the early church was not a "full-time" preacher, even though everyone shared the Gospel.

Who, then, should be encouraged to become this special worker for God? Someone who has tried everything else and could not succeed? Someone who has the gift of gab? Someone who is out of a job and believes preaching would be a fairly easy work? Someone who wants the power to stand before others and tell them what to do and not to do? Hardly. Many other chapters of this book deal with who the preacher really is and what he is to be. It should be clear that everyone is not expected or blessed with the gifts necessary to be a preacher, but others are and they need to be encouraged.

One group that needs special encouragement is new converts. Many of them have lived lives far away from God. When they receive forgiveness, they want to share the same opportunity with others. Some who "grew up in the church" often do not have the same urgency and drive as new converts. However, if new converts are not encouraged to act while they are so appreciative, time seems to steal away that sense of excitement and urgency they had as new Christians. This same encouragement should be extended to Christians who have fallen away and have then been restored to that wonderful relationship with Jesus, as they often share the same feelings as new converts.

We need to identify those who show special potential for serving as ministers. While our observations won't always be right, we need to encourage those who appear to have potential. We need to be aware that some we may not think could ever "make it," will also turn out to be faithful preachers of the Gospel. Some of us might not have picked Peter to be an elder, but there is no limit to what God can do with a man who will let God use him. We need to try and look beyond the physical only and see man as God sees him (cf. 1 Sam. 16:7).

Methods of Encouragement

If we want more full-time, dedicated, qualified, spiritually-minded preachers, we must encourage our young men to become preachers by training them through our local Bible classes. While classes are good for all ages, it is also valuable to offer classes to help develop men to make an educated decision as to whether or not they would desire to preach. One-on-one meetings with current preachers and church leaders are also valuable.

Someone once asked, "What if we got preachers the same way we get elders?" By that he meant that the congregation would look around among its members, find people whom they thought fit the basic scriptural requirements, put their names up for a couple of weeks, and if there were no objections they became the new preachers. This does not seem to be a good idea, but we do need to look at training men in our congregations. This is basically the concept on which "schools of preaching" were based. With a view toward applying 2 Timothy 2:2, they use the local congregation as a basis for educating and training men to preach. At one time 51% of all preachers in the United States had graduated from a school of preaching. A local congregation need not feel that it must have its own school of preaching, but it ought to consider how it will fulfill 2 Timothy 2:2.

Another way encouragement can be given is by getting every capable, experienced, local preacher to choose one man to train to be a preacher. Many of our present ministers were educated and trained like this. This method has the double advantage of showing the chosen individual how much confidence the experienced preacher has in him and providing on-the-job training. If thousands of preachers would take the time to choose and train just one man per decade, think how much encouragement would be provided back to the man, the congregation, and the lost who were converted by these preachers.

One of the most effective ways to encourage men to think about preaching is to actually let them preach for the congregation. There have been many whose first thought about becoming a full-time preacher came after someone asked them to "fill-in" for the local preacher. This is not to be confused with just allowing them to "give a devotional talk" at some gathering, although sometimes this too can be a beginning. If an offer is extended to present an entire sermon, and guidance is given in preparing and delivering it, many young men will be encouraged to consider preaching for the Lord on a regular basis.

Conclusion

One author said there is no shortage of preachers, just a shortage of good preachers. It certainly is true there is a severe shortage of full-time, faithful preachers throughout the world. Some statistics say that 70% of the world's population is without a Bible, let alone a preacher. With this in mind, the need to encourage more to preach is seen not just as a good idea but as a necessity.

At present many see the need for more preachers, but something has been holding large numbers of men back from responding to the call. For example, during the five-year period from 1983-1987, there was a 40% decline in enrollment of Bible majors in Christian colleges and universities in the United States. Special offers of scholarships, new bible buildings and increased recruiting have helped stay the decline. However, without vision, purpose and encouragement, the decline is apt to return.

There seems to be looming on the horizon a greater need for even more preachers tomorrow than there is today. The most obvious reason is population growth. World population increased from 3 billion people in 1960 to 5.5 billion in 1992. The Lord's church herself has not kept up the same ratio of growth nor kept up the needed increase in ministers and missionaries to evangelize the added souls.

As we move into whatever time is left for us on earth, let us with faith learn to encourage potential ministers wholeheartedly, understanding that without this new fervor on our part, there may well be no response on their part.

Warren Wilcox attended Abilene Christian University (B.A., M.A.). He has served as instructor, director and academic dean at the Bear Valley School of Biblical Studies in Denver, Colorado, since 1966.

MAN of GOD

Part 4 — His Study

The Preacher As a Man of the Word

Earl D. Edw.

To understand the role of the preacher portrayed in the New Testament it seems best to consider the letters Paul wrote to Timothy and Titus.

Timothy and Titus were frequent traveling companions of Paul and he used them as messengers to various churches (2 Cor. 6:6-7; 8:6-17; Titus 1:5; 3:12). Certainly if any of the evangelists of the New Testament ever enjoyed a position of confidence and trust it was these two. Therefore, if there is any difference in the authority possessed by an evangelist today and these two men, the balance would tip in favor of them as having more authority or more ample powers because of their close association with Paul.[1]

The Assigned Work

Two key passages aid in understanding what Paul wanted them to do:

Preach (*keruxon*) the word; be ready (*epistethi*) in season and out of season, reprove (*elegxon*), rebuke (*epitimeson*) and exhort (*parakaleson*) — with great patience (*makrothumia*) and instruction (*didache*) … But you be sober in all things, endure hardship, do the work of an evangelist (*euangelistou*) fulfill your ministry (*diakonian*) (2 Tim. 4:2, 5).[2]

> Until I come, give attention to public reading (*anagnosei*) of the
> Scripture, to exhortation (*paraklesei*) and to teaching
> (*didaskalia*) ... take pains with these things; be absorbed in them,
> so that your progress may be evident to all (1 Tim. 4:13, 15).

It is important to note in the latter of these two passages it is said
these are the things Timothy is to be absorbed in. These things con-
stitute his work as the apostle defined it. If one can understand the
single elements of these admonitions, he will have understood
Timothy's mission.

First, Paul tells Timothy to "do the work of an evangelist (*euangelistou*)" (2 Tim. 4:5). In giving the specifics of his duty he tells him
to "preach (*keruxon*) the word" — that is, do the work of a preacher
(2 Tim. 4:2). It seems necessary to observe that the two terms are,
from a practical standpoint, synonymous.[3] Timothy's mission is that
of preaching the Word. He must continually be about his task. In
fact, the word translated "be ready" (*epistethi*) means "be on hand."[4]
He must be ready to go into action at all times accepting every
opportunity to preach the Word.

Timothy is to "reprove" (*elegxon*) which means to correct in the
sense of refuting.[5] He is to refute what does not correspond to the
Word he is preaching.

He must also "rebuke" (*epitimeson*). This is a strong verb. Some
translators have even translated it as "menace" or its equivalent,[6] but
the proper idea indicates that one speaks a serious warning to prevent an action.[7]

Timothy was duty bound to "exhort" (*parakaleson*) which means
to "appeal to."[8] The action envisioned is much gentler and milder
than rebuke. The evangelist must know how to adapt his tone to the
precise need of the moment, at times being very firm when such is
necessary, and in other moments using a more gentle approach.

Paul taught Timothy to carry these duties forth "with great
patience" (*makrothumia*) and "instruction" (*didache*). Patience is
forbearance toward others which means to be long-suffering.[9]
Vincent affirms that "long-suffering is to be maintained against the
temptations to anger presented by the obstinacy and perverseness of
certain hearers; and such are to be met, not merely with rebuke, but
also with sound and reasonable instruction in the truth."[10]

Anger and threatenings serve no good purpose. To fulfill his duty
as an evangelist, Timothy needed to be ready and willing to endure
hardship. Further, Timothy's mission included: public reading of
Scripture (*te anagnosei*) and teaching (*te didaskalia*). The King James

Version has "reading," but the New American Standard Bible is more precise in translating it "public reading." Though the word sometimes refers to just any reading, it is also used in the New Testament to refer to the public reading of the Scriptures,[11] especially in the Jewish synagogues. Since Timothy was to "preach the word" it makes sense that he was to do a lot of "public reading of the scripture."

Timothy is told to give attention to exhortation and to teaching. This, too, is likely public teaching. In fact, it is difficult to distinguish between the terms "preaching" and "teaching" in numerous biblical contexts.[12]

Man of the Word

These are the principal elements of the mission of Timothy and Titus. It needs to be emphasized that every aspect of their work had meaning only as related to the Word. Indeed, the preacher as Paul describes him in these epistles is a man of the Word whose mission consists of spreading the Good News everywhere. It is logical that Paul tells the evangelist to guard that message carefully and to continue in what he has learned, proclaiming only sound words. Paul's gospel message was clearly a perfect one. The man of God has the duty of presenting it without even the slightest change. He will be a good servant only if he continues to warn the brethren of the grave danger of departing from the Word (1 Tim. 4:1-6).

Kerux

Notice the titles and descriptive terms applied to the group of men under discussion. In this manner it will be possible to understand their mission more fully. The New Testament commonly uses three terms to describe public proclamation. The three are *katangeleus*,[13] *euangelistes*[14] and *kerux*. This study will include only the word *kerux*. It is being singled out because it is deemed to be the most significant for our understanding of the role of the preacher.

Kerux appears, in its various forms, three times in the New Testament. One of these is in 2 Peter 2:5, where Peter speaks of Noah as a "preacher (*keruka*) of righteousness." The other two occurrences are in the epistles under investigation (1 Tim. 2:7; 2 Tim. 1:11).

In the first of these Paul affirms that he himself "was appointed a preacher (*kerux*) and an apostle," and in the second he repeats that he was appointed a preacher (*kerux*), an apostle, and a teacher." Several translations, including the New International Version, render *kerux* in both of these passages with the term "herald."

In these passages Paul is not only an apostle, but also a teacher and a herald. Apostles, inasmuch as they preached, could also call themselves evangelists, but certainly there were many evangelists who were not apostles in the more limited sense of the term apostle.[15]

Though *kerux* is not used to describe Timothy or Titus in these epistles, it is applied to Paul to describe a particular work he did which was identical to that work assigned to Timothy and Titus.

Work of Timothy and Titus

Kerux is defined as one "whose duty it is to make public proclamations ... in a religious sense, preacher, one who proclaims."[16] Beyond this simple definition, the historical background offers insight into New Testament usage of the term.

From Greek literature we learn that the *kerux* had to submit to a voice test to see if he had a deep resonant voice so that his message, which he frequently had to cry out from a distance, could be heard.[17]

An important fact about the work of the *kerux* is seen in the laws of Plato:

> If anyone, while acting as an ambassador or herald (*kerux*), conveys false messages from his state to another state, or fails to deliver the actual message he was sent to deliver, or is proved to have brought back, as an ambassador or herald, either from a friendly or hostile nation, their reply in a false form — against all such there shall be laid an indictment for breaking the law by sinning against the sacred messages and injunctions of Hermes and Zeus, and an assessment shall be made of the penalty they shall suffer or pay, if convicted.[18]

This kind of warning became necessary because of the abuse of certain heralds who claimed authority inserting their own ideas in the message, whereas a true kerux would not be guilty of such.[19]

In the Septuagint one gains insight into the office of the *kerux*.[20] The term appears four times. In Genesis 41:43 *garah* refers to servants of Pharaoh who went before Joseph's chariot to cry out to the people to bow in submission. In Daniel 3:4 it is used to describe a servant of Nebuchadnezzar's who calls upon the people to worship the king's image. In the Pseudepigrapha book of 4 Maccabees 6:4, it describes a similar servant of the King Antiochus IV. Finally, in the Apocrypha book of Sirach 20:15, it is used figuratively for raising one's voice.

The *kerux,* in the Greek world, was a man with a good speaking voice who was given the responsibility of delivering the message of someone in authority. It should be noted that he was to see that it was delivered exactly as he received it.

The biblical *kerux* does not correspond to this description in every particular, but this picture of the *kerux* does have a great deal in common with the *kerux* of the New Testament. The message of the biblical *kerux* is a message from God. Second, the message is sent to persons estranged from God who need reconciliation (Rom. 5:8-10). It is therefore extremely important that not one iota of that reconciling message be changed. God's thoughts, not those of the *kerux*, must be communicated. The preacher is to be a man of the Word. He is to preach what God wants preached and not what he or his audience might desire.

Conclusion

The preacher must understand that to be a man of the Word he must resist the tendency to give the kind of entertainment that some audiences desire. The protestant preacher, William M. Willimon, asks why it is out of style to preach expositorily on a biblical text. He answers, "people want to be entertained rather than converted."[21] To the person who responds that Jesus also used stories in his preaching, Willimon responds, "When Jesus preached in stories, he meant to convict, to convert, to subvert. We mean to entertain and amuse. Intention is everything."[22] Preachers, who are serious about being men of the Word will do as Paul instructs and preach the Word (2 Tim. 4:2).

Endnotes

1. Cf. Donald Guthrie, *New Testament Introduction* (London: Tyndale Press, 1963) 215. It is stated that Timothy and Titus were not only evangelists, but "apostolic delegates" as well. He assumes they had more ample powers than their modern-day counterparts.

2. 2 Tim. 4:2, 5. All quotations of the biblical text will be from New American Standard Bible (Nashville: Holman Publishers, 1960) unless otherwise stated.

3. Later in this essay it will be necessary to discuss the term *kerux* (herald or preacher), although it is never applied to either Timothy or Titus. In the New Testament it is applied only to Noah (2 Peter 2:5) and to Paul (1 Tim. 2:7; 2 Tim. 1:11), but it seems clear that any evangelist is, at the same moment, a preacher or herald (*kerux*). Therefore, to get the fullest picture possible of this office or function, it seems necessary to discuss both terms.

4. Bauer, *A Greek-English Lexicon*, p. 330. Cf. its usage in 2 Tim. 4:6; Acts 28:2.

5. Bauer, 249. Cf. its usage in Matt. 18:15; Luke 3:19.

6. Cf. Fulvio Nardoni, *La Bibbia* (Sancasciano Val di Pesa, Italy: Editrice Fiorentina, 1968) who translates the word "minaccia" (English—menace).

7. Bauer, 303. Cf. its usage in Mark 8:32-33.

8. Bauer, 617. Cf. its usage in Titus 1:9.

9. Bauer, 488. Cf. its usage in Col. 3:12-13.

10. Marvin R. Vincent, *Word Studies in the New Testament*, vol. 3, (New York: G. Scribner's Sons, 1990) 319.

11. Bauer, 52. Note also its usage in Luke 4:16, Acts 13:15; 2 Cor. 3:14. Cf. the *New English Bible* (Cambridge University Press, 1970) which also translates "public reading" in this passage.

12. *Katangeleus*. Cf. Alford, *The Greek New Testament*, vol. 3, p. 382 where the author comments that it is difficult to distinguish between "teaching," "evangelization," and "preaching." Some have tried to make a clear distinction between preaching (to sinners) and teaching (to Christians). Leroy Garrett sustained that it "is utterly impossible to preach the gospel to the brethren ... the N.T. says nothing of preaching to the church" (Teaching and Preaching," *Bible Talk* [Jan. 1953]: p. 51), but that was well refuted by J.W. Roberts ("The Located Preacher," *The Firm Foundation* [24 April 1953]: 1ff.) who pointed out that both Paul (Acts 20:27 — *anangello*), and John (1 John 1:5 — *angello*) preached to people who were already Christians.

13. Used only in Acts 17:18 and translated "proclaimer."

14. Used only three times in the New Testament: Acts 21:8; Eph. 4:8-12; 2 Tim 4:5. It is generally translated "evangelist."

15. Timothy (2 Tim. 4:5) is one example, and Philip (Acts 21:8) is another.

16. Bauer, 431.

17. Demosth. *Orat*. 19, 338, Loeb Classical Library (Cambridge: Harvard University Press, 1926).

18. Plato. *Leg*. 12. 941, Loeb Classical Library (Cambridge: Harvard University Press, 1926).

19. Cf. Carroll D. Osburn, *How Much Authority Does the Preacher Have?* (The Firm Foundation, 1979): 70.

20. This translation was made in Alexandria, Egypt, and was concluded around 150 B.C.

21. "Preaching—Entertainment or Exposition?," *Christian Century* 28 Feb. 1990: 204

22. "Preaching," 204.

Earl D. Edwards began preaching in 1952. He holds degrees from David Lipscomb University (B.A.), Harding Graduate School of Religion (Th.M.) and Trinity Evangelical Divinity School (D. Miss.). He served as missionary in Italy (1960-76). He was professor and dean at the Florence Bible School in Italy, professor of Missions at Harding University, assistant professor of Bible and Missions, dean of the School of Biblical Studies, and now as director of Graduate Studies in Bible at Freed-Hardeman University. He is the director of the Freed-Hardeman Church Leaders' Forum.

The Importance of Biblical Languages

Jack P. Lewis

The necessity for the study of the biblical languages — Hebrew, Aramaic and Greek — by the preacher is stated convincingly by the writer of the prologue to Ecclesiasticus:

> For what was originally expressed in Hebrew does not have exactly the same sense when translated into another language. Not only this work, but even the law itself, the prophecies, and the rest of the books differ not a little as originally expressed.

Haddon W. Robinson compared the reading of the Bible in the original languages and in translation to the difference in watching color and black and white television. The show is the same, but the vividness and precision is different.[1]

It is standard procedure in universities that a person who is working on a dissertation must be able to read the languages in which his primary sources occur. He must often also read French and German. Anyone can see that a serious student of Luther must know German, and a serious student of Shakespeare must know English.[2] Perhaps indeed the sons of this world are wiser in their generation than the sons of light.

Can a preacher study his English Bible and preach without learning Hebrew and Greek? Certainly he can. But the answer to be given to the question is largely dependent on how he and his audience define his work.

CHAPTER TWENTY-ONE

Here at the end of the 20th century — when counseling, social work, church administration, church growth, missions and a host of other disciplines demand preparation time — it is very persuasive to assume that knowledge of languages is a luxury, not a necessity. Biblical languages get short changed in the present theological curriculum.

If the preacher is the cheerleader of the congregation, its counselor, its social worker or its current social theorist, he probably can do all of those tasks without knowledge of the original biblical languages. If a preacher's sermon is to be a mere summarization of what has appeared in the popular journals and books, he probably will not need biblical languages. A lot of current preaching has little to do with the biblical text. One said of current preaching:

> We are no longer going to save the world by "the folly of what we preach"; we are going to save it by efficient church administration, pastoral psychology, liturgical esthetics, social pronouncements, and the like. We are so busy with the mechanics of church life that we throw our sermons together from ideas culled from the latest books and fail to take seriously the Book of books. The popularity of topical preaching over biblical preaching is one evidence of this.[3]

If, on the other hand, the preacher, like Ezra, sets his task as studying the law of the Lord, doing it and teaching His statutes and ordinances in Israel (Ezra 7:10), the languages become essential. If one is to be an expositor of Scripture, then he matures in that through a life-long study of the languages of Scripture.

A translation (old or new) by its very nature is an interpretation of the original, and its use perpetuates that interpretation. The committee that made the translation was not in total agreement about what that interpretation should be in numerous details. One can expound the interpretation the majority chose, but to challenge its accuracy at any point one has to know the languages. Without languages one can only compare it with translations he has known before, while assuming that they are a reliable standard. He has no way to know if a certain translation is defective.

Our age is an age that pragmatically seeks instant results. If I want a pie, I can buy a ready-made crust, ready-mixed pie filling and ready-mixed meringue. I can put them together, add heat and feel that I have baked a pie; but the outcome is quite different from learning to cook and making a pie, as any taster knows.[4] The modern preacher wants what he can use before Tuesday morning. While the authorities he is dependent on went through the discipline of learning the languages, he seems to think he can short-cut the process and obtain equal depth without the pain of discipline. It just cannot be done. The lack of depth is obvious.

Let us consider some of the values to be gained in studying Hebrew, Aramaic and Greek.

Learning His Own Language

Every student who has learned either Hebrew or Greek will attest that he learned more English in the process than he did of either of the languages. One has only to listen to preachers a few minutes to know that many of them do not know the difference between nominative and accusative pronouns in English. They have not learned subjects, predicates and modifiers. Yet preaching is communicating through the use of language. There is no way to preach without skillful use of one's own language. A curriculum committee of the Presbyterian church reported in 1959, "There is a direct relationship between the knowledge of English grammar and facility in the study of Greek and Hebrew."[5]

The Pronunciation of Names

Both the Old Testament and New Testament are full of names which one hears slaughtered when read from the pulpit, not to mention when read by the person in the pew. English Bibles usually transliterate these names, but they have come third-handed. First there was transliteration into Greek, then Latin and finally English. New Testament names not taken from the Old Testament have the last two of these stages. Modern translations translate many names that the KJV transliterated, but some still remain — "Akeldama" (Acts 1:19), "Abaddon" and "Apollyon" (Rev. 9:11), and "Armageddon" (Rev. 16:16). Once one has learned the original languages, the pronunciation of names becomes simple.

Beyond the proper names, there are also transliterated words. How many ways have you heard Jesus' words from the cross read (Mark 15:34)? Yet they are clear Semitic words. Words like *Corban* (Mark 7:11), *Talitha kumi* (Mark 5:41), *Ephphatha* (Mark 7:34) and *Maranatha* (1 Cor. 16:21) are pronounceable and explainable Semitic expressions.

Evaluating Translations

There are now more than 25 English translations of the Bible in circulation, as well as many paraphrases. No two are exactly alike.

How, other than being able to check the wording in its original, can one know which is preferable on a specific passage? Shall one check the new translation by the KJV or ASV and condemn everything that differs? Such a procedure can only be based on the erroneous assumption that the KJV or ASV were perfect, a claim which their producers never made. Shall one check his favorite commentary and follow its lead? No two commentaries are exactly alike. Shall he trust the opinion of his favorite teacher or preacher?

There is no way to know which translation is the more accurate other than by checking it by what the writer originally wrote in Hebrew, Aramaic or Greek. So-called "dynamic equivalence" is popular now in translation; but how can one judge whether the equivalence actually exists? Paraphrase is also popular, in which the paraphraser attempts to state in different words from those used by the writer the concepts the writer set forth. How is one to judge the accuracy of the paraphrase? How is one to know that the KJV translation of the word "Easter" (Acts 12:4) is incorrect.

Biblical Languages In Order To Know

Even with all the other demands on his time, the preacher still should consider himself first and foremost an expert in the Word of God. The Gospel — not cross cultural studies, not counseling, not church administration, not social work — is the power of God unto salvation. The proper meaning of Scripture deals with people's eternal welfare. Shall one pass himself off as an expert, saying to people, "You can trust your souls on what I say," when he can only read that Word in translation? Shall I be dependent only on those I think knew?

John Reuchlin said in pre-Reformation times:

I would have you know that nobody of the Latin people has been able to give an exact explanation of the Old Testament without having first had knowledge of the language in which it was written.[6]

Martin Luther agreed:

While a preacher may preach Christ with edification though he may be unable to read the Scriptures in the originals, he cannot expound or maintain their teaching against the heretics without this indispensable knowledge.[7]

Flacius, a post-Reformation figure expressed the same idea:

The first [understanding seeks to ascertain] how the readers understood the individual words. This demands the best possible command of the sacred languages, above all of Hebrew, and then also of Greek. Without that, O Reader, you are necessarily dependent on the judgement of others, or you must guess at the meaning. Along with that if you do not at once take notice of what he had in mind or of how in the passage in question he has used or misused his words.[8]

This view of the value of biblical languages for meeting error is not limited to Reformation times:

Theological education which neglects the study of Hebrew is like a house built on sand and the flood of the various theological views, the many religious and secular claims, can easily lift it from its foundations and sweep it away to destroy it in the tides of the times. Only genuine and concerned study and understanding of the Old Testament, which is undergirded by a knowledge of Hebrew, can provide and serve as a sure foundation and bulwark against the flood of claims, e.g. ancient and modern Gnosticism, antinomianism, Jesusolatry, or Christomonism and against the various forms of anti-semitism, which mark Christian history.[9]

A.D. Nock, pleading for a thorough knowledge of the Greek language, said:

Even a reasonable mastery of language gives a key that unlocks not only much beauty that would otherwise be hidden but also modes of intellectual approach, and a reasonable mastery of Greek might save a man from easy verbalizations about abstract questions. It is of course not enough to know the Greek alphabet and to identify the words of the Authorized Version in the Greek, like the student who gave what was a correct version of the story of the head of John the Baptist being brought on a charger, but did not know what a charger was. I hope that we shall always here insist that graduate students of the New Testament learn something more than Biblical Greek.[10]

The available translations are good and are adequate enough for a person to learn the general message of the Bible, but when it comes to fine points, more accuracy is needed. No other literature in the world has had such careful work expended on it as the Bible. Yet any biblical word has more than one meaning. Any English word has more that one meaning. There is not a 100% equivalence in moving from one language to another. Suppose the translator selects meaning number three as the likely meaning of a Hebrew or Greek word in a particular setting and as equivalent to meaning two of an English word. The reader, however, knows meaning number four for that English word. He will miss the true import of the passage. A person once asked me if being sealed with the Spirit meant that one was filled with it. He reasoned that one seals a full bottle not a part empty one. It had not occurred to him that his meaning for seal was not the one Paul was using.

One cannot conduct an analytical study of the Bible without a knowledge of languages; he cannot engage in a word study; he cannot adequately deal with a biblical concept. Such basic tools as the *Theological Dictionary of the New Testament*, the *Dictionary of New Testament Theology*, and the *Theological Dictionary of the Old Testament* are closed to him. Even an elementary work like *Vine's Expository Dictionary of New Testament Words* will have much that he has no way to grasp. He can consult lexicons, but he has no adequate equipment for choosing between options they offer.

Knowledge of biblical languages is for understanding, not for impressing the Sunday audience by how many foreign words are sprinkled into the message. With languages, as in other areas, a little learning is a dangerous thing. Take the English word "mark" which is most widely known in the meaning of "brand." So in sincerity one deduces the duty to brand every person whom one supposes is an erroneous teacher. But the original did not say that at all. *Skopein* (Rom. 16:17; cf. Phil. 3:17) merely means "take notice of." If one is to know whether the man in Thessalonica was "disorderly" (1 Thess. 5:14; 2 Thess. 3:6, 7, 11) in the sense of breaking rules or was the "idle" man, either he is going to have to be able to read the original language for himself or he must trust someone who will tell him.

In English "a man," "the man," and "man" are three distinct concepts. Yet the translations have not been consistent in inserting or omitting the article. "Great tribulation" (Matt. 24:21; Rev. 2:22) is a different concept from "the great tribulation" (Rev. 7:14). How can one know that Paul wrote "there is no male and (*kai*) female (Gal. 3:28) rather than "neither male nor female" as the KJV and RSV have it?

When English used "man" for both humanity and for the male, how can one, apart from a knowledge of Greek, really know whether a passage is speaking of everyone or speaking of males? With gender inclusive language "man" is no longer used for humanity except in the word "human." In Greek *aner* (cf. 1 Tim. 2:8, 12) is the male, but *anthropos* can be inclusive.

In conveying their messages, the Hebrew prophets played on words as a literary technique.[11] Plays on words cannot be translated from one language to another. Footnotes of our translations try to transliterate some of the plays, but the effort is futile to the person who does not know the original language enough to appreciate them. From the summer fruit (*gayits*), Amos derives the idea that the end (*gets*) of Israel is at hand (Amos 8:2). Jeremiah sees a rod of almond (*shaged*) and is informed that the Lord is watching (*shoged*) over his word to perform it (Jer. 1:11-12). The people ask is there any oracle (*massa'*) from the Lord, and Jeremiah seems to reply, "you are the burden (*massa'*)" the Lord has to endure (Jer. 23:33). When Jeremiah says that the opposing prophets become wind (Jer. 5:13), the Hebrew reader knows that he is playing on the fact that their claim of spirit guidance is being pointedly denied, for the words spirit and wind in Hebrew are both *ruach*.

Every biblical question ultimately has to be answered by consideration of what a writer wrote in Hebrew, Aramaic or Greek and by what he meant by those words. Those who can read the languages are in a position to work on the question. Others are dependent on those who can read the original language.

Literary Style

Each writer of the Bible has his own vocabulary and his own style of expressing himself. Only in limited ways can these be conveyed in translation. Hebrew has its distinct, colorful idioms to be grasped only by those who read Hebrew. The Hebrew says, "the Lord uncovered my ear"; English has "the Lord revealed to me." Hebrew says "Bless God and die" (Job 2:9) and "Naboth blessed God and the king" (1 Kings 21:10, 13). English says, "Curse God and die" and "Naboth cursed God and the king." The word "curse" had a force in the Hebrew mind not to be released by pronouncing the word; hence, a euphemism is used. Hebrew used the very expressive "God lifted up my face"; English says, "God forgave me."

Hebrew poetry is not composed of rhymed syllables as is often the case with English poetry. Rather it is a matter of stressed syllables in a line that is usually divided into two halves. One particular type of meter is the *qinah* meter used for funeral dirges; but one learns that from Hebrew. Coupled together with rhythm is the phenomenon which is known as parallelism, of which there are various types. These features cannot be duplicated in English. But the Hebrew reader knows that when he reads a parallel he is not to make mountains of difference in theological meaning between its variants. When he preaches on "Therefore the wicked will not stand in the judgment, nor sinners in the congregation of the righteous" (Psalm 1:5), he will recognize the type of parallel used.

The acrostic psalm is based on the Hebrew alphabet, not on the English one. Psalm 119 has 22 sections each of which is composed of eight lines each beginning with the successive letters of the Hebrew alphabet. All that the translator can do with this feature is to transliterate the names of the Hebrew letters at the beginning of the sections.

Most Old Testament names have a meaning connected with the reason for which they are given. They are not always arrived at by strict etymology. Samuel meant "God heard" because his mother asked for him from the Lord (1 Sam. 1:20). Eli's grandson was named Ichabod because his dying mother said, "The glory is departed from Israel" (1 Sam. 4:21). Few people know what "Ebenezer" (1 Sam. 7:12) really means when they sing of it, but it is simple to the Hebrew student.

While these and some other names are explained in the text, others have a meaning which is not explained. The last king of Judah had his name changed by Nebuchadnezzar from Mattaniah, which meant "the Lord gives," to Zedekiah , which means "righteousness of the Lord" (2 Kings 24:17); however, Zedekiah certainly did not prove to be that. There are those figures whose names were at first combinations of the name of Baal — like Ishbaal, Meribaal and Baalyada — that later become a combination of "bosheth" ("shame") when the revolt against Baal worship had taken place.

Vocabulary Implications

Vincent long ago said:

Even as nature fills in the space between the foreground and the background of her landscapes with countless details of form and color, light and shadow, so the rich details of the New Testament words, once apprehended, impart a depth of tone and just a relation and perspective to the salient masses of doctrine, narrative, and prophecy ... .How often a picture or bit of history is hidden away in a word, of which translation gives and can give no hint.[12]

There are theological words in both Hebrew and Greek which have no specific equivalent in English. A word like *chesedh* which occurs 245 times is the subject of much study.[13] Greeks seldom used *charis* for it, for which English uses "grace." Coverdale gave us "lovingkindness" as its translation. But it is not the exact equivalent of any of these. *Shubh* is translated as "repent." But it really means to turn around and go the other direction. It is behavior far more weighty than just being sorry for past actions.

From English one would never know that the word *zera* (KJV: "seed") at times takes feminine modifiers in the Old Testament (Gen. 16:10; 24:60), so that the argument that women do not produce seed becomes a fallacious argument when connected with Genesis 3:15. One would also not know that *nephesh chayyah* (KJV: "living soul"; Gen. 2:7) is not a unique description of man (cf. Gen. 1:24; 9:10). The English reader could never know that the Hebrew feminine word *'almah* (Isa. 7:14) has its masculine equivalent in *'elem*, which merely designates a young man, not his prior sexual experience or lack of it (1 Sam. 17:56; 20:22).

To this point our illustrations have been from Hebrew and Aramaic because even to the preacher who may have dabbled in Greek, knowledge of Hebrew is considered an optional luxury which he never intends to spend time acquiring. When the theological curriculum is cut, it is always Hebrew that goes first. This attitude has been true through most of Christian history, so those scholars of the early period who knew Hebrew are few indeed. Justin Martyr, Origen, Jerome, and a few others put themselves through the Hebrew discipline. Jerome commented:

> I set myself to learn the Hebrew alphabet and to study a language of gutteral and heavy-breathing words. Much effort as I had expended and many the difficulties I had suffered, how many times in desperation did I not break off from a study which the stubborn desire for knowledge made resume again afterwards I alone can testify, I who have toiled so hardy, and with me those who then shared my life. And I render thanks to God for any delicious fruit I now gather from so bitter a sowing.[14]

There are many theological questions whose solution must rest on Greek. Take an expression like "from faith to faith" (*ek pisteos eis pistin*; Rom. 1:17). How many proposals have been made! Yet, there are Greek parallels of the use of the same two prepositions such as translated "to one a fragrance from death to death, to the other a fragrance from life to life" (2 Cor. 2:16). The idiom suggests an intensification.

How is one to know that the verb for care for the church (*epimelestai*; 1 Tim. 2:5) is a different verb from that used for one leading his house (*prostenai*) if he knows no Greek? How can one know that this verb occurs elsewhere in the New Testament only for the care given the wounded man in the Samaritan parable (Luke 10:34-35)? How can he know that the word *exousia* never occurs in the New Testament for the relationship of elders to their people? How can he know that elders are described as being "overseers" in the church (*en ho*; Acts 20:28) rather than "overseers" over the church, as the KJV had it?

How apart from checking the Greek can one be made conscious of the fact that *martys* ("witness"; Heb. 12:1) is never used in the New Testament in the sense of "spectator"? Sermons usually seem to stress the "witness" idea. Another pet sermon vanishes in favor of truth when one realizes that *chazon* of Prov. 29:18 speaks of prophetic insight without which people perish, not of human foresight.

Translation

A missionary of admirable dedication and motives revealed that he and his associates were making a translation of the New Testament into the language of their area. His question was, "Would it be better if we translated the KJV or the RSV? I asked if any in his group knew Greek, and he answered negatively. The goal was admirable, but the process, no matter how carefully done, was doomed to inaccuracy. Each step intervening between the original and the product merely moves the outcome from true representation of what the Holy Spirit inspired.

If these various illustrations, which could be multiplied in an unlimited way, have not convinced the reader of the necessity of biblical languages, perhaps he might be benefited by remembering that there are values in art known to the artist which the non-artist does not know exists. There are values in music known only to those who have put themselves through the discipline of music.

For a preacher to say, "I never studied Hebrew or Greek, and I never missed it," only reflects on the preacher, not on the values in knowing Hebrew or Greek. No person who ever spent enough effort to learn to read his New Testament in Greek or even to check its passages in Greek, and no person who did the same for the Hebrew of the Old Testament would ever make such a statement.

There are about 1600 languages or dialects in which there is still no written Scripture. Some should prepare themselves to make those translations. Others will be needed to make better English translation in the twenty-first century. The door of opportunity opens only to those who are equipped. The preacher cannot learn biblical languages after he has been asked a hard question. If he does not already know, the opportunity will pass by.

Endnotes

1. Haddon W. Robinson, *Biblical Preaching* (Grand Rapids: Baker Book House, 1980) 59.

2. Walter L. Michel, "Why Study Hebrew?," *Dialog* 18 (Winter 1979): 62.

3. Thomas P. Lindsay, "Are the Original Languages Worth Studying?" *The Princeton Seminary Bulletin* 54 (February 1961): 25.

4. E. Earl Ellis, "Language Skills and Christian Ministry," *Reformed Review* 24 (Spring 1971): 162.

5. B.M. Metzger, "On the Study of Hebrew and Greek," *The Princeton Seminary Bulletin* 54 (February 1961): 31.

6. E. G.Rupp, *The Bible in the Age of the Reformation in The Church's Use of the Bible, Past and Present*, Ed. D.E. Nineham (London: S.P.C.K., 1963) 74.

7. B. Ramm, *Protestant Biblical Interpretation* (Grand Rapids: Baker, 1970) 54-55.

8. W.G. Kummel, *The New Testament: The History of the Investigation of Its Problems*, trans. S. McLean Gilmour (Nashville: Abingdon Press, 1972) 29.

9. Michel 62.

10. A.D. Nook, "The Necessity of Scholarship," *Official Register of Harvard University: Harvard Divinity School* 47 (April 1950): 42.

11. Robert B. Chisholm Jr., "Wordplay in the Eighth-Century Prophets," *Bibliotheca Sacra* 144 (January-March 1987): 44-52.

12. Marvin R. Vincent, *Word Studies in the New Testament*, Vol. 1 (Grand Rapids: Eerdmans, 1946) ix.

13. H.J. Zobel, *"chesedh"* in *Theological Dictionary of the Old Testament*, Ed. G.J. Botterweck (Grand Rapids: Eerdmans, 1986) 44-64.

14. Epistle 125.12.

Jack P. Lewis has served as local minister, elder and professor for many years. He is especially noted for his scholarship in the areas of biblical languages and translations. He studied at Abilene Christian University (B.A.), Sam Houston State University (M.A,), Harvard University (Ph.D.) and Hebrew Union College (Ph.D.). He is the author of numerous periodical articles, articles in encyclopedias and books.

The Preacher in His Study

Shawn D. Mathis

The Need for Study

There is a growing tendency for the man of God to be less than a diligent scholar of the Word. At the core of our spiritual passion for Christ should be daily preparation for the life of ministry. Far too many men are content to preach warmed over sermons from years past without ever digging deep into God's Word to develop fresh exegesis.

Of equal consequence is the minister who says, "I don't have time for study. I've got a congregation to care for." A prospective minister was told by an established preacher that many men have misunderstood the work of a preacher as that of being a student (his estimation of a student was one who studied more than 5-10 hours per week). Based on his conviction that there is no real middle ground, he commented: "Either the man studies so much that he cannot work with the people or he works with the people so much that he cannot study and produce a masterpiece every Sunday." As a result he has committed to meeting the needs of the congregation through visitation without practicing serious study. When asked to teach the book of Revelation the preacher responded, "You'll never catch me teaching that book here or anywhere else."

This example represents the problems of a need for discipline in study, an unbalanced approach to ministry, a lack of integrity in dealing with God's Word, and laziness. All of these result from a primary problem: A lack of intense mental discipline in the study of God's mind. Good preaching requires time, energy and hard work.

One great ecclesiastical deficiency is the battered pulpit created by abusive preachers who have failed to comprehend the true nature of our work. God's most honorable arena to herald His work of salvation is the pulpit. To desecrate the pulpit forsakes the supreme work of the man of God — preaching. God forbid that any man make a sacrilege of this noble forum. The birth of this profanity is the disregard and neglect of the Book of God. Knowledge of God's Word is found through exacting study.

The Purpose of Study

The responsibility of study should not cause distance between us and our people, or harm our ministry. If either occurs it may be that we have not properly balanced our ministry.

The purpose of study is to create within the man a special bond with God which causes him to turn toward people in a compassionate and gentle manner. Thank God for people who love the Lord enough to allow us to devote our energy to the proclamation of the teachings of Christ. Study enables us to effectively minister to the people who have made this special time available to us.

Another purpose of study is to wrestle with difficult texts, that there may be simplicity in the pulpit. Personal, first-hand work on the text will equip you to explain it clearly. This form of study brings the preacher's mind, as a messenger of God, into "sympathy with his work as the work of God."[1] Be proud that we have been commissioned to serve God as preachers of the gospel.

The most needed reformation in modern preaching is a heightened interest in expositional preaching. After hearing a preacher quote 60-70 scriptures in a 25-minute sermon, one individual quipped, "He literally went everywhere preaching the Gospel." Proper exegesis and precise exposition of Scripture requires more than a shotgun approach to preaching. "In almost every case you will find that the man who does effective expository work in the pulpit has learned to enjoy the work of the study."[2] Expository preaching demands that the preacher systematically work his way through a passage of scripture with care, thought and considerable time. The preacher should begin studying the Book at a relaxed pace months, even years, before preaching on it. This lays the groundwork. The richest nuggets lie buried in the deepest recesses just waiting to be mined.

The Preacher as a Student

The greatest challenge of the preacher is to be a faithful student of God's Word. Every minute of study is an effort to digest God's inspired revelation. Long hours of careful exegesis based on reverent research and sound scholarship will guide us and our people away from theological and biblical malnutrition. Diligent study serves as a discipline to prepare us for the work at hand.

The preacher must be well studied. It has been said of the studious preacher that "the ordinary preacher becomes a great preacher"[3] and that "great preachers are great students."[4]

We need to possess deep respect for those men who have given their lives in study. Adam Clarke gave forty years of his life in writing his *Commentary on the Bible*.[5] His habits of study, eventually causing the loss of his eyesight, included several hours of writing before daybreak and many hours in the night. Albert Barnes began his massive commentary with the intention of completing only the gospels. His persistent work in the early morning hours serves as an incredible stimulus to be a diligent student. He rose between 4 and 5 o'clock in the morning, writing until 9 o'clock each morning. He then devoted his efforts to the ministry of a large congregation, avoiding any neglect of his ministerial duties. He ascribed his opportunity of writing to,

> the habit which I had formed of spending the early hours of the day in the study of the sacred Scriptures. That habit, continued, has carried me forward until I have reached the end of the New Testament.[6]

Each honest man will commit to a life of intense work in the Sacred Text of God. As we plunge into our study, we will emerge as men of God. Burn with the desire to preach just as Jesus did because you have the distinct privilege of being a man of God (Mark 1:38).

What the Preacher Studies

W.A. Criswell writes that the preacher should, "always preach through some book of the Bible."[7] If this is the case, our study system is clearly planned ahead of time. We will not spend hours rehashing the same old routine of trying to determine what to preach. Systematic exposition demands that a preacher work diligently through a book, milking the text of its riches. If we are to be effective expository preachers we will study scripture with that structure in mind. Approach the Bible book-by-book, persistently studying some particular book for exposition. In the past few years I have preached through Matthew 1-7 with careful emphasis upon the Sermon on the Mount, selected expositions in the gospel of John, James, Genesis 1-11, and the Pauline letters to the Ephesians, Colossians and Philippians.

Using the biblical languages on a daily basis will greatly improve your effectiveness. It is only proper that we engage in daily exegesis of the text, initially focusing our work in the original language. Translation work forces us to become intimately acquainted with our chosen text for exposition.

The Effect of Study on the Preacher

A man of God is to so balance his ministry that sufficient time is available to equip his mind for each message. The Christian preacher earns the mastery of biblical exposition through careful and intense study from many resources; therefore, we must be diligent exercising precision in our preparation.

It is crucial for the man of God to immerse his mind in Scripture. Our ultimate task in life is to know God's Word and to communicate His message into the lives of people. The Bible is our primary area of study. G. Campbell Morgan urged an honorable goal for the preacher by saying that a man should have, "a personal acquaintance that involves first-hand study. God help the man who, when some occasion demands this, has got to go to his concordance to find a text."[8] Too many preachers know much about the Bible and little of the Bible itself. Our primary task is to "master portions of it in exquisite detail and all of it in its general outlines. Moreover, his knowledge of the book should grow until the Bible becomes more precious to him even than life itself."[9]

It is wise to shield time away from the pressures of daily ministry to give devotion to serious reading or study. Our critical arena is not the public assembly but our own private room. This is the workshop where our private habits of systematic study take place. Be rigorous in preserving uninterrupted study time. Most situations that arise do not require immediate attention and can wait until the important time of communion with God is sufficiently cared for that day. Our congregations will love and respect our time with God because they know we are working hard to gain knowledge of the Word. If we are to be good ministers, we must have times for study just as we have times when we work directly with people.

Daily time with God will add a healthy and vigorous agenda for investigation of Scripture. The preacher who plans to remain fresh and strong through the long years will continue vibrant study of the Word. He will resolve to do scholarly exegesis of God's Word. The New Testament preacher would do well to heed the advice of Austin Phelps, who wrote of his own personal struggle of study:

> I speak the less unwillingly to you of that chapter of my life, because there was nothing in my experiment which was the fruit of genius, or in any way exceptional. In kind it was a success which any one of you may achieve, I hope in much greater degree. I beg you to try the experiment for yourselves. Supply your libraries at the outset with the best works in biblical literature. Do not spare your purses in so doing. Wear the old coat, and buy the new book. Incur any hazard or hardship, but those of debt or dishonor, to get your outfit of tools to work with. You must have them early in your ministry, if you are ever to use them. Your wedding can wait, but your library can not. Then systematize your biblical studies, and give yourself to them religiously. Let the garden go unweeded, and let the potatoes rot in the ground. Get rid of church councils, and building committees, and executive miscellanies, so far as you honorably can. Leave social dinners, and the pleasure-parties, and the regattas, and the operas, and the fast horses, to those who need them. Say you, with Nehemiah, to the messengers who tempt you to such things, `I am doing a great work, so that I can not come down: why should the work cease whilst I leave it and come down to you?' Cultivate a stern unity of purpose in your calling of God, and hold to it to the death. Come thus to your biblical sermons with a full mind which aches to deliver itself. Get yourself into a state of biblical production in which your materials for the pulpit shall always crowd you, you never hunting them.[10]

Persistent study is indispensable if one is to minister adequately. One of the most difficult tasks in the life of the preacher is to find adequate time for personal study; nevertheless, we must set study at the top of the priority list in our lives, for close study of Scripture is the life of our preaching.

The ministry is one of the few professions which will insist that we continue daily growth through study in our field. Lawyers and doctors must continue to study, but they do not immerse themselves in this task every day. Textbooks for the lawyer and the doctor change daily, but our textbook remains the same. The Bible, being the only indispensable book in the preacher's library, is the textbook which reveals God's dealings with mankind. We must feel compelled to saturate our minds with the thoughts of the Divine Spirit communicated in the Sacred Text. If we do not possess an insatiable appetite for the Word, then we were not meant to be preachers. This appetite, certain to develop a deeply passionate reverence and awe for the Word of God, will spiritually gird us for the tremendous task of preaching.

The Preacher's Study

The most important development in my spiritual life was the decision to use time daily for simple Bible reading. My practice is to read through the actual text of the Bible two or three times per year. The impact on my life has been immeasurable and I commend the practice to all.

A quiet study, away from the demands of the daily activities at the church building, is a great tool. It is important that the study be that place most suited for communion with God. Congregations often do not trust the preacher enough to grant this important place and time for intense fellowship with God.

For years I dreamed of that perfect study. My congregation was sensitive to my need for a private study away from the church building. Ron McCance, my spiritual friend and partner in ministry, was the master carpenter for the project. It is a place of private study. The benefit is that I am able to go the office to do office work and go to the study to do just that, study. The whole purpose of the room is to study.[11] Arranging exclusive time for study is difficult, however, study is the "main artery of preaching."[12]

The study is my personal sanctuary, a quiet room and sacred place. I feel comfortable in this special place created for time with God. We meticulously selected the mood for the study: the desk longs for the arrival of that intimate friend who once again shares an interlude with Deity, six adjustable flood lamps line the ceiling to offer suitable lighting, the breeze of a ceiling fan circulates the room, bookshelves trail the wall, and an inclined ledge follows its course awaiting the opportunity to hold the thoughts of the ages in book form. This is a special place designed for communion with the mind of God.

My study is a refuge where I find solitude with God and His blessed Scripture, a respite away from the pressures of the world, a retreat for the moment with my God, and a haven of rest to meditate upon the power of God in our lives.

Locked behind the door is the opportunity to go to my knees and bow in the presence of God Almighty. Here I enter His throne room. I beg God for strength to labor in the field, petition Him in behalf of family, and entreat him to forgive my sin that I may enter the pulpit as a pure man of God with a message for spiritual Israel. In God's presence I ask that He will move in the lives of the people I serve. This special time is offered as an opportunity for communication with God and to place our burdens in the palm of his hand.

The preacher is like Moses, who descended from the mountain to instruct God's people. After spending hours of careful study, preparation and prayer over God's Word, we will be ready to descend from our study into the presence of our people with a living message from God.

The preacher is a guardian of the mysteries of God. He studies the truths of the Sacred Text that are known through the revelation of God. In his study the Christian preacher lives and moves in the realm of the supernatural. Preachers are sometimes told they are too other-worldly. Yet when we lose this quality we cease to abide in our true calling of God. We must abide in this spiritual realm until the message of God becomes a passion that burns within us. We must descend the mountain of God to tell the people of Jehovah God.

The Preacher's Schedule

Plan times of serious reading and study from your schedule. One writer said that the preacher was to "burn his weary eyes with study" and "wreck his emotional poise with worry for God."[13] Deep, serious, hard study can produce a man of sound scholarship. Set aside specific times of study which will not allow those disrupting pressures to befall you. Make a conscious effort to plan your study into regularly occurring blocks of uninterrupted study time.

Personally, I find that I need a routine time where I know that I will be in concentration on the Scriptures. The demands of ministry require that I block out sections in my daily calendar two weeks in advance for study. Of course you will need to be flexible. The early hours are least likely to be infringed upon, but daily ministerial needs may occasionally necessitate afternoon hours. I reserve from 5 to 8 a.m. as a time for serious exegesis and writing; from 9 a.m. to noon as a time for office work at the building, ministerial visitation, letter writing, etc.; and from 1 to 5 p.m. I return to the study to learn more of God's Word. The evenings are used for both ministerial and family activities. This schedule is designed to encourage mental intensity with the Word. I feel spiritually deficient if I am unable to maintain a regularly planned nutritional diet of God's Word.

Conclusion

Find the time that is best to produce the most effective study. My dad taught me that it does not matter how many books you read per week or how fast you can read. It is rather a matter of what you learn. His advice was to "be persistent and deliberate in your study."

Decide upon a specific time and place to study, being interrupted only for true emergencies. The study must be quiet and comfortable. Find a comfortable chair and a place to lay your Bible. Make sure you have good lighting.

Guard your time alone with God. This special time is one of the best remedies for spiritual staleness in the man of God because it is here that you seek the face of God. John Stott wrote: "Only a constantly fresh vision of Christ and his commission can rescue us from idleness and keep our priorities correctly adjusted."[14] "Under God, the preacher is an artist."[15]

Endnotes

1. Austin Phelps, *The Theory of Preaching* (New York: Charles Scribner's Sons, 1903) 66.

2. Andrew W. Blackwood, *Expository Preaching for Today* (New York: Abingdon-Cokesbury Press, 1953) 192. The author was the great scholar from Princeton Theological Seminary. This is a practical guidebook about expository preaching.

3. W.A. Criswell, *Criswell's Guidebook for Pastors* 66.

4. Sam E. Stone, *The Christian Minister: A Practical Approach to the Preaching Ministry* (Cincinnati: Standard Publishing, 1980) 81.

5. Adam Clarke, *Clarke's Commentary* (Nashville: Abingdon Press, 1824).

6. *Barnes' Notes on the New Testament* (Grand Rapids: Kregel Publications, 1962) 1521.

7. Criswell 60-61.

8. *Preaching* (Edinburgh: Marshall, Morgan, & Scott, n.d.) 45. Morgan writes concerning methods of preparation for expository preaching. His inspirational writing sets preaching in the supreme

place as a sacred work. One of the most inspirational books on preaching is Phillips Brooks' book *Lectures on Preaching*.

9. Samuel T. Logan Jr., ed., *The Preacher and Preaching* (Phillipsburg: Presbyterian and Reformed Publishing Company, 1986) 95. This is one of the better books on preaching written from the Reformed background.

10. *The Theory of Preaching* (New York: Charles Scribner's Sons, 1903) 218-219.

11. David Alan Black, *Using New Testament Greek in Ministry* (Grand Rapids: Baker, 1993) 61.

12. C. Sumner Wemp, *The Guide to Practical Pastoring* (Nashville: Nelson Publishers), 237.

13. Floyd Shafer, "And Preach As You Go," 1961 *Christianity Today*.

14. John R.W. Stott, *Between Two Worlds* (Grand Rapids: Eerdmans, 1982) 209.

15. Andrew W. Blackwood, *Preaching from the Bible* (New York: Abingdon Press, 1941) 46. Blackwood writes on numerous methods of approaching expository preaching.

Shawn D. Mathis earned degrees from Freed-Hardeman University (B.S.) and David Lipscomb University (M.A.R.). He has served as a minister since 1986. He is also Book Review Editor for *Christian Bible Teacher*.

MAN of GOD

Part 5 — Preaching

Preaching's Place in Christian Doctrine

Duane War

"Why do we continue the practice of standing one man before an audience for a monologue in our churches? If teaching is our objective in the sermon, why do we not use more effective teaching methods?" The question came from a teacher, and it was a good one. Here is the substance of how I attempted to answer my friend: "Teaching is not the only thing, perhaps it is not the most important thing, the sermon is about. Preaching is also worship, which is to say, it is the congregation uniting together in common adoration of God. When the preacher proclaims the essentials of what Christians believe and do, it is an expression of the church's devotion and praise. In its own way, the proclamation of the Word is the church affirming its collective belief in the saving truths of the Christian faith."

Of course, I did not fully answer my friend. His question and my answer were produced extemporaneously. That aside, he raised an important question: From a biblical perspective, what is the sermon to be? What is its function in the life of the church? In the New Testament it appears that preaching, teaching, mutual encouragement and common praise is basic to the Christian's sense of fellowship with the Savior and with others who share his faith.

This organic sense of fellowship is necessary for real preaching and common worship; it is at the heart of

Christianity. Through the years, educated Christians have left the great religious authors on their shelves and come to churches to listen to mediocre preachers because, from a person among persons, they were getting what they could never get alone.[1]

The testimony of the ages, and of the New Testament itself, is that preaching is not an appendage fastened to church life by tenuous threads; it is part and parcel with the meaning of Christians functioning together as a fellowship of believers.

The common sense that teaching is not the sole function of the sermon is illustrated by a remark one hears fairly often in church circles. Of a given person someone may say, "He is an excellent teacher, but not a very good preacher." The one who makes the remark may not have thought it through carefully, but he likely means that the person under consideration has a great deal of information to impart and that in a discussion-like class setting he communicates effectively. Why, then, is he not also a good preacher? Perhaps when he speaks he does not compel interest, stir emotions, motivate to action or excite to praise and adoration. Whatever the preacher's shortcoming, the remark is an acknowledgement that we expect something different from a sermon than simply teaching.

Unless Christians have some idea of what purpose the sermon serves, how will they be able to decide whether preaching is merely a long standing, and hence dispensable, tradition in the church or somehow vital to its life? Anyone who either listens to sermons or delivers them has an obligation to define what he expects when the preacher speaks or, more importantly, to explore the function God has given to the sermon within the framework of the life of the church.

Preaching Confronts the World with Jesus Christ

The apostle Paul asks the questions rhetorically, "But how are men to call upon him in whom they have not believed? And how are they to believe in him of whom they have not heard? And how are they to hear without a preacher?" (Rom. 10:14). The preacher announces to the world that God, now, at the end of the ages, has become incarnate in the form of a servant. God's purpose, as announced beforehand through his prophets, has been that His servant should take the sins and offenses of the world upon Himself and pay the penalty for them. Further, the particular form His servant took was in the person of Jesus of Nazareth. This function of the sermon is illustrated by Paul's work in ancient Thessalonica, when he was "explaining and proving that it was necessary for the Christ to suffer and to rise from the dead, and saying, 'This Jesus, whom I proclaim to you, is the Christ'" (Acts 17:3). Notice the two elements. First, it was necessary that the Christ suffer. Scripture proclaims a suffering Messiah. Second, Jesus is the Christ.

Through preaching God has determined that men should know His grace, justice and mercy. Paul, Peter, John, Barnabas, Timothy and scores of others stood in the market places, synagogues and wherever else they could find an audience to declare the forgiveness of sins through the atoning sacrifice of Christ. Paul concludes his sermon before the synagogue in Pisidian Antioch by saying, "Let it be known to you therefore, brethren, that through this man forgiveness of sins is proclaimed to you, and by him every one that believes is freed from everything from which you could not be freed by the law of Moses" (Acts 13:37-38). Because God has revealed that His mercy is for all creation, because He has given His church a commission to proclaim His mercy, the church preaches. The sermon is first a proclamation. It announces what is — Jesus is the Christ. He has "died for sins once for all, the righteous for the unrighteous, that he might bring us to God" (1 Peter 3:18). When it has announced, the sermon may proceed to reason and persuade, but first it announces God's grace has appeared to all.

What are we to say to those who object that the sermon is ineffective, that people are indifferent to religion, or that preaching is tantamount to forcing one's opinions on somebody else? We answer only this: God has revealed himself in Jesus Christ and His grace is offered to the world. We cannot but speak what we have seen and heard. With no apology we announce, and we will continue to announce, the Lord is risen and He will come again. If the church is to be a preaching church it can and will do nothing less than the Lord commissioned it to do in Matthew 28:19-20 and Mark 16:15-16.

What an odd paradox that preachers themselves are often the most severe critics of preaching. What is the meaning of this denigration? It is not only to Christians that its incongruity is striking. In 1948 the French Dominican monks of Latour-Maubourg asked Albert Camus, famous literary figure and avowed atheist, to address them on the topic, "What Unbelievers Expect from Christians." To call his speech interesting is an understatement. Among other things, Camus mentioned hearing a priest who caved-in to a Marxist lecturer by saying that he too was anticlerical. Camus then adds, "Well, I don't like priests who are anticlerical any more than philosophers who are ashamed themselves."[2] In the spirit of Camus, I don't like preachers who disdain preaching, who seemingly are ashamed of what they do. The design of God is that through preaching His grace should be announced. A church confident that it has a message from God will not hesitate to declare it with with steady determination.

Preaching Molds the Saved into the Kingdom of God

When Christ is proclaimed some will believe, and by grace through faith some will meet the Lord in baptism and have their sins washed away (Acts 22:16). They will experience God's grace and be saved, but there is more to be said. When the first believers had put on Christ in baptism, they were formed by Christ into a community. To this community the Lord added those who were subsequently saved (Acts 2:47). To be saved is to partake of the church. Having proclaimed Christ, the preacher, relying on the revelation of the Word, instructs the church on how it is to behave and what it means to be a Christian. Another function of preaching is to mold the saved into a kingdom over which Christ is Lord and Savior.

The Bible consistently pictures communion with God as taking place in company with other believers. To be a Christian is to struggle with personal needs and weaknesses in a context of mutual exhortation, caring and support. It is within the community of the saved that the kingdom of God is realized. It is there that, "The wolf shall dwell with the lamb, and the leopard shall lie down with the kid, and the calf and the lion and the fatling together, and a little child shall lead them" (Isa. 11:6). In the words of David Buttrick, "Christian preaching not only reveals, it continues the work of Christ by calling, liberating, and forming a new humanity."[3] We observe that for the most part, Jesus' own preaching was directed toward men and women who were well acquainted with the God of Israel. It was not that they needed to know God, but they needed to know Him better.

James Thompson offers good evidence that the letters of Paul are, among other things, models of early Christian preaching.[4] If his assessment is accurate, the preaching of apostles and other church leaders devoted a great deal of attention to instructing and encouraging the church concerning the practical implications of having owned the name of Christ. In Romans and Ephesians the apostle instructs the church in the rudiments of Christian doctrine. In Corinthians he addresses a litany of questions the church had put to him concerning the conduct of Christians in a world that did not share their values and ideals. He urges Christians to love one another, to dwell together in unity, to turn away from sins of the flesh, to care for the poor, and to live honestly and honorably before all men.

Whether confronting the world with Jesus Christ, or molding the church into the kingdom of God, the preacher must teach — he must impart information to those who hear him. He wants his hearers to know some things after he has spoken that they did not know beforehand. However, effective preaching must do more than impart information. The preacher wants to stir emotions; he wants to build bonds of love and commitment between the risen Lord and his people; he wants to inspire and motivate. To do this requires not only the preacher's words; it requires his life. When he preaches well, the preacher is a recipient of the grace of God. He speaks from who he is and from his own relationship to Christ. John Stott observed, "No man can be a great preacher without great feeling. It is a matter of universal observation that the speaker who would excite deep feeling must feel deeply himself."[5] To excite deep feeling is an element of what the sermon must do if it is to build up the church and confront the world with the Savior. To some extent, the preacher is always saying, "Be imitators of me, as I am of Christ" (1 Cor. 11:1).

It is instructive to notice how unabashedly Paul appeals to his personal conduct. To the Thessalonians he says, "For we never used either words of flattery, as you know, or a cloak for greed, as God is witness. ... But we were gentle among you, like a nurse taking care of her children" (1 Thess. 2:5, 7). To the Corinthians he adds, "We have renounced disgraceful, underhanded ways; we refuse to practice cunning or to tamper with God's word, but by the open statement of the truth we would commend ourselves to every man's conscience in the sight of God" (2 Cor. 4:2). The nature of preaching is such that the person cannot be separated from message. If preaching had only to teach, the preacher himself would matter little. If preaching is to mold the church into the kingdom of God, the character of the preacher is a crucial factor.

Preaching Affirms the Common Faith of the Christian Community

Many sermons are preached which impart new information to few in the congregation. The church hears what it has heard many times before and in response utters its "Amen." Peter says that his objective in his second letter was "to arouse you by way of reminder" (2 Peter 1:13). The sermon serves as a device for the church to assert its shared values and its common faith, to arouse and to remind one

another of what it means to wear the name of Christ. Elizabeth
Achtemeier reminds us that preachers forget the theological tradition
in which they stand only at great peril. "There is a basic Christian
understanding of who Jesus Christ is; of what his relation to the
Father and the Spirit is; of what has taken place in the sacred, biblical history; of what the goal of human history will be; and of how
the Christian is incorporated into the purpose of God."[6] Among the
reasons for the sermon is for the church as a body to affirm the basic
Christian understanding of God, existence and personhood.

When preaching is done well, the preacher will not hesitate to
insert old, familiar truths into the substance of his message. Fred
Craddock observes, "There is a fiction abroad among preachers that
the familiar is without interest, without power, and without prophetic edge."[7] Recall the sermons in the Bible that rehearse the history of
God's dealing with his people. Does anyone suppose that Stephen
began his sermon to the Jewish high council with God's appearance
to Abraham in Mesopotamia because they were unfamiliar with it?
Does Paul instruct the Ephesians on the nature of the church because
they had never heard it before? When the preacher tells of Adam and
Eve in the garden, of Moses leading Israel from Egypt, of David's
sin with Bathsheba, of the temptation of Jesus in the wilderness, of
the betrayal of Judas Iscariot, the church says, "Yes, yes we have
heard the stories before and they are true. They are words of life. The
generations come and go, but God remains forever." Christians have
heard the stories before. They see in them their spiritual ancestry,
and in them they reaffirm their confidence in the promises and the
blessings of God.

Preaching Makes a Statement About God's Nature

The very act of proclaiming the Gospel makes a statement about
the nature of God. Far from being a malevolent force or an abstract
power in the universe, God is a person. Because God is a personal
being He loves, and He desires to be loved in return. It is incredible
that the only infinite God of the universe should love the human family. But what is more incredible is that He should desire that men and
women return love to Him. Moses said, "Hear, O Israel: The Lord
our God is one Lord; and you shall love the Lord your God with all
your heart, and with all your soul, and with all your might" (Deut.
6:4-5). In Mark 12:28-31 a scribe puts the question to Jesus, "Which
commandment is the first of all?" Without hesitation the Lord
repeats the words of Moses. "Hear, O Israel: The Lord our God, the

Lord is one; and you shall love the Lord your God with all your heart, and with all your soul, and with all your mind, and with all your strength." It is because He is a person that God speaks to His people, for there can be no love in silence. He has commissioned those who love Him to speak of his love to others. When one proclaims the word he affirms that God loves and that God desires the love of his creation.

Preaching affirms more about the nature of God. It declares that He is a God of holiness and justice. Because He is just and holy, God cares what men and women do. When men brought disgrace on themselves and on their creator, God sent His Son to bear the guilt and burden of sin on Himself. We have been redeemed. To preach is to affirm that God's holiness and justice has not been compromised by the shedding forth of His grace. Paul remarks, "For our sake he made him to be sin who knew no sin, so that in him we might become the righteousness of God" (2 Cor. 5:21). To its infinite harm the modern church often finds it expedient to pass over such great doctrines as the atonement in favor of more "practical matters," like building strong marriages or feeling good about oneself. Let no one dismiss affirmations on the nature of God as dry doctrine of only academic concern. It is her great doctrines that have driven the church for its two thousand year history. The practical concerns of the Christian church will dry up like the fig tree cursed by the Lord when it no longer speaks of its doctrine. In the words of George Sweazey, "What you believe about who Christ is will determine how you live and who you are."[8]

When the preacher proclaims the Word, and the church consents to and encourages its proclamation, a statement is being made about God's choosing a people to be his own. One of the great doctrines of the Old Testament is that God came down to Egypt, chose a slave people, put His name on them, and claimed them for Himself. Israel might never quite understand why the only God of the universe, the God of all being, had chosen them to be peculiarly His, but they could never forget it. Moses must have felt the mystery of it all when he wrote, "Behold, to the Lord your God belong heaven and the heaven of heavens, the earth with all that is in it; yet the Lord set his heart in love upon your fathers and chose their descendants after them, you above all peoples, as at this day" (Deut. 10:14-15). It was not only that God had chosen their fathers, God had chosen them. The only explanation that Moses could offer was that God had loved them. But why them of all peoples on the face of the earth? To that there was no answer. God loved them because He loved them. One does not question love; one only basks in it. God loved Israel and He chose them.

Far from giving up on the concept of a chosen people, the New Testament affirms it with new confidence. To Jew and Gentile who share in the grace of God, Paul affirms, "He chose us in him before the foundation of the world, that we should be holy and blameless before him" (Eph. 1:4). He adds, "We are the true circumcision, who worship God in spirit, and glory in Christ Jesus, and put no confidence in the flesh" (Phil. 3:3). The preaching church affirms there is a people chosen by God; indeed, the choosing is done by the very Word which we preach.

Preaching affirms that God is a personal God of love, that He is a God of holiness and justice, that He has chosen a people, and that He is coming again. C.H. Dodd captures the spirit of New Testament preaching when he writes:

> The more we try to penetrate in imagination to the state of mind of the first Christians in the earliest days, the more are we driven to think of resurrection, exaltation, and second advent as being, in their belief, inseparable parts of a single divine event. It was not an early advent that they proclaimed, but an immediate advent.[9]

Near the end of his letter, James reminds his readers, "Establish your hearts, for the coming of the Lord is at hand" (James 5:8). Peter comforts Christians who face persecution and suffering for his name, "The end of all things is at hand" (1 Peter 4:7). In the daily stress of dealing with immediate problems faced by believers, Paul writes, "The appointed time has grown very short" (1 Cor. 7:29).

Were the apostles and the early church mistaken in their expectation of the immediate return of the Lord? Not at all! In every age, first century and twentieth, the church looks for His return. To preach Him is to affirm that the time is at hand. Not only is the Lord going to return, He is going to return soon. The church longs for His appearance. He came once to suffer; He has ascended to God's right hand; He is coming again. Every time we preach Him, every time the church hears His name called, and every time God's people look to Him for instruction it affirms that He is coming soon. To know that He is coming soon puts a new perspective on the world and all the things that occupy our thoughts and time. The Lord reigns and when He wills it, He will call to an end this world.

Preaching Offers Up the Praise of the Church to God

Preaching is worship, and worship by its nature is praise. It is not only that God speaks to His church when the Word is faithfully proclaimed, but in the sermon the church returns to God its praise and thanksgiving. Praise is an integral element in almost any extended statement made by almost anyone in the Bible. Praise permeates the Bible. When Solomon dedicated the great temple he had built in Jerusalem, he ended by standing aside meekly and accepting its inadequacy: "Behold, heaven and the highest heaven cannot contain thee; how much less this house which I have built" (1 Kings 8:27). Neither the temple nor our skyscrapers nor our cathedrals can contain Him. Like Solomon we cannot speak of God without His praises being on our lips. As the prayers and the hymns of the church praise, so the sermon praises. In the words of the old English hymn, "All people that on earth do dwell, Sing to the Lord with cheerful voice; Him serve with fear, His praise forth tell, Come ye before Him, and rejoice."

The preacher speaks of Him whom the heavens declare and the earth proclaims. The sermon affirms His sovereignty over human life and history. When the preacher speaks of His majesty and glory and the church adds its amen, God's people are offering up "a sacrifice of praise to God, that is, the fruit of lips that acknowledge his name" (Heb. 13:15). It seems this is an aspect of preaching often overlooked. When we asked the question, "What is preaching to do," the answer, at least in part, is, "The sermon is to offer up the praise of God's people to the eternal Creator and the author of our common salvation."

Preaching Is Affirmation That the Christian Canon Is God's Word

In the Christian canon — the Bible — there is a phenomenon unlike that in any other book of the world. Through human language and in the context of human historical experience, God has spoken definitively to his people. Through the centuries Christians have struggled with the concept of canon. How was the canon formed? What historical criteria were used to decide the books that were to be included as canon? What is the relationship between the human and the divine in any given statement from Scripture? How is the authority of a Word written to a different people who lived in different circumstances in a different world to be applied to the modern church? The questions are complex, but it is not necessary for the preacher or the church to answer them to the satisfaction of all for it to proclaim its faith that in the Bible God speaks to his people across the ages.

The act of proclaiming a message that calls on Scripture to guide the life of the modern church is an affirmation that the Bible is authoritative. Preaching affirms that no individual can assert his special revelation and set it over against the authority of the Bible, regardless of what extraordinary claims he might make. In a recent anthology, Sinclair Ferguson, of Westminster Theological Seminary in Philadelphia, wrote the following:

> Involved in the view that such gifts as prophecy and tongues have ceased is the fact that the New Testament regards certain gifts as signs of the apostle and evidence of the apostolic nature of the church (2 Cor. 12:12; Heb. 2:3b-4). But also implied is the conviction that, as revelatory, these gifts were exercised prior to the coming into being and universal recognition of the entire New Testament canon. Insofar as prophecy and tongues plus interpretation were regarded as divine revelation, they served an interim function prior to the inscripturating of the apostolic message.[10]

To proclaim that the Bible is authoritative is to say that the church finds in Scripture its way life, its worship and its doctrine. Authority is not a pretty word for those who want infinite freedom, no restraints on what they consider religious experiences or practices. The real world, including the real word of the relationship between God and man, lives within the restraints of authorship and fact. Commenting on art, G.K. Chesterton observes:

> If you draw a giraffe, you must draw him with a long neck. If, in your bold creative way, you hold yourself free to draw a giraffe with a short neck, you will really find that you are not free to draw a giraffe. The moment you step into the world of facts, you step into a world of limits.[11]

If one would honor and serve God, he too must step into a world of limits. The people of Israel found that trampling on courts, offering sacrifices and engaging in the formal practice of religion offered no honor to God. God expects a certain behavior from His people. He sets forth the limits of the behavior that pleases Him in the canon.

Preaching affirms that faith comes in a context of duty, submission and obedience. It is amazing that some Christians will gladly affirm duty in moral and civic realms, but chaff when duty is mentioned in the context of religious faith. Careful thought suggests that only the Christian, with a living faith in God, can speak meaningly of duty. William James expressed an important truth:

> Once dismiss the notion that certain duties are good in them-selves, and that we are here to do them, no matter how we feel about them; once consecrate the opposite notion that our perfor-mances and our violations of duty are for a common purpose, the attainment of subjective knowledge and feeling, and that the deepening of these is the chief end of our lives,—and at what point on the downward slope are we to stop?[12]

The statement by James is admirable, but after one reads his essay, it is not clear at all why duty should stir the interest of anyone. Preaching affirms duty because it affirms authority, because it affirms canon.

Conclusion

To some degree it might be argued that teaching underlies all the functions of preaching we have discussed. Teaching is clearly an important function of preaching, but preaching does much more. Let me return to the question my friend asked when we began this study. The preacher stands before the congregation and proclaims a mes-sage because proclamation is able to do what the simple impartation of knowledge, what we are calling teaching, could not by itself do. The sermon can hardly be dismissed as a child of the Reformation or a development of modern church tradition. The proclamation of the Word is basic to the fabric of church life.

Endnotes

1. George E. Sweazey, *Preaching the Good News* (Englewood Cliffs, NJ: Prentice-Hall, Inc., 1976) 6.

2. Jaroslav Pelikan, ed, *The World Treasure of Modern Religious Thought* (Boston: Little, Brown, and Company, 1990) 30.

3. David Buttrick, *Homiletic: Moves and Structures* (Philadelphia: Fortress Press, 1987) 451.

4. James Thompson, *Surmounting the Obstacles: Studies in II Corinthians* (Parkersburg, WV: Ohio Valley College, 1989) 6.

5. John R. W. Stott, *Between Two Worlds: The Art of Preaching in the Twentieth Century* (Grand Rapids: William B. Eerdmans Publishing Company, 1982) 273.

6. Elizabeth Achtemeier, *Preaching as Theology and Art* (Nashville: Abingdon Press, 1984) 11.

7. Fred Craddock, *Preaching* (Nashville: Abingdon Press, 1985) 45.

8. Craddock, 227.

9. C. H. Dodd, *The Apostolic Preaching and Its Development* (Grand Rapids: Baker Book House, 1980) 33.

10. Sinclair B. Ferguson, "How Does the Bible Look at Itself?," *Inerrancy and Hermeneutic: A Tradition, A Challenge, A Debate*, Havie M. Conn, ed. (Grand Rapids: Baker Book House, 1988) 61.

11. G. K. Chesterton, *Orthodoxy* (New York: Doubleday and Company, 1959) 40.

12. William James, *Essays on Faith and Morals*, Ralph Barton Perry, ed. (New York: World Publishing Times Mirror, 1962) 171.

Duane Warden is professor of Bible and Biblical Languages at Harding University. He served as chairman of the Division of Bible and Religion at Ohio Valley College in Parkersburg, West Virginia. He is a graduate of Freed-Hardeman University (B.A.), Harding Graduate School of Religion (M.A.R.) and Duke University (Ph.D.).

The Preacher: A Man of Balance

Clarence De

Christianity is the religion of revelation and has been divinely communicated in the book we call the Bible. Christianity revolves around a person, but the message about that person must be proclaimed or preached.

However, preaching has fallen on bad times. We live in a time of sophisticated technology. The media entertains us with color graphics and pictures. Preaching appears to be out-dated, bland and boring. Even some in the church do not feel that it has much influence in the modern world.

John Stott has correctly observed:

> This has become the age of sermonettes — and sermonettes make Christainettes. The uncertainty of our age about the Gospel and the mission of the church is due in large part to a generation of preachers who have lost confidence in the Word of God.[1]

There is no indication from above that God has changed his mind with reference to the priority of preaching. Paul's affirmation as to the place of preaching still stands: "It pleased God by the foolishness of preaching to save them that believe" (1 Cor. 1:21).

When the fullness of time came for God to send the Redeemer, He could have sent him as an engineer, a scientist or a politician — but he chose instead to send him as a preacher. Mark states, "He came ... preaching" (Mark 1:14).

He was Truth, and He came with a message of truth. He was "the teacher sent from God," and man has the responsibility to hear, receive and respond to that Truth (John 14:6; 8:32; 3:2; 6:44-45).

Whether traced from cause to effect, or from effect to cause, saving faith requires preaching (Rom. 10:13-17). However, much more is involved in preaching than sweating, shouting and waving a Bible. Much of the preaching in modern times is theatrical, sensational and little more than bombast, falling far short of the biblical ideal.

The focus of this chapter is the need for balance in the preacher. One may preach but fail to be effective simply because he lacks balance. Balance is the quality of equilibrium and symmetry that avoids extremism. It suggests decisiveness, proportion and moderation.

God is a God of balance. Such is beautifully displayed in nature. The universe demonstrates a precise balance in planetary operation and the earth reflects it in her seasons. God often called His people to balance, exhorting them not to turn from the Law to the right hand or to the left (Josh. 1:7; Deut. 17:20).

Jesus: The Example of Balance in Preaching

The balance that makes preaching powerful and effective is exhibited in the New Testament. The greatest example for biblical preaching is displayed in the New Testament. What greater role model than the Master Teacher? What greater model than the teaching of Paul?

In Jesus one sees the marvelous balance between commitment to truth (content) and genuine interest in people. One may come to love preaching more than those to whom he preaches. That is dangerous and wrong. Our Lord came with a message, He said, "My teaching is not Mine, but His that sent Me" (John 7:16).

He delivered that message faithfully and without compromise. But while committed to that message, He was also a people person. Preaching, to Jesus, was more than a presentation of theological propositions. He was always out with the people seeking to save the lost. You see Jesus in the temple court (Matt. 21:23), the synagogue (Matt. 4:23), and throughout the towns and villages (Matt. 11:1). He preached in Galilee, Judea and Samaria.

Jesus' message was made applicable to his audience. He spoke to the needs and situations of His hearers. A meal in a home provided an opportunity to share great insights into life. Some audiences were composed of multitudes, but most of his teaching took place where two or three were gathered. He walked on busy roads and down village paths. He dared to go to those whom society had forgotten. At the workplace He called people right off the job. Because He identified with people, the common people heard Him gladly. He understood their hearts and empathized with their hurts. He saw their fears, frustrations and doubts. He heard the plea of mothers and the anguish of fathers. He disputed with religious leaders, talked to women and even ate with sinners (Matt. 23; John 4; Luke 15). He demonstrated respect and compassion for humanity and never sought to manipulate or exploit any person. Throughout His ministry He took risks that endeared Him to some, marked Him as foolish to others, and made Him appear courageous to yet others.

Jesus never asked His disciples to do anything He was unwilling to do. He prayed, toiled and ate with all kinds of people. These things impressed His disciples. Even Luke began his historical narrative in Acts by calling attention to "all that Jesus began to do and teach" (Acts 1:1).

Jesus did not go along with accepted ideas or practices in order to get along with others or gain easy acceptance. When the tide of popular opinion turned against him, he changed neither His message nor His mission. That is the essence of balance.

Jesus' awareness of people is seen in the sources of His illustrations. He drew from life experiences. He was acquainted with nature, business, domestic activities, agricultural practices and political life.

Those who preach now must not lock themselves in studies at the expense of contact with people. Many an able student has been ineffective because of his lack of contact with people. We need to present truth — but truth that relates to people and addresses their needs. Truth is both propositional and relational.

Balance in the Scope of Jesus' Message

An analysis of the Sermon on the Mount (Matthew 5-7) reveals balance between content and relationship. The sermon begins with "being" (Beatitudes; attitudes of being) and concludes with "doing" ("whoever does these sayings of mine"). The order is significant: being before doing, not doing before being. We often rush into doing without being what we should be. The result is frustration and shallowness. The Beatitudes focus on right relationship with God, others and self. The key to Christian service is a close, committed relationship with God.

Today, when discussing church growth, we tend to stress programs, budgets and facilities; but the key to true church growth is repentance and changed lives. People whose being is right will have an influence like "salt and light" in the world (Matt. 5:13-16).

The subject matter in Jesus' preaching is a model of simplicity, pointedness, comprehensiveness and balance. It was both propositional and relational. He was compassionate toward the distressed and hurting, while at the same time strenuously denouncing sham and pretense in others. Jesus spoke of false teachers as threats, revealing their clever and deceptive manner. He even mentioned their destiny (Matt. 7-13-23).

Jesus' Balance Impressed His Disciples

When John, who loved Jesus dearly, summarized his life and preaching, he said, "We beheld his glory, as of the only begotten of the Father, full of grace and truth" (John 1:14). He noted the grace and dignity of Jesus' manner and the commitment and faithfulness of His message. That is balance. There must be consistency between lip and life; talk and walk. Peter explained that our Lord gave us an example to walk in His steps (1 Peter 2:21).

Every gospel preacher should closely scrutinize the preaching of Jesus. He ought always to follow Christ's conversational skill when talking one on one. He would do well to look at Jesus' method of dialogue and debate when confronting religious leaders. He should seek to fathom the Lord's tenderness when dealing with the hurting. A sincere gospel preacher should observe and emulate that warmth and easy accessibility which made children feel comfortable in His presence.

Matthew emphasizes what Jesus said. His emphasis is upon the kingdom and in particular the teaching of the King. Matthew 11 illustrates the kind of balance needed in preaching. The chapter begins with Jesus preaching in the cities; however, he was never too busy to encourage one who needed his support. Parenthetically, Matthew records an instance of Jesus taking time to speak to visitors who had come with questions from John the Baptist who was in prison. John's voice had been silenced. Jesus answered John's questions, praising and encouraging him as one of God's greatest servants. In our preaching, let us not overlook the ministry of encouragement. Then, following that demonstration of compassion, Jesus severely denounced the cities of Bethsaida and Chorazin because they had greater opportunity but did not repent. The chapter closes with a tender and compassionate invitation.

Lessons emerge from this chapter that have serious implications for preaching. The preacher must encourage. Any preacher who sees his

work as a constant barrage of brow-beating, bashing and berating will
see as the result a demoralized church. There is a time to condemn. Sin
must be denounced, error must be repudiated and false teachers must
be exposed. But caution must be exercised while uprooting the tares
lest the wheat be destroyed too. Our words and our manner must
always exemplify a sincere passion to see the lost saved.

Balance and Soundness

The word "sound" is used by Paul in his letters to Timothy and
Titus. A cognate of this word is often used in connection with Jesus'
ministry of healing. It means healthy and whole. Paul spoke of
"sound doctrine" (1 Tim. 1:10), "sound words" (2 Tim. 1:13) and
"sound speech" (Titus 2:8).

A preacher who is sound is one who is whole, complete, healthy
and balanced. He is not an extremist. He keeps a careful watch over
both himself and the doctrine (1 Tim. 4:16). He is effective. He does
not seek to be controversial, but he does not steer away from controversy when truth and principle are at stake. His major interest is
serving God and building the church.

I am convinced that God has a great host of preachers whose
names are seldom heard. They work hard, serving God and man.
They have no axes to grind, no agendas to serve, and no names to
build except that of Jesus Christ.

Balance as Exemplified in Paul

Most would agree that, next to Jesus, Paul was the greatest
preacher Christianity has produced. During his work with the church
in Thessalonica, Paul's balance was evident. Paul described his work
with three metaphors in 1 Thessalonians 2.

First, Paul described himself as a steward faithfully discharging a
trust (1 Thess. 2:4, 13). As an earthen vessel Paul delivered the treasure of the Good News to them. They received it as the Word of
Truth and were saved by it. Thus, their Christian life was begun.

Second, he continued to nourish them as a nurse provides for her
children. He was like a mother to them, showing patient understanding as he nurtured them in the Lord.

Third, Paul challenged them as a Father charges his sons. Here we
see the element of high expectation for the future.

What an example for all who preach Christ. We must faithfully
present the facts, the commands and the promises of the Gospel.
This is essential if lost people are to learn how to be Christians.
These are commonly called "the first principles."

Next, new Christians must be nourished and their faith must be confirmed. As Jesus said, "teach them all things I have commanded" (Matt. 28:19).

Then comes the deeper challenge of going on to the meat of the Word. We must encourage and lead others toward a richer, fuller, spiritual life.

A Practical Plea for Balance

We have all known preachers who seem to display the balance discussed in this chapter. It prods us to emulate their example in so far as they follow Christ. Even Paul said, "Be imitators of me, even as I follow Christ" (1 Cor. 11:1). Again he said, "Examine everything carefully, hold fast to that which is good" (1 Thess. 5:21). We would do well to mimic him.

Preachers, we are involved in serious business. It is a high calling, an awesome responsibility. Yet good men of talent and motivation can be neutralized and made ineffective by imbalance.

We can be plain without being cruel. Dignity is always in order. Words can be pointed and specific without being cruelly blunt. Words should be carefully chosen to be bold without being brazen. Paul urged that, "speech be seasoned with salt" (Col. 4:6), not pepper. There is never justification for being unkind. We must never preach an angry Gospel. Souls are fragile, so we ought to handle with care — "speaking the truth in love" (Eph. 4:15).

A balanced preacher will guard against beating one subject to death. God has given us plenty of material to preach. Explore the great possibilities of expository preaching covered elsewhere in this text. It will save you from yourself. A preacher striving for balance will learn to manage his time well so as to have adequate periods for study and spiritual growth; but, he must not forget to get out among the sheep and goats to sense and serve their needs.

By all means, do not neglect your family. People closely observe the genuineness of your faith by your relationships. Preachers are scrutinized and judged for integrity and trustworthiness. The public notices how family members, neighbors, members, and business are treated. That exemplary walk with others has more influence than the grandest eloquence displayed in the pulpit. A balanced preacher will be decisive and distinctive where God has spoken but remain pliable on matters of judgment and methods of outreach.

It is imperative that a balanced preacher manifest a caring spirit even when preaching on tough issues and prevalent moral evils. The

Gospel is good news and should always be presented as such. God never delights in the destruction of the wicked; rather He wants all men to come to the knowledge of truth. So must we who represent Him.

In all things, we should seek to exemplify in our lives what we enunciate from the pulpit. Remember, we are imperfect men working in the midst of imperfection. So the grace we preach is desperately needed in our own lives.

We must never seek to dominate. Being submissive will enable us to work in harmony with God's ordained leaders and servants. Preaching is not an ego trip but a mission of service. By all means we should avoid competition with others who preach. Lighthouses do not compete. We are servants; privileged but responsible.

We need to remember to preach on: Old and New Testaments; heaven and hell; grace and faith; the sovereignty of God and the responsibility of man; broad principles and specific applications; the Man and the plan. We need to remember to tell men what God has done before telling them what God wants them to do.

May God grant those of us who preach the wisdom to be balanced (James 1:5). Extremism destroys while balance builds. Preachers unquestionably set the tone for a local church. Balanced preachers produce balanced churches. Our ministry is a grace to be used with fear and trembling (Eph. 3:8).

As young or old we must be balanced. If we lean forward or backward too far we lose balance. When the center of gravity is lost something or someone goes down!

Endnotes

1. John R.W. Stott, *Between Two Worlds: The Art of Preaching in the Twentieth Century* (Grand Rapids: Eerdmans Publishing Co., 1982).

Clarence DeLoach Jr. began preaching at the age of 15. He has conducted more than 350 gospel meetings, campaigns in Guyana and Suriname, and radio and TV programs. He has authored three books and two video series. He has taught at Ohio Valley College and done local work in Tennessee, Georgia, Ohio and West Virginia.

The Golden Age of Expository Preaching

Earl West

It was the year 1826 and two young men stood in the doorway of James Challen's parents home in Lexington, Kentucky. They had recently made a momentous decision that would effect the rest of their lives. But chill winds blew, as one of them expressed it, when trenchant tongues sliced away at them in undignified disapproval. The resolute youths, James Challen and Jacob Creath Jr., were convicted that they were standing on the Word of God. They would not be shaken.

Thirty-four years later Creath remembered that Challen's parents cried over the vigorous adolescents for accepting "Campbellism." When the two youths had strolled to the meeting house, they would long remember that people ran out into the street and stared at them as though they were strange creatures from outer space. By the time they had finished their sermons that day, the building was full of a passionate audience.

Even when the two youths were later turned out of a Baptist Association in Harrison County, Kentucky, they, as Creath expressed it, "felt much confidence in the Bible and the cause we were in, as I do today, and were cut off and publicly denounced, and everything was done to ruin our characters." But as they reaffirmed, they had faith in God Almighty's truth: "Had it not been for that — every pulsation of our hearts would have ceased, every throb in our spirits would have been silenced, would have been hushed, and all the energies of our souls would have been paralyzed. But placing ourselves upon the eternal foundation of Christ, pledging ourselves to the truth as it is in Jesus Christ, preaching it when it was like preaching against a dead wall, preaching it with the confidence that it was a truth, and He would own it, we went on." [1]

The confidence of two young men, that the cause they had espoused was God's divine revelation, came in the pre-Civil War days to be shared by more than 300,000 believers. That conviction drove those confident disciples to rally around the central truth that Jesus was the Son of God, that human creeds and the doctrines of men should be discarded, and that all unauthorized names and plans should be rejected. Truth was the polar star that directed their course. Since that truth was embedded in the sacred Scriptures, the challenge was to understand those writings and present them accurately and clearly from the pulpit.

The reformation of the nineteenth century lured hundreds of talented preachers to hoist on the frontier a flaming beacon of hope. There was John T. Johnson, "the evangelist of the restoration movement," as John Rogers once called him. Elder Ben Franklin, John Allen Gano, T.M. Allen and many others would become household names in their times. As the century bore on, J.W. McGarvey and T.B. Larimore would adorn their own names with a certain radiance. They all had one thing in common: Each had mastered the art of expository preaching in his own style. Each one, too, found an archetype in a masterful teacher — Alexander Campbell.

The Bethany preacher, Campbell, attached great importance to understanding the Scriptures and in presenting them flawlessly and attractively to inquiring listeners. He expressed it once:

It is a matter, therefore, of vast importance with me to understand the words found in these sacred writings in the very identical sense of these writers; and I am assured that when this is done all doubts on the subject of religion will vanish, and the New Testament will be perfectly understood. [2]

By planting himself upon these two purposes, it is small wonder that Campbell became the foremost expositor of the Bible in the nineteenth century. But he was more than a framer of majestic stanzas: the range of his attainments stretched through fields of religious, intellectual and spiritual perceptions that continue to strike the admiration of Christian leaders in the present day.

Beginning in the year 1810, this 22-year-old Irish giant buried himself in the study of Protestant platforms of church union to determine what his own duty to God and man would be. "I devoted several years to a very strict and rigid study of the whole Bible, but more especially to the Christian religion," he later recalled. Many Scriptures he now studied were those he had previously memorized. He now concluded that all Protestant doctrines had more or less usurped the divine Scriptures. This observation he would often repeat through his entire life.[3]

Moreover, from the earliest days of his studies this future role model came to agree with James Hay Beatie, that the Christian religion was a "simple thing, intelligent to the meanest capacity; and what, if we are at pains to join practice to knowledge, we may make ourselves acquainted with[,] without turning over many books."[4] To deliver a clear expository sermon based on the Scriptures, Campbell well understood he must first begin with a clear understanding of the Bible passages.

Campbell was no "legalist," because he declared the necessity for men to translate biblical commands into obedience. As Beatie defined it in his *Elements of Moral Science*, "law" was "the declared will of a person or persons, in authority."[5] Since the Heavenly Father and His Son both possess innate authority over man, their commands could not be mere suggestions but divine and compulsory guidelines for human conduct.

Nor was there ever any question in Campbell's viewpoint that God addressed His directions to men in human language that could be understood by ordinary human reason. As Campbell understood it:

> The fact that God has clothed his communications in human language, and that He has spoken by men to men, in their own language is decisive evidence that he is to be understood as one man conversing with another.[6]

When, therefore, God gave commands to Adam and Eve in the Garden of Eden, both understood perfectly what God said. Their disobedience to God constituted the misconduct that compelled God to exclude them from the home He had divinely provided for them. The principle was easily transferred down into the Christian religion. As Campbell noted:

> The apostles were commissioned by the Lord to teach the disciples to observe all things he had commanded them. Now we believe them to have been faithful to their master, and consequently He gave them to know His will. Whatever the disciples

practiced in their meetings with the approbation of the apostles, is equivalent to an apostolic command to us to do the same. To suppose the contrary, is to make the half of the New Testament of no effect. For it does not altogether consist of commands, but of approved precedents. Apostolic example is justly esteemed of equal authority with an apostolic precept.[7]

As Campbell's exertions continued toward his goal of possessing a most lucid understanding of the Bible, impressive principles of hermeneutics fell in line. He trod a discreet path in grasping the truth that no sinner in Holy Writ was ever justified by any one principle, thought, volition, act or deed apart from any other. Sinners, he noted, are justified by grace, faith, the blood of Christ and baptism among other commands. Likewise, they are saved by the name of Christ, by the working of the new birth, and by baptism. "Are we ashamed or afraid, or so priest-ridden," he inquired, "as to fear to read, and to preach, and teach these perspicuous declarations of God's own book?" He reduced these principles succinctly by articulating:

> Thus, we are saved by grace, as the originating cause; by Christ and His blood, as the meritorious and God, the justifying cause; by faith, repentance, and baptism, as instrumental causes , and by good works, as the consummating and God-honoring causes.[8]

Valuable insights into understanding the Bible also occurred when Campbell once received a letter from a Kentucky German Baptist — a "Dunkard." This reader of *The Christian Baptist* informed Campbell that he approved of his taking the words of the apostles, but was surprised that Campbell did not accept washing of feet and the kiss of charity. In reply, the Virginia editor pointed out that men must always distinguish in any institution between what is circumstantial and what is the essence of the institution itself. He maintained that it was bad logic to draw a general occurrence from a particular one. He inquired if one could say that because Paul immersed a jailer in the wee hours of the night, that modern Christians could only baptize at the same hour. Too, must the Lord's Supper be taken at night because it might have been when Jesus instituted it and when the Christians at Troas later partook of it.

On another occasion Campbell was charged with denying "experimental religion." He searched his Bible and found nothing about it. When he asked a friend, he was told there were two kinds of religion

— "head" and "heart." "As the New Testament is my religious creed, I appealed to it again," he wrote. But it was as silent as the grave on all these distinctions, he noted. Consequently, he urged his readers to study their Bibles: "From all these scenes of raging enthusiasm, he admonished, my friends, to open your Bibles and to hearken to the voice of God, which is the voice of reason."[9]

Campbell's diligence for perspicuity in the Scripture's teachings prepared the way for his vivid expositions of passages in sermons that ran from one and one-half hour to three hours. Meanwhile audiences sat spellbound as he unfolded divine truths to them.

Moreover, Campbell was cool to the idea of allowing his sermons to be printed, permitting this only once when D.S. Burnet recorded, "The Riches of Christ" in the *Christian Teacher*. On the other hand, an experience in Louisville in the spring of 1835 has proved most revealing of the great preacher's sermonic procedure. If this occasion be typical of others, it is clear that Campbell did not possess total originality in his expository preaching. As a Seceder Presbyterian in his younger days, like his father, Campbell's religious roots went back to the Puritans. In his debate defending Protestantism against Bishop John B. Purcell. Campbell stated, "I claim a very intimate relation with the Protestant family. It was then my family that first settled this country."[10]

Much is known today of the Puritan style of expository preaching. The similarity with Campbell's is striking. The general procedure was simple. In an effort to appeal to the popular audiences, Puritan preachers carried into the pulpit only the heads of sermons. Three steps were followed. First, read the text out of Scripture and then clarify it by explaining the context. Puritan preachers called this "opening" the text. Second, the preacher would proceed to collect a few and "profitable points of doctrine." Puritan preachers called this "dividing" the text. Third, the speakers then applied the doctrines rightly collected to the life and manners of men in simple and plain speech. Puritans called these the "uses" of the Scripture.[11]

Speaking in the Unitarian building in Louisville, Kentucky, for one hour and fifteen minutes on the night of April 5, 1835, Campbell provided an appealing style of preaching. The editors of the *Western Messenger* were delighted with this "bold and powerful preacher of rational and liberal views in religion." They explained that western people "have a real taste for oratory" and enjoy "long harangues," but the editor considered Campbell as better than any of them. As he saw it:

Many are more imaginative and sublime in their language; he keeps a pretty even flight in this respect, never soaring very high. Many excel him in the inflections and management of voice and gracefulness of gesture.[12]

They viewed Campbell as he stood upright with his head tilted a little back and his right hand leaning on a cane. His few gestures were made with his left hand. They found his sermon on this occasion highly impressive.

The great excellence however of Campbell's delivery, consists in the feeling which it inspired of his manly independence, entire conviction of the truth of what he says, and entire understanding of his whole subject. He is plain, forcible and self-possessed; he is not hurried away by his words or by his thoughts but has command of both.

The Louisville Unitarian journal described in great detail Campbell's sermon. The distinguished preacher spoke, as he frequently did over his lifetime on "Christian Union," quoting from the early verses of Ephesians 4. Emphasizing that the Bible should not be read piecemeal, he underscored "that the Bible should be read like other books, with the use of our reason." He accented that the basis of Christian union was "one Lord, one faith," etc. He highlighted that opinions were not faith, which led him to defining faith. He concluded by stressing that men must give up their own opinions and traditions and go only by the teachings of the Word of God.

Here was expository preaching on a theme close to Campbell's heart. He laid the pattern for coming generations of expository preachers to understand the Scriptures through diligent study, and to present appealingly those divine truths needed by every generation.

Endnotes

1. "Semi-Annual Convention of The A.C. Missionary Society," *American Christian Review* 15 May 1860: 78.

2. Alexander Campbell, "Reply to 'Extract of a Letter from a Friend in North Carolina, to the Editor, September, 1826'" *Christian Baptist* 4 Dec. 1826: 2911-2993.

3. Alexander Campbell, "Dr. Jeter's Campbellism," *Millennial Harbinger* March 1856: 163-69.

4. Alexander Campbell, "Dr. Beatie's Opinion of the Christian Religion," *Christian Baptist* 3 August 1823: 10.

5. James H. Beatie, *Elements of Moral Science*, II, 112. Quoted in Lunger, *Political Ethics*, 69.

6. Alexander Campbell, "Tracts for the People — No. III," *Millennial Harbinger*, 3rd ser. 2, January 1846: 18.

7. Alexander Campbell, "A Restoration of the Ancient Order of Things, No. VII," *Christian Baptist* 5 Sept. 1825:180-182.

8. Alexander Campbell, "Tracts for Tennessee Baptists," *Millennial Harbinger* Sept. 1854: 493-511.

9. Alexander Campbell, "Address to the Readers of the *Christian Baptist*, No. IV," *Christian Baptist* 1 March 1824:48.

10. *A Debate on the Roman Catholic Religion: Between Alexander Campbell of Bethany, Virginia and the Right Rev. John B. Purcell, Bishop of Cincinnati* (Cincinnati: n.p., 1861) 333.

11. William Haller, *The Rise of Puritanism* (New York: n.p., 1938) 134.

12. J.F.C., "Alexander Campbell at Louisville," *Western Messenger* June 1835: 60.

Earl West is professor of church history at Harding University Graduate School of Religion. He holds the Ph.D. from Indiana University. He has written numerous books and articles in the field of restoration history and speaks frequently at Christian college lectureships.

The Exposition of Scripture

C. Michael

Many of the sermons I have heard could be termed "pop psychology" or "here's-how-to-be-a-success." Unfortunately I have seen very little evidence of careful study of the biblical text. Sermons seldom arose from what God, through the human author, was saying to His people. About the best one could hope to find was scripture as the "jumping-off-point" for the preacher's homiletic excursion. A colleague described this process of sermon preparation as "jacking up a passage and running the sermon under it." It was then that I concluded something needed to be done to avoid facing real problems.

Long ago God warned the people through the prophet Amos, "The time is surely coming, says the Lord GOD, when I will send a famine on the land; not a famine of bread, or a thirst for water, but of hearing the words of the LORD" (Amos 8:11 NRSV). That may well be the dilemma of the church today.

Many have argued that sermons are a thing of the past. Bible classes where people seriously study the Bible are increasingly rare. They reason that if the church is to survive, it must be more consumer conscious. If there are to be sermons, they must be practical, warm and light. Bible classes must build fellowship and good feeling. The careful exposition of Scripture is simply inappropriate in the worship assemblies and classes of the late 20th century and will become increasingly so in the 21st century. Expository sermons and textually based Bible classes are at their best mediocre and at their worst boring. If there is one thing that a modern man or woman cannot abide, it is anything that is boring.

While the preacher is obliged to concern himself with his audience and their felt needs, God still must be allowed to speak through the Scriptures. If one is convinced that the power to change lives comes from God Himself, from His Word, His revelation of Himself, and His will for His people, then the preacher becomes simply a conduit for that message. The power is always in the message and not in the one who bears message. If that thesis is correct, then the minister must seek ways to clarify the message and, at the same time, stay out of its way. Expository preaching and teaching are an attempt to do just that. "The expositor is only to provide mouth and lips for the passage itself so that the Word may advance."[1]

Greidanus has said,

> The outstanding characteristic of expository preaching is that it uses the Bible as the source for its preaching; it seeks to give an exposition of a biblical passage. By contrast, non-biblical topical preaching presents neither text nor exposition. Although it is possible to preach topical sermons that are biblical in actual practice they often turn out to be flights of fancy which have little or nothing to do with biblical thought.[2]

Expository sermons and classes need not be boring. Church leaders and preachers have wrongly assumed that careful study and application of the biblical text to the lives of caring people will be of no interest.

The preacher has two primary obligations as he approaches a biblical text in his study on Monday, in the pulpit on Sunday, and at any Bible study setting. The recognition of these obligations will keep the preacher on course.

Obligations to the Text

The preacher must first live with the text. One cannot hope to be fair to a biblical text that is examined only on the day the minister hopes to compose the sermon or prepare a class lecture. Reading an epistle through at a single setting, examining again material that surrounds a narrative, and simply spending time with a text will provide some degree of objectivity.

The minister must diligently seek the message that the human author and God had in mind for the original audience. Put simply, "What was the intent of this passage?" Getting into the mind of the original author and his audience is never an easy task, and it is by no means a foolproof endeavor. Yet, the Bible student must undertake that task. As Fee and Stuart have said, "A text cannot mean what it never meant."[3] Put another way, a biblical text can never say what it never could have said to its author and his audience. One cannot simply pick up a text, get a feeling, and be satisfied that he has the message God intends. Bible classes cannot be the pooling of ignorance, the mere sharing of feelings. God must be allowed to speak. The only safeguard to guarantee that God's will is being sought rather man's is the attempt to seek out first what God said to the original readers before finding His message for today's readers. One must seek the historical context for any and every passage. The preacher must seek to understand the genre of the passage he intends to share. All of the Bible is not the same. It is all the Word of God, but one cannot read every text the same way. That only makes sense; one does not read the newspaper the way he reads a technical journal, poem or novel. The Bible is a collection of works and genres in which God speaks to His people. One cannot read Revelation as he would Genesis, or Genesis as he would the Psalms, or the Psalms as he would Paul's epistle to the Romans. One must seek literary context both in terms of the immediate context of the book, paragraph, psalm, etc.; in terms of the literary genre as a whole; and, to some degree, in terms of the Bible as a whole.

The preacher must allow each text to speak for itself without moving to explore dozens of other passages. That is not to say that parallel passages should never be consulted. At times a simpler text must be allowed to clarify a more difficult text; on other occasions one must explore how apparently divergent or contradictory texts may be reconciled. It does, however, indicate that texts should stand on their own. As one student put it, "When the Corinthians got their letter from Paul, they did not have James, Galatians or Matthew. First Corinthians must make sense on its own." God did not speak in "gobbeldy-goop." He intended for those of right heart to understand His message. Sermons and Bible classes that link together dozens of passages may unintentionally reinforce those in the pew taking passages out of their literary context. They may be seen as modeling bad exegesis and thereby providing hearers with a faulty view of Scripture and its use. This is not to suggest that such sermons and

Bible classes propounded heresy. They do, however, often derive lessons which are not the point of the texts cited.

The preacher must begin by applying the message discovered in the text to his own life. He has no right to preach or teach a text unless he allows the text to speak to him.[4]

Obligations to the Audience

The minister and teacher have an obligation to model for their audiences the methodology they have used to arrive at the meaning of the text. This does not mean that one will share all the nitty-gritty, verb-parsing, historical-research details of his study. The one who shares the Word of God has a responsibility to give the biblical text to his audience and to allow the text to move them. He is obliged to give his listeners some sense of how he arrived at his conclusions. Bible study must be seen as being within the reach of the person in the pew. Many who teach preaching today and do not encourage this approach reenforce the feeling that either the persons in the pew are inadequate to interpret the Scriptures on their own or that one really can read and use a text in almost any manner.

The modern audience needs to sense how the original audience would have received the biblical text under consideration, what their situation was, how they would have felt, how God's Word would have touched their lives, and how they would have understood it. Helping the students to walk in the shoes of the original recipients is a challenging task. The modern world is drastically different from the world of biblical times, but before modern listeners can hear the message for their lives, they must hear and feel the message for the original reader. The preacher must apply the message to his audience. Exegesis, the study of what the text said to its original audience, could be simply an abstract exercise in history and, therefore, boring. But hermeneutics, the application of the text to the modern hearer, apart from that exegesis lacks any control and becomes an exercise in subjectivity. As Fee and Stuart put it, "The only proper control for hermeneutics is to be found in the original intent of the biblical text."[5] One must move beyond what Paul said to the Corinthians to where the person sitting in front of him finds himself and what God is saying to him today. The preacher or teacher must have his Bible in one hand and today's newspaper in the other. He must know his people and how they think. He must lead them to see the implications of the word of God for their lives.

Advantages of Expository Preaching and Teaching

Expository preaching and teaching allow God to speak in ways that the preacher or teacher on his own cannot. After arriving at a new congregation, the minister began a series of sermons from Ephesians. When he came to the text on spiritual leadership in Ephesians 4:11-16, he spoke of the pastors function as teacher and the responsibility of leadership to prepare the congregation for ministry. He was met at the back door by one sister who said that she thought he was awfully brave to preach that sermon so soon after coming. His response was, "That's where I was in Ephesians." Amazingly the Bible can speak and the one who teaches its message can stay out of the way. After all he is simply moving through a text. His sermons and classes are not as likely to be seen as his pet peeves, his opinion or his agenda.

Similarly expository preaching and teaching that work through a biblical book or a series of related texts on a topic gives the teacher both a sense of direction and comfort. The general organization comes from Paul, Amos, David or Moses. Sermons and classes can easily be planned for months in advance. No longer is there the struggle, "O no! Now what am I going to preach? What shall I teach?"

The outline for an expository sermon or class is simple. It arises from the text. Its content, emphasis, structure, purpose, message and tone are identical to the content, emphasis, structure, purpose, message and tone of the original text.[6] That in no way removes opportunities for creativity in discussion or presentation. But it does guarantee a serious attempt to get the God-intended message. I can remember being told by my preaching professor that I had to preach an expository sermon. My first two sermons for him had been topical and were quite easy to put together. I struggled with a text from Philippians trying to determine Paul's message. I struggled to organize that sermon in a way that would make sense to me and to my professor. I wanted a unique approach but was stuck with Paul's organization. I was not sure this style of preaching was for me. Now I would not dream of preaching in any other way. Learning to preach a good expository sermon or a class is at first difficult. It requires serious study. It cannot be done in a few minutes or even a few hours. It is not a matter of deciding what you want to say and then looking for biblical texts to support those points. When the task is mastered, amazingly it provides the minister with the most simple and straightforward method of preparing a sermon or class.

The careful exposition of Scripture is the logical product of an affirmation of the doctrine of the priesthood of all believers. Keeping the text at the center provides the listener with the opportunity for the text to speak, allows the listener to evaluate alternative interpretations, and moves the preacher or teacher out of the limelight.

The preacher wears many hats. He is counselor, comforter, promoter, organizer, office manager and general helper. But his foremost task must always be the exposition of Scripture and the application of that message to the lives of his audience. That task can never take a back seat to the other tasks that beckon the preacher and devour his time. The man of God lives with, lives by and lives to share the Word of God; and he must do so responsibly.

Endnotes

1. Gustaf Wingren, *The Living Word: A Theological Study of Preaching and the Church*, trans. V.C. Pogue (London: SCM, 1960) 201.

2. Sidney Greidanus, *The Modern Preacher and the Ancient Text: Interpreting and Preaching Biblical Literature* (Grand Rapids: William B. Eerdmans Publishing Co., 1988) 15.

3. Gordon Fee and Douglas Stuart, *How to Read the Bible for All Its Worth*, 2nd Ed. (Grand Rapids: Zondervan, 1993) 26.

4. In recent years there have been numerous works that educate the minister as exegete. In addition to the books above, note the following: William W. Klein, Craig L. Blomberg, and Robert L. Hubbard, *Introduction to Biblical Interpretation* (Dallas: Word Publishing, 1993); Grant R. Osborne, *The Hermeneutical Spiral* (Downers Grove: InterVarsity Press, 1991); W. Randolph Tate, *Biblical Interpretation: An Integrated Approach* (Peabody: Hendrickson Publishers, 1991).

5. Fee and Stuart 25.

6. Although now out of print, Donald G. Miller's book, *The Way to Biblical Preaching* (Nashville: Abdingdon Press, 1952) is an excellent call for allowing the text to shape the sermon.

C. Michael Moss attained degrees from David Lipscomb University (B.A.), Harding Graduate School of Religion (M.A.) and Southern Baptist Theological Seminary (M.Div., Ph.D.). He began preaching in 1968. He has worked with several congregations in Nashville, currently serving as pulpit minister for the Central Church of Christ.

Expository Preaching

Stafford N

Many preachers are seeking the means to do preaching which enables them to keep the audience focused on a Bible text during the entire sermon, allows Scripture to be the guide in the selection of issues for preaching, and allows ready application of Scripture to life. Expository preaching accomplishes these goals.

Unfortunately expository preaching has been defined in more than 25 ways and many sermons given the "expository" label do not deserve it. Some think of expository preaching as simply reading a verse, explaining it and repeating that process for as long as time lasts. Others think of it merely as preaching through a book of the Bible, whatever the style of sermon organization.

Our study of expository preaching begins, then, with a definition to clarify our view of expository preaching, presentation of a number of samples for demonstration, consideration of the steps for developing expository lessons, and suggestions on how to make these lessons effective.

A Definition of Expository Preaching

Expository preaching is a method for finding in a passage of Scripture the fundamental message the Bible writer desired to convey, capsuling that message so it can be easily grasped, and elaborating on that message primarily with material from the passage itself.

In Ephesians 5:21-6:9, for example, Paul is clearly focused on a message about submission. Everything in these verses is connected with that theme. But what is Paul's message about submission? He explores three different relationships in which some Christians are to submit and others are to receive the submission. We might capsule the message by saying, "Whether you lead or follow, meet your responsibility in every relationship." To elaborate on this theme, we would take the three different relationships Paul mentions and discuss the responsibility he gives both the leader and the follower in husbands and wives, parents and children, and masters and slaves. Thus we have found the fundamental message of a passage, have capsuled the message in a strong statement, and have elaborated on this theme through the content of the passage itself.

The Process of Preparing an Expository Sermon

To prepare an expository sermon, the preacher first analyzes a passage to find a central truth the Holy Spirit put there to meet a need of his audience. He then finds several parallel thoughts from the passage which "expose" this central truth to light. Then, primarily with quotations and illustrations from the passage, from elsewhere in Scripture, and from life, the preacher shapes the message to inform and motivate the listeners.

Usually the preparation of an expository sermon will move through the following process: The preacher will choose a section of Scripture, usually a paragraph, which appears to be a unit; he will study the passage carefully to state its basic theme, message, lesson or proposition as a thesis for his sermon; and he will find the main points that passage teaches about the theme.

The expository sermon, then, is typically built around few verses, rarely more than a chapter. The theme of the verses is crafted into a powerful statement, and the teaching of the verses about the theme is summarized in parallel main headings. Each of those headings is developed, first, from the passage and then, as necessary, from elsewhere. Either as a part of each point or in the conclusion, the preacher should make very clear application of the message to the needs of the audience.

A way of viewing an expository sermon is to think of the basic theme of the passage as a net drawn through the passage to catch the lessons or points the passage reveals on that theme. Thus, from the passage comes the theme and the analysis of the theme into easily grasped thoughts. Each of these main concepts would be developed first by explaining how the passage makes the point and then by illustrations from the Bible and from life.

Approaches to Expository Preaching

Once a theme is determined, the preacher must look for main ideas which cluster about that theme. These main ideas may come from several possible approaches.

First, the preacher may find ideas in characteristics of the theme. In Revelation 20:11-15, for example, John writes of the judgment of God at the end of the world. As we look at this passage, we can ask, "What different characteristics does the writer provide for that judgment?" The passage suggests that judgment is certain, fair, merciful, final and eternal.

Acts 2:1-12 is another passage that lends itself to using characteristics. Here we have the only instance recorded in the Bible where the act of speaking in tongues is described in detail. So from this passage, we seek to learn the characteristics of tongue speaking. A study of the passage reveals that tongue speaking is made possible by the Holy Spirit, is uttering "known" languages recognized by natives in that language, and is exercising a sign to demonstrate the approval of God. These characteristics of speaking in tongues become the main headings of a sermon on this theme.

A final example of using the characteristics of a theme to shape a sermon is Revelation 21-22. In this passage John has a vision of heaven, the New Jerusalem, coming down where he could view it. He saw a city of a perfect cube, 1500 miles on a side, with 12 foundations of precious stones. A red, jasper wall 210 feet high encompasses the city, with 3 gates on each side. Those in the city get their light from God and Christ, living in the very presence of God and of the redeemed of all ages. They walk the street of gold and eat of the tree of life, which gives a different fruit every season. They have no pain, suffering, disappointment or death. After giving such a description, the preacher may distill all of these details into four qualities of life for those whose names are written in the book of life and who, therefore, can enter the New Jerusalem: They live in a place of perfect fellowship, perfect protection, perfect provision and perfect joy.

The passage, through its various figures, has revealed the real message — heaven will be perfect in every respect. The expository analysis, then, has looked for the characteristics of the theme as revealed in the passage.

Second, organization may grow from lessons about the theme. A study of Galatians 5:16-26 would suggest that the theme is "Live by the Spirit and not by the flesh." But what does the passage say we should do to attain this goal? It suggests you recall when you crucified the flesh (v. 24) and keep your life in step with the Spirit's teaching (v. 25). A sermon built on this analysis would elaborate on each of these lessons with explanation, quotations and illustrations.

Third, the preacher may search for reasons for the theme. In 1 Corinthians 13, the theme is certainly "Love." Yet a study of the context reveals that in both the chapter before and the chapter following, Paul discusses spiritual gifts. So the fundamental message of 1 Corinthians 13 must be connected with spiritual gifts. Its theme, as indicated by 12:31, is "love is superior to spiritual gifts." What reasons does Paul give for this superiority? In verses 1-3, he shows that love is more important than spiritual gifts because spiritual gifts are of no value without love, while love is of value without the gifts. In verses 4-7, he shows that love is more beneficial than spiritual gifts because love improves the character, while spiritual gifts often create undesirable personal qualities. In verses 8-13, he shows that love is more lasting than spiritual gifts since the gifts pass away, while love outlasts even faith and hope. Thus, we can reveal to our audience Paul's theme through asking, "What reasons does the writer give for his point?"

Fourth, finding persons or groups in the passage that relate to the theme is another approach. Our earlier example on submission from Ephesians 5-6 illustrates this approach of finding groups related to the theme: husbands and wives, parents and children, masters and slaves. Another example is the parable of the prodigal son, where the theme is, "Have the proper attitude toward the lost." One may consider this theme from the viewpoint of the lost toward themselves (prodigal son), the attitude of God toward the lost (Father), and the attitude of the saved toward the lost (elder brother).

Fifth, steps in the process may provide organization. Luke presents the story of the conversion of the jailer from Philippi in Acts 16:25-34. One may look at that story and ask, "What did the jailer do to be saved?" That is certainly the theme of the story. The analysis would show that the jailer took the following steps: he believed in the Lord Jesus, he repented of his sins, and he was baptized the same hour of the night.

Sixth, analysis or sub-division of the theme is another approach. An example of this approach comes from James 3:13-18. The topic of the passage is obviously "wisdom to live by." A careful study of the passage reveals that it deals with three aspects of such wisdom: the source of the wisdom (from above or from the devil), the nature of the wisdom (pure or sensual, peaceable or jealous.), and the outcome of the wisdom (good life or confusion). Notice that the passage does not deal with these aspects in order, but rather in a somewhat mixed fashion. A careful analysis, however, can separate these ideas into each element.

These six are but a few of the approaches one might take to study the passage or theme, but they illustrate the process of expository analysis.

Steps in Preparing an Expository Sermon

An excellent way to summarize information about expository preaching is to look carefully at all the steps in preparing an expository sermon. While some of the items in this list would fit any type of sermon, the list is prepared with expository sermons in mind.

I. Find the passage for the expository sermon.
   A. Find a passage with a theme which links God's message with man's needs.
   B. Ask whether the prospective message deals with an issue that is both significant and practical.
   C. After an initial look at the passage, draft a preliminary statement of the theme of the passage.

II. Explore the passage.
   A. Read several translations of the passage. Note particularly key words that differ.
   B. Study the passage in the original language to the extent you are able.
   C. Study the context before and after the passage to insure you recognize its connection with the section and the book of which it is a part.
   D. Outline the passage to note carefully its central theme and the points it expresses about the theme.
   E. Consider related passages from elsewhere to insure that your interpretation of the passage is in harmony with Bible teaching elsewhere on the same topic.

III. State the theme of the passage concisely in a way that relates the meaning of the passage to the needs of the audience.
   A. Word the theme as a subject sentence — short, strong and memorable.

B. Be sure the lesson is potentially biblical, interesting, practical and significant. If it does not qualify on any one of these four criteria, look elsewhere for a sermon topic.

IV. Word the main points.
   A. Analyze the theme, as stated in the subject sentence, into its constituent parts.
   B. See that these points all bear the same relationship to the subject sentence — all should flow from it as lessons, challenges, steps, elements, parties involved, reasons why or some other consistent set of headings.
   C. State these headings in complete sentences which are striking and parallel.
   D. Check each point to see that it is true to the meaning of the text.

V. Develop the main points with supporting materials.
   A. Find supporting materials of a wide variety such as quotations, comparisons, factional information, and examples.
   B. Especially use examples — both from the Bible and from life. Stories of people doing what you want the audience to do are usually the most powerful support for a point.
   C. Use explanation as sparingly as possible.
   D. Be sure your points and their support are biblical, interesting, practical and significant.

VI. Add the introduction and conclusion.
   A. The introduction should gain attention to the subject, gain good will for the speaker, and give necessary background information for the subject.
   B. Be sure the introduction emphasizes the need of the audience you are meeting and has material that will capture interest.
   C. The conclusion should summarize and give the final motivation and appeal.
   D. The conclusion is a good place for a strong final positive example and for bringing the practical applications to a climax — "This is what you should do." Often this is called the "So What?" of the sermon.

VII. Consider the climax and transitions.
   A. The sermon should have rising action, peaks and falling action. Normally you should have a sub-climax near the

end of each of the main points and the major climax in the early part of the conclusion.

   B. Be sure transitions make clear the movement from point to point and keep the audience always aware of the point you are developing.

VIII. Check the emotional appeal in the sermon.

   A. While you should have been including materials with emotional appeals as you have developed almost all the previous steps, it is useful to ask at this point if the sermon has the right level of emotional appeals.

   B. Ask whether your appeals are honest, fair and to the appropriate drives. Will the audience be moved, challenged and inspired?

IX. Make a final check for the interest level all the way through the sermon.

   A. Does your supporting material have good variety?

   B. Are there enough good examples?

   C. Are there practical applications and are they relevant to the lives of those in the audience?

   D. Have you drawn the audience into the sermon so they feel a part of the experience.

Suggestions on Expository Preaching

Be sure you are getting the message out of the text and not forcing one into it. Search and dig until you are sure that the message you are presenting is God's message for the audience's need and not a thought of your own which you have pushed into the passage.

Use expository preaching to leave the audience with a better understanding of a passage. Every time in the future your listeners encounter the passage of your expository lesson, they should recall the sermon about it. If you deliver a series of expository sermons on a book, you can both present useful and practical lessons Sunday-by-Sunday, and at the same time leave your congregation with a better grasp of the entire book you are preaching. Preaching through a book also allows the topics God put into that book to be brought to the audience.

Explore a number of possible approaches to the text before settling on the one you consider the best. It is not likely that the very first option that comes to your mind will be the best. Try several sets of points before you settle on one. It is also important for you to hone the statement of the subject sentence or theme and the main points until they are short, striking and memorable. "Value Yourself" is much stronger that "It is very important that each one of us should place a high value on his own existence." In identifying your theme and main points, be sure you are true to the context of the larger passage and the book from which you are preaching.

While an expository sermon draws its theme and main headings from one passage, illustrations, examples, narratives and cases must be added and may come from outside the passage. To make your expository sermons practical, interesting and compelling, you must use good illustration. It is easy for a expository sermon to be primarily explanation of the text with heavy reliance on word studies, a comparison of versions, and restatement of the wording.

Since most people are so "story oriented" from television, books and magazines, a preacher must use frequent illustrations. Some examples may be analogies. Other examples may be negative cases, stories of those who have not done what the passage teaches and have therefore encountered problems. The strongest illustrations will be those which tell stories of people doing exactly what you want your audience to do. If your lesson is on personal work, tell of Christians who are doing personal work. If your lesson is on honesty, you may tell of people who have lied and gotten in trouble, but also tell of people under pressure to lie who told the truth.

Be sure applications are clear and forceful. As you study a passage for an expository sermon, keep asking what needs will be met. Most of us are not very good at making applications to our own lives. If we see the application at all, we will likely think of someone else who needs this teaching. You must, then, be direct in application. Ask yourself, "What temptations this passage can help the audience meet? What dangers can it help them face or trials to overcome? What Christian service can this passage prepare the listeners to do? How can it make them to be better husbands or wives, parents or children? How can it help them go to heaven?"

Use some help on expository analysis if you need it, but be careful. Some commentaries are especially good for help on exposition. *The Pulpit Commentary* has a section on each passage with thoughts that can be good starters. Commentaries by William Barclay and Warren Wiersbe often have a useful expository analysis. While such sources can give beneficial ideas, you should develop your own skill at expository analysis and not rely heavily on others. Rarely should you take another's exposition without adapting it to your own style, your own audience, and your own personal experience.

Do not limit yourself to expository preaching alone. While this method is often the best approach and should be the most frequent type of lesson a preacher uses, there are times when a subject-based sermon or a textual sermon many be the best way to deal with a need of the audience. Sermons are sometimes needed that combine the teaching of many passages in different places on topics like grace, baptism, worship in song, repentance or the work of elders.

Conclusion

Expository preaching is a powerful way to apply the message of God's word to the needs of Christians and non-Christians alike. It can get people to bring their Bibles to church and begin studying through the text with the preacher. It can teach them how to dig into a passage so that, in their own study and in their own Bible teaching, they will be better students of the Word.

Expository preaching is a valuable method for allowing a preacher to become the conduit by which God delivers the message which He provided in His work to people in need. Every preacher should know how to use exposition well.

Stafford North began preaching in 1948 and has served churches in Louisiana, Florida, Texas, Oklahoma and Kansas. He has been an elder of the Memorial Road Church of Christ since 1972. A frequent speaker and writer, he has specialized in the books of Daniel and Revelation. Since 1952, he has been associated with Oklahoma Christian University of Science of Arts. He holds degrees in speech from Abilene Christian University (B.A.), Louisiana State University (M.A.) and University of Florida (Ph.D.).

Use of the Old Testament in Preaching

Terry Briley

The Need to Preach from the Old Testament

The preacher faces a daunting task, so he needs all the help he can get. Unfortunately he often neglects the support he can gain from the Old Testament. It has been my observation that many ministerial students come to school convinced the Old Testament has little relevance for them or that their congregations are not interested in hearing the Old Testament preached. They give little emphasis, therefore, to preparing themselves to properly understand and apply the message of the Old Testament. Interestingly, those who have been out in the field for a while, having faced the challenge of preparing 100 sermons per year, more often recognize their need for this resource and seek to make up for their earlier lack of preparation.

It is understandable that Christian preachers would seek to emphasize the New Testament message. I have no intention of persuading anyone otherwise. I am convinced, however, that it is extremely difficult to understand and proclaim the New Testament message unless both the preacher and his hearers have a good grasp of the Old Testament message. If my premise is true, the Old Testament has both a direct and an indirect function in our preaching.

Our frequent indifference to the Old Testament has a theological basis. As Leonard Allen has pointed out in *The*

Cruciform Church, an extreme emphasis on the distinction between the covenants leads to the conclusion that the former covenant has nothing to say to those of us who are under the new.[1] It is possible to blur or even obliterate the distinction between the covenants, which would have serious consequences. It is not necessary to do so, however, in the quest to apply the Old Testament today.

The neglect of the Old Testament by many modern preachers is ironic in light of the extensive use of it in apostolic preaching. It has frequently been noted that the Old Testament was the only Scripture available to the earliest Christians. The sermons in Acts, as well as most of the books of the New Testament, are packed with Old Testament quotations and allusions. According to one calculation this material constitutes almost one-third of the New Testament.[2] Although a completed canon of Scripture was anticipated and needed, there is no indication that the earliest Christians were simply "settling" for the Old Testament until the sequel came out.

In 2 Timothy 3:16-17, Paul reminds Timothy that all Scripture is inspired of God and is profitable for thoroughly equipping the man of God for every good work. In the preceding two verses, however, Paul refers to Timothy's Jewish upbringing, which included instruction in the sacred writings from childhood. The reference to "all Scripture" in verse 16, therefore, refers in part, if not primarily, to what we call the Old Testament. Similarly, in Romans 15:3-4, Paul tells his readers that the things which were written in earlier times were written for our instruction, referring to Jesus' fulfillment of Psalm 69:9. Paul firmly believes this principle, for he repeatedly backs up his arguments with references to the Old Testament.

In addition to the quotations, allusions and explicit reference to the value of the Old Testament in the New Testament, there are more subtle but equally important reasons to appreciate the Old Testament. One would be hard-pressed to understand Hebrews without a good understanding of the priesthood, sacrifice, sanctuary and other Old Testament teachings. One of the reasons many Christians struggle with Revelation is because it is written in "Old Testament language," with 518 allusions to the Old Testament even though it contains no direct quotations.[3]

The area of the prophetic fulfillment of the Old Testament in the New Testament is obviously of great interest. There are rather straightforward passages, such as Micah 5:2 which predicts the birth of the Messiah at Bethlehem and the numerous verses which identify the Messiah as a descendant of David. Many others, however, are not so simple. They require sensitivity to the prophetic passage's context if they are to make sense. Good examples of such passages are the four Old Testament references around which Matthew 2 is structured. For example, what is the relationship between the "entrance" of the infant Jesus and his family into Egypt and the reference to Hosea 11:1, "Out of Egypt I have called my Son?"[4] One is hindered from grasping one of the most basic elements in the New Testament — the fulfillment theme — without a good understanding of the Old Testament. In Luke 24:27, Jesus explained to the disciples on the road to Emmaus "what was said in all the Scriptures concerning himself." In a sense, then, one cannot proclaim the New Testament message without at the same time proclaiming the Old.

On an even deeper level, the Old Testament presents foundational concepts which the New Testament assumes. The purpose of creation, the nature of God, man, sin, redemption and many others are covered in the Old Testament, often in greater depth. For example, when Jesus was questioned about divorce He referred back to the creation account. When Paul dealt with the relationship between men and women in marriage and the church he referred back to creation and the impact of the first sin.

Given the close connection we have observed between the Old and New Testaments, it is impossible to hold on to the New while rejecting the Old. Many Christians fail to fully appreciate that God has not changed, nor has the basic nature of His relationship to His people changed. When Paul discussed justification by grace through faith, he felt it was important to demonstrate that this has always been the way of salvation (cf. the example of Abraham).

The relationship between the Old and New Testaments might be compared to the relationship between French I and French II, or Algebra I and Algebra II. The latter is built on the foundation of the former, and we would not think of placing someone in the advanced class who has not learned the basics of the foundational one. There is therefore much for the Christian to learn and for the minister to preach from the Old Testament.

How to Preach from the Old Testament

First, I would like to examine some general considerations for preaching from the Old Testament and then look more specifically at the different types of materials found in the Old Testament and how to approach them.

Perhaps the most important consideration in preaching from the Old Testament is how to relate the material to the Christian. More attention will be given to this subject in relation to specific types of Old Testament literature, but in general we must not move to this goal too quickly. In other words we should always strive first to view any passage from the perspective of its original participants and hearers. This is true whether we are dealing with an explicitly prophetic text or one we may apply in principle.

The preceding caution addresses a basic principle of the proper handling of biblical texts. One should recognize the relationship between what a text said to its original recipients (often referred to as "exegesis") and what it says to its current audience ("interpretation" or "hermeneutics"). If one does not base interpretation upon exegesis the end result is likely to be flawed. This is true of New Testament texts as well, but the danger is even greater with the Old Testament.[5]

In attempting to read the Old Testament initially without our New Testament "glasses," we realize that there is an ever-developing understanding of God and His purpose within the Old Testament (progressive revelation). We must first, therefore, seek to place what we are reading on the continuum of awareness of God's purpose in that time. This helps us understand God's tolerance of polygamy, for example. Similarly we evaluate to some extent the laws given at Sinai against the background of the people of that day.

Ultimately, our goal is to apply the message to the believer today in light of New Testament revelation. In so doing we keep in mind the matters of continuity: the nature of God, man, etc. We next consider matters of discontinuity. We might have to distinguish, for example, between the situation of an Israelite in a theocratic state and a believer under American government. As we do this we are in a better position to fairly and legitimately apply the passage to the Christian today.

Literature is not all of the same type. We normally adjust our method of reading to the type of literature with which we are dealing. There are different "rules" for reading a newspaper article, a work of fiction, a technical manual and a book of poetry. It is helpful to realize that the Bible is made up of a number of types, or genres, of literature.[6]

When one examines the literature of the New Testament, it basically falls under three headings: history/narrative (the Gospels and Acts), epistles and apocalyptic (Revelation). There is more diversity, however, in the Old Testament. We will briefly examine five major Old Testament genres and how to approach them in order to proclaim their message effectively.

Old Testament Narrative

Probably more sermons are preached from the narrative, or historical, portion of the Old Testament than from any other genre. There is great value in recognizing that the Old Testament is consumed to a large extent with telling a tremendous story. A major issue in preaching from portions of this story is understanding the overarching plot. The main character of the Old Testament is God. In other words, the Old Testament is not ultimately about Abraham, Moses or David, but God. Sermons from Old Testament narrative often take the form of moralizing from the lives of Old Testament saints or sinners. This misses the fact that the primary emphasis is upon how God relates to and works through these individuals.

Emphasizing God's role in the Biblical story also reduces the tendency to resort to allegorizing the text, a common abuse in preaching from the Old Testament. This occurs when one takes an incidental detail of the text and gives it some deeper significance. Part of the problem of allegory is the fact that it is so subjective that almost anything can be proven by it. As with all types of material in Scripture, the sermon should be derived from, not imposed upon, the text.

Old Testament Legal Texts

If most Old Testament sermons come from the narrative portions, probably the fewest are based upon legal texts. The exception to this generalization would be the Ten Commandments. These continue to receive emphasis because they are seen, for the most part, to have an abiding relevance. The rest of the Mosaic Law is widely considered to be both irrelevant and obscure. How many who have committed to read the entire Bible have bogged down or quit somewhere between Exodus 21 and Deuteronomy 34, or simply skipped this material? The result of this attitude is unfortunate, for if we will take the time to understand the Law we will find much of value.

God has not changed. We are in a covenant relationship with him now as Israel was then. With regard to the Law, we have stressed the discontinuity between the covenants almost to the exclusion of their continuity. We have tended to simplistically conclude that the former covenant was based on law whereas the new is based on grace. There is grace in the Old Testament, however, just as there is law in the New. The preface to the Ten Commandments (Ex. 20:2) illustrates the principle of grace: "I am Yahweh your God who brought you out of the land of Egypt, out of the house of bondage." Redemption thus preceded legislation. Similarly, Deuteronomy repeatedly emphasizes that God did not call Israel to be His people because of their numbers or might or righteousness, but because of His love for them and the promise He had made to Abraham.

An additional problem in our attitude toward the Law is the word "law" itself. It tends to have a negative connotation. The Hebrew word *torah*, however, is better rendered "instruction" or "guidance." It is a positive term when viewed properly. In Psalm 19, God's commandments are seen to restore the soul and rejoice the heart; they are more precious than gold and sweeter than honey. Since the New Testament, and Paul in particular, reacts against improper approaches to the Law, we tend to view the Law as inherently negative. The New Testament contains God's instruction just as clearly as the Old, and there is no more a basis of salvation in one than the other. God's instruction tells those redeemed by His grace how to live in order to maintain fellowship with Him and to glorify Him by fulfilling His purpose for His people.

Even if we have a proper appreciation for the Law and its role in Scripture, we still must face the fact that the ritual elements of the Law of Moses have been fulfilled in Jesus, and the elements governing Israel as a theocratic nation do not directly apply to the nature of the kingdom of God today.[7] In examining these laws we can more clearly understand the work of Christ, the nature of a holy people, and the mind of God. We must look for the underlying principles of God's laws for Israel.

The New Testament describes the work of Christ within the framework of priesthood and sacrifice, brought out most clearly in the highly neglected book of Leviticus. In the first seven chapters we have a treatment of the various types of sacrifice which collectively picture Christ as our sacrificial substitute. In Leviticus 8-10 we find the institution of the priesthood and the sacred nature of that institution. The two concepts are brought together powerfully in chapter sixteen, which treats the Day of Atonement. We cannot adequately appreciate and understand the fulfillment without acquainting ourselves with that which it fulfills.

Israel's ritual purity laws are obscure and mysterious to us, and most believers are relieved that they no longer apply. They still have something to say to us, however. Even though we may not understand the rationale for all of these laws, we are able to understand their larger purpose. They were to mark Israel as distinctive, set apart for God. The comprehensiveness of these laws is striking. They deal with birth, death, food, marriage, sex, work and more. All of life was to be viewed in connection with one's relationship with God and the desire to honor and reveal Him. In a sense they correspond to Paul's prayer in 1 Thessalonians 5:23, that we be sanctified entirely — spirit, soul and body.

God's laws governing Israel's civic life, along with their penalties, reveal something to us about what is important to God. There were numerous capital offenses that may be divided into three categories: those which are directly against God (idolatry, blasphemy); those which undermine the family (adultery, rebellious child); and disrespect for life itself (murder). Even though we are not compelled to carry out these punishments today, they should tell us something about how God views such matters.

The motivation for capital punishment is twofold: to remove evil from the community and to discourage others from repeating the offense. There was to be a strong sense of community. Individuals were responsible for dealing with sins which they witnessed. Execution was normally by stoning. Although the witness was to cast the first stone, the entire community was to participate. Though we are not called upon today to execute, but hopefully to redeem, the offender, there is still to be a sense of community and the responsibility which goes along with it. The widely neglected New Testament teaching on church discipline parallels Israel's community relationships.

Finally with regard to Old Testament legal texts, we have an opportunity in them to aid our understanding of a key subject in the New Testament — the proper relationship between law and grace. Deuteronomy, especially the first eleven chapters, is probably our best source in this area. Moses sets the Law clearly within the framework of a covenant relationship. He emphasizes the graciousness of God and the motive of love. It is from Deuteronomy 6:5 that Jesus derives the "great commandment" of loving God with all of one's being. We would have a much healthier concept if we would go back to God's original intention for the Law.

Psalms

The book of Psalms is quoted in the New Testament more often than any other Old Testament book. It has also retained its popularity with Christians more than most portions of the Old Testament, being frequently bound with pocket New Testaments. The use of Psalms in preaching, however, still requires some special considerations. One issue is the highly poetic language of the Psalms. This vivid imagery is part of the power and appeal of Psalms, but it must not be pressed too far. For example, when David in Psalm 51:5 proclaims that "in sin did my mother conceive me," he is not addressing the matter of original sin but affirming how deeply-rooted he felt sin to be in his life.

This diversity of experience is demonstrated by the various types of psalms. Hymns are expressions of praise and adoration to God. Thanksgiving psalms offer gratitude to God for some deliverance or fulfilled promise. However it is the laments, or complaints, which make up the largest category of Psalms.

Walter Brueggemann has reclassified these three categories of psalms. He calls the hymns songs of orientation; the laments he sees as songs of disorientation; and he considers songs of thanksgiving to deal with reorientation.[8] This is meaningful terminology and provides a healthy perspective on the relevance of Psalms to the Christian. The laments in particular show us how we can be brutally honest with God about our feelings of pain and despair and yet not give up our faith (Psalm 22). We gain tremendous insight on prayer, perspectives not given to nearly the same extent in the New Testament. The personal nature of Psalms makes it a meaningful source for preaching. We normally conceive of the movement of Scripture as from God to man, but here the movement is more from man to God. It is the ability of the later reader to identify with the psalmist which accounts, at least in part, for the abiding popularity of Psalms.

Psalms also teaches us about the nature of worship. Psalm 100 singles out the importance of praise in worship. Those whose perspective is shaped by the New Testament alone will have a deficient framework for understanding this issue. Although there are external differences between worship in the Old and New Testaments, the fundamental nature and purpose of worship has not changed.

Wisdom Literature

Like many of the Psalms, Old Testament wisdom literature portrays the struggle to apply God's truth to everyday life, particularly to dilemmas such as the suffering of the righteous. The books which are traditionally categorized as wisdom literature, however, are not all of the same type. Some consideration must be given to the nature and purpose of each work before we can preach effectively from them.

Proverbs, as the title suggest, consists of a collection of concisely stated truths. By their very nature they are generalizations rather than ironclad rules. A clear example of this is found in Proverbs 26:4-5. In consecutive verses we are told first not to answer a fool according to his folly and then to answer a fool according to his folly. This is not a contradiction, but rather a recognition that wisdom does not dictate the same policy in every situation. We should keep this in mind when we deal with Proverbs.

For example, Proverbs 22:6 says, "Train up a child in the way he should go, and when he is old he will not depart from it." To take this as an absolute guarantee not only contradicts experience but it also removes the child's freedom of choice. Needless pain has been inflicted upon good parents by the abuse of this text. This does not deny the validity of the wisdom in Proverbs which is applied to many vital subjects, but recognizes its limitations. It is true that the likelihood of a child following the proper path as an adult is greatly enhanced by proper training from his parents.

We live in a world which has a great deal more knowledge than wisdom. Proverbs has much to teach us about what wisdom is and how it manifests itself in our attitudes and practices and relationships. In presenting this material, it is best to glean the material topically throughout the book. This gives us a broader perspective and minimizes the possibility that we will misconstrue an isolated proverb.

A somewhat different strategy must be followed when dealing with Job and Ecclesiastes. Each of these wisdom books tells a story. In fact, they may be compared to mystery novels in the sense that one cannot fully understand the elements along the way until the conclusion is reached. Since they deal with some of the most fundamental and timeless dilemmas of life, they are worthy of our efforts.

Job is normally understood to address the problem of the suffering of the righteous. There is an even deeper issue, however, relating to the justice and fairness of God. Most Christians are aware of at least the broad outline of Job's story. In the end, God confronts Job and makes it clear that human beings are incapable of fully understanding their Creator and His ways. There is a temptation to conclude that we should not question God and simply to say "all's well that ends well." However this does not resolve the question of why God allowed Job to suffer. The key to understanding the book of Job, in addition to the concluding chapters, is the response of Elihu in chapters 32-36. He had been hesitant to speak up because of his youth, but finally he could restrain himself no longer. He was angry

with the three friends because they could not find grounds to condemn Job but did so anyway. More significantly, he rebuked Job
"because he was righteous in his own eyes" (32:1) and "because he
justified himself rather than God" (32:2). It is this awareness, plus
God's confrontation, which led Job to confess, "I have heard of you
by hearing of the ear, but now my eye sees you. Therefore I abhor
myself and repent in dust and ashes" (Job 42:5-6). This confession
marks Job's last words before God restores his fortunes.

Although Job may have been innocent of any great outward trans-
gression, prideful elevation of self over God made Job incapable of
truly knowing God and thus seriously jeopardized his relationship
with God. Job's sufferings were part of a purifying process. This is
in keeping with the New Testament teaching on God's discipline of
His children and forces us to recognize that we cannot expect to
understand God's ways in every case.

Ecclesiastes addresses a broader spectrum of human struggles,
and is also largely dependent upon the conclusion for a proper
understanding. The apparent theme of despair, illustrated by the
repeated refrain "Vanity of vanities; all is vanity," has caused many
to question the book's value and validity for believers in God at any
time. To many, the conclusion that one should fear God and keep his
commandments (Eccl. 12:13) seems totally out of character with the
rest of the book. Liberal scholars erroneously consider this conclusion a later addition designed to redeem what precedes it. However
Ecclesiastes has a unified message and is one of the most significant
books in the Bible for today's world, which daily questions whether
one can find meaning and purpose in life.

In Ecclesiastes 2:24-26, for example, it is pointed out that the ability to enjoy life must come from the hand of God (cf. Eccl. 3:11-13;
5:18-20). As painful as it is to examine the bleak realities of life
without God, it is important to do so in order that we might appreciate and communicate to others the joyful alternative.

The challenge of preaching from both Job and Ecclesiastes is one
must either preach an overview of the entire book, or at least deal
with individual passages in light of the overall message. One must
be cautious, for example, in preaching from the speeches of Job and
his friends in the central portion of the book. Although there may be
much truth to be found there, we know from the conclusion that they
were also mistaken on some basic points. Similarly, we should not
preach that "all is vanity" in an absolute sense, but only when considered apart from God.

The Song of Songs (or Song of Solomon) is also normally categorized as Wisdom Literature. It is certainly one of the most challenging books in Scripture from which to preach. The key issue is the overall interpretation of the book. Is it a song in celebration of the intimate love of a man and woman for one another, or is it an allegory of God's love for Israel or the church? Although many interpreters through the ages have felt compelled to opt for the latter in order to legitimize the book, that decision probably says more about the interpreters that the Song of Songs itself.

I find no justification within the Song of Songs for seeing it as anything other than what it appears to be, a love poem. While its frankness may be unsettling to us, we find similar language in Proverbs 5:15ff. From the beginning, God instituted the sexual relationship, within the proper context, as a gift to human beings. Although the more explicit passages would not be suitable for public discourse, a passage such as Song of Songs 8:6-7 would be appropriate for the promotion of the love between a husband and wife.

The Prophets

There is a common tendency to view the Old Testament prophets as primarily foretellers of the future. While the predictive element was certainly a significant part of their work, their main task was more like what we would consider preaching. They have been aptly described as "covenant enforcement mediators."[9] They were largely involved in calling people back to the covenant stipulations which defined their relationship with God. The covenant clearly outlined what would happen if Israel was unfaithful to the covenant. The predictive element thus focused on the times and agents of God's judgement, as well as future restoration.

Since the message of the prophets is so closely tied to the former covenant, we must take that into consideration when preaching from them today. For example, the prophets are often used as a basis for preaching on social justice. There are legitimate texts for addressing matters of justice and fairness in society, but we must remember the differences between the structure of Israel's society and our own.

Since there is a great deal of continuity between the former and new covenants in their fundamental nature, the prophets are valuable in their reflection upon the nature of covenant life. While the legal texts define the nature of the covenant and the consequences for faithfulness and unfaithfulness, and the historical books illustrate these principles in the real world, the prophets give us insight into the heart of God as he relates to His people. In this process we see both the righteousness and the love of God revealed. God holds His people accountable for their sins (cf. Amos 2:6-16; 3:1-2), but His faithfulness and compassion will not allow Him to forsake them (cf. Hosea).

The prophets, like many of the psalmists, deepen our appreciation of the meaning of worship. Old Testament worship was not to be merely external ritual. Proper worship demands the incorporation of a life submitted to God and his purposes (cf. Isa. 1:10ff; Hosea 6:6; Amos 5:21ff; Micah 6:6ff). The prophets also enhance our understanding of the one we are to worship. Part of this comes through the messianic expectation which elevates our regard for our redemption (cf. Isa. 53).

There are, of course, many other important subjects addressed in the broad scope of the prophetic message. Jeremiah 18:7-10 describes the conditional nature of God's promises and warnings. Ezekiel 18 emphasizes individual accountability for sin. Habakkuk demonstrates a faith that overcomes uncertainty about God's actions. The prophets may sometimes be difficult to understand due to their extensive use of poetic imagery and the need to know the historical background of each writer, but the effort yields a rich reward of insight.

Conclusion

There is great value to preaching from the Old Testament. Extra work may be required to allow us to effectively incorporate preaching from the Old Testament into our ministry, but rich rewards will be gained from looking at all of Scripture. Our understanding and appreciation for the redeeming work of Christ will be enhanced through a better understanding of the Old Testament. Each preacher, as a "man of God," must arm himself with the whole counsel of God in order to most effectively equip the saints and reach the lost.

Endnotes

1. C. Leonard Allen, *The Cruciform Church: Becoming a Cross-Shaped People in a Secular World*, 2nd ed. (Abilene: ACU Press, 1990), pp. 52ff.

2. Andrew E. Hill, *Baker's Handbook of Bible Lists* (Grand Rapids: Baker, 1981), pp. 102-104.

3. Eugene H. Peterson, *Reversed Thunder: The Revelation of John and the Praying Imagination* (San Francisco: Harper & Row, 1988), p. 23.

4. For a good discussion of the Old Testament references in Matthew 2 and the subject in general, see Walter C. Kaiser Jr., *The Uses of the Old Testament in the New* (Chicago: Moody, 1985).

5. See Gordon Fee and Douglas Stuart, *How to Read the Bible for All Its Worth*, 2nd ed. (Grand Rapids: Zondervan, 1993) for an excellent treatment of biblical genres.

6. Ibid., pp. 78ff.

7. Israel's laws are sometimes divided into three groups: moral, civil and ritual. These categories overlap, and they might have sounded strange to ancient Hebrews who viewed things from a more holistic perspective. They still have value, however, for the purpose of our discussion.

8. Walter Brueggeman, *The Message of the Psalms* (Minneapolis: Augsburg, 1984).

9. *How to Read the Bible for All Its Worth*, pp. 167ff.

Terry Briley holds a degree in Biblical Languages from David Lipscomb University (B.A.) and degrees in Hebrew and Cognate Studies at Hebrew Union College (M. Phil., Ph.D.). He now serves as an assistant professor of Bible at David Lipscomb University. He has lectured at regional and national conferences, including the conferences of the Christian Scholars Conference and the Society of Biblical Literature.

Use of the New Testament in Preaching

Burt Groves

In the name of relevance and eloquence, contemporary preaching is seeking to attract large audiences by rhetorical power. Instead of relying on human ingenuity, however, the man of God should use Scripture as the basis of all preaching. God's Word has power.

New Testament Use of Scripture

Jesus quoted from Scripture, employing it to establish truth. Tempted by the devil in the wilderness, He responded from the Law; He quoted Malachi to identify John the Baptist, and He explained why the Jews rejected Him with reference to Isaiah 6:9-10. The Lord rebuked the scribes and Pharisees by applying Isaiah 29:13 to them. When He drove the merchants from the temple, Jesus explained His conduct by quoting both Isaiah 56:7 and Jeremiah 7:11. He applied Psalm 118:22-23 to explain that the Jews were forfeiting the kingdom for rejecting Him. Jesus and His inspired biographers quoted from Scripture because all things had to be fulfilled "which were written in the law of Moses, and in the prophets, and in the psalms" (Luke 24:44).

Preaching Jesus

Man of God, be cautious to draw your listeners to the Savior rather than to yourself (1 Cor. 2:11). Paul warned

Timothy about people who would seek teachers who would please them rather than teach them the truth (2 Tim. 4:3-4).

Paul answered the question of what to preach by saying, "I determined not to know any thing among you, save Jesus Christ, and him crucified" (2 Cor. 4:5).

Paul did not place his trust in scholastic credentials. One does not see in Paul the charisma of great contemporary preachers nor the programs which attract thousands to hear them. Paul's preaching in Corinth pointed to Savior and not himself (1 Cor. 2:3).

Worldly perspectives prevent accurate appraisals of the blessings enjoyed in Christ — wisdom, righteousness, sanctification and redemption (1 Cor. 1:30-31). The believer cannot, in the name of relevance, turn from the inspired text to preaching messages that originate in philosophy, psychology or sociology. The power of positive thinking may enhance egos but it cannot save souls.

A compromised message causes those who hear it to be lost. Most Jews found the message of the crucified Christ offensive and most Greeks heard no moving appeal to their popular philosophies (1 Cor. 1:23). Only the message of the suffering Servant can save. One cannot preach Christ while ignoring His doctrine. The teaching of Christ embraces all of the Gospel, instructing sinners how to be saved and saints how to live (Rom. 1:16; 16:25-26).

Preaching the Word

The New Testament offers the authentic account of the only message that can reconcile the sinner with God. The Bible is more than a book — it provides the Message who became the messenger (John 1:14). No wonder Paul urged Timothy, "Preach the word; be instant in season, out of season; reprove, rebuke, exhort with all longsuffering and doctrine" (2 Tim. 4:2).

The man of God knows the use of the New Testament is vital to preaching (1 Peter 4:11). Preaching should be presented to listeners in a manner that makes the truth understandable. An ideal sermon communicates a single idea supported by Scripture. Expository preaching best accomplishes this task.[1]

Handling the Text

Expository preaching does not require isolation of the text from other passages which address the same subject. True exposition of Scripture gets out of the text what God put in it; putting something into the text which God did not place there is called imposition. A knowledge of all the New Testament helps prevent one from resorting to subjective preaching.[2]

Those who object to the complete use of the New Testament in preaching must believe that man communicates better than the Holy Spirit. One cannot preach the Word without presenting the teachings of the New Testament. Paul's practice must be followed: "For I have not shunned to declare unto you all the counsel of God" (Acts 20:27)

Preaching All of the New Testament

Matthew, Mark, Luke and John provide perspectives into the nature of the God-man (John 1:1-18). Jesus is the Bread of Life, the Light of the world, the Door, the Good Shepherd, the Resurrection, the Way, the Truth, the Life, and the Vine. Christ fulfilled the law and the prophets, brought grace and truth to people alienated by sin, challenged their tradition, and saved sinners through his own death. Jesus gave insight into God's love in the parable of the prodigal son and declared God's justice in the rich man and Lazarus. All four writers record the heart of the Gospel — the death, burial and resurrection of Jesus.

The book of Acts provides us with insight into the practice of early Christians. This early history describes how people were converted, how they supplied one another's needs, the primary mission of the church, and how they organized according to God's will. Because the apostles were binding and loosing as the Holy Spirit directed, what they approved then continues to be approved today. What they preached then should be preached now. We learn about elders, the Lord's supper, and how the early Christians cared for one another.

Prior to his ascension, Jesus commissioned the apostles to preach the Good News to all nations. Preaching from the epistles, letters to groups of Christians, helps us know that churches today face many of the same problems of first century churches and how we should address these problems.

The letters to the Corinthians address division resulting from following man-made teachings, sexual immorality, selfishness, unapproved marriages and idolatry. Other lessons from this book that are relevant today include conduct in worship, the nature of miracles and their proper use at that time, and the definition of mutual love.

The presence of false teachers caused Paul to warn against another gospel which would have caused the unwary to fall from grace

(Gal. 1:8-9; 5:4). While in the custody of Roman officials Paul wrote concerning the exalted Christ to the church at Colosse and to Philemon. One finds many texts almost identical in Ephesians and Colossians, but in Ephesians the church is presented in her splendor as Jesus' bride, while the divine nature of Jesus is emphasized in Colossians. Preaching Ephesians allows congregations the opportunity to hear a description of how unity can be enjoyed.

The gospel preacher will find no text presenting better challenges to the congregation that those in the letter to Philippi. One such lesson is the warning against self-seeking rather than Christ-seeking. We need to hear the message sent to the Thessalonians: patiently endure persecution, practice church discipline, and pray.

The letters to preachers, Timothy and Titus, provide instruction about work in the kingdom. Congregations with a knowledge of these letters will better understand the work of preachers, elders and deacons. They also remind us of the threat of heresy, the need to warn Christians of danger, and the need to teach men to pray.

Hebrews demonstrates the superiority of Christ's priesthood. Stories of those who had great faith inspire people to live more faithful and dedicated lives.

Preaching James will help a congregation to develop practical faith. James vividly illustrates saving faith, the importance of preparing to teach, the brevity of life, and the importance of patience.

In preaching from the letters of Peter we see both the inheritance of the faithful and the omnipotent will of God. We learn that no sinner can purchase salvation, but the sacrifice of God's Lamb makes salvation possible for those who through obedience become holy. Through Peter, Christians learn about their identity as God's chosen people, living stones in His spiritual temple, a royal priesthood that sacrifices self, and strangers passing through a wicked world. Peter also teaches us that suffering is part of the Christian life, a difficult message for comfortable churches.

John's writings teach about fellowship with God. Such preaching brings joy of salvation for those who walk in the light. Gospel preaching warns against the danger of selfish conduct (1 John 2:15-17). Preachers can identify with John, whose greatest joy was the faithfulness of others. In a day when men imagine that truth is relative and faith subjective, John's warning against encouraging false teachers is essential (2 John 9-11).

Jude is a short book with an important message of urging God's children to struggle for the faith.

The symbolism in Revelation is sometimes difficult to preach but the message is clear — Jesus is victorious and the faithful will share in his glory. The letters to the seven churches are easy to apply to us today.

Our Commitment

Gospel preachers cannot echo the teachings of the world (Titus 2:1). We must preach the teachings of the New Testament to impress upon people the need to please God.

Man of God, never confuse your hearers concerning the New Testament with your opinion about it (Rev. 22:18-19). Make the message plain by the Scriptures you preach and the life you live.

Endnotes

1. Robinson, p. 33, 19.

2. Gus Nichols, *Crowning Fifty Years*. ed. J.D. Thomas (Abilene: Abilene Christian College, 1968) p. 201.

Burt Groves is the author of two books about the life of Christ, editor of a teaching periodical, and a minister of the Lord's Church for more than 35 years. He is presently in his 12th year at the Pleasant Grove Church in Dallas, Texas.

Suggestions for Further Reading

The Man of God in the New Testament
Stan Smith

Blamires, Harry. *The Christian Mind*. Ann Arbor: Servant Books, 1978.

Blenkinsopp, J. *The Men Who Spoke Out: The Old Testament Prophets*. London: Darton, Longman & Todd, 1969.

Bullock, C. Hassel. *An Introduction to the Old Testament Prophetic Books*. Chicago: Moody Press, 1986.

Graham, William C. *The Prophets and Israel's Culture*. Chicago: U. of Chicago, 1934.

Heschel, Abraham J. *The Prophets*. 2 vols. New York: Harper & Row, 1962.

Leslie, Elmer A. *The Prophets Tell Their Own Story*. New York: Abingdon, 1939.

Lewis, Jack P. *The Minor Prophets*. Grand Rapids: Baker, 1966.

Peterson, Eugene H. *Run with the Horses*. Downers Grove: InterVarsity, 1983.

Phillips, J.B. *Four Prophets*. New York: The Macmillan Company, 1963.

The Whole Man
J.J. Turner

Bell, Donald (1970). *How Get Along With People In The Church*. Grand Rapids, Mich: Zondervan Publishing.

Boren, Maxie B. (1964). *Problems Faced By Young Preachers*. Texas: Self published.

Horne, Chevis F. (1975). *Crisis In The Pulpit*. Grand Rapids, Mich.: Baker Book House.

Matthews, Dewitt (1976). *Capers of The Clergy*. Grand Rapids, Mich.: Baker Book House.

Paul, Cecil R. (1981). *Passages of a Pastor*. Grand Rapids, Mich.: Zondervan Publishing.

Phelps, Arthur S. (1958). *Public Speaking for Ministers*. Grand Rapids, Mich.: Baker Book House.

Rassieur, Charles L. (1976). *The Problems Clergymen Don't Talk About*. Philadelphia: Westminister Press.

250

Stephens, R. E. (1969). *The Courteous Clergyman*. Elizabeth City, N. C.: Roanoke Press.

Turner, J. J. (1979). *How To Make It As A Preacher*. Chino Hills, CA. Penman Productions.

Turner, J. J. (1973). *Standing Before An Audience*. West Monroe, La. Central Printers & Publishers.

The Spiritual Life of the Preacher
F. Furman Kearley

NOTE: The Bible in many versions and many languages. Perhaps the greatest spiritual growth I experienced came to be as a serendipity. I began reading my Bible, a chapter a day, in Hebrew, Greek, Latin, French, German and English to master my required languages. However, this type reading opened my eyes and helped me to see the many dimensions of God's Word as it was expressed in so many different ways in different languages. Since then I have continued to read the Bible in parallel versions and polyglots of Hebrew/English New Testament, Greek/English, Spanish/English, German/English and such like.

Ash, Tony. "The Minister's Spiritual Life" in *The Minister and His Work*. Ed. Michael R. Weed. Fort Worth: Sweet Publishing Company, 1970.

McMillan, E.W. *The Minister's Spiritual Life*. Austin, TX: Firm Foundation Publishing House, 1959.

Expectations of the Man of God
Larry D. Mathis

Baird, James O. "Preachers May Have Roles Confused," *Gospel Advocate* July 1987: 393.

Goebel Music. "Is Christian Consideration Too Much to Ask?" *Firm Foundation* Jan. 1987: 16[48]-19[51].

Price, Al. "What Worries Preachers," *Gospel Advocate* Oct. 1991: 7.

Smith, Dennis R. "Let Your Preacher Be What God Intended Him To Be—A Man!" *Fulton County Gospel News* n.d.: 3-4.

Turner, J.J. "The Right Motivation May Prevent Burnout." *Gospel Advocate* Sept. 1988: 54-55.

Smith, J.M.P. *The Prophets and Their Times*. Chicago: U. of Chicago, 1941.

Stott, John R.W. *Between Two Worlds: The Art of Preaching in the Twentieth Century*. Grand Rapids: Eerdmans, 1982.

Young, Edward J. *My Servants the Prophets*. Grand Rapids: Eerdmans, 1952.

Day-to-Day Ministry
Cecil May, Jr.

Blackwood, Andrew W. *Planning a Year's Pulpit Work*. Abingdon Press, 1942.

Claerbaut, David. *Urban Ministry*. Grand Rapids: Zondervan, 1983.

Dugan, Dave. "Organization can Help a Preacher." *Christian Bible Teacher* May 1992:188.

Hodge, Charles. *Your Preacher*. Fort Worth:Star Bible Publishers, 1972.

Huffard, Everett W. "Preaching and Church Growth." *Gospel Advocate* 1 Feb. 1991:18.

Jarrett, Paul E. "Do You Do Anything Just Because You Are a Christian?" *Carolina Christian* Sept. 1991:8.

Jowett, John Henry. *The Preacher, His Life and Work*. N.Y.: Abingdon, 1912.

Malone, Avon. "Preaching of Paul." *Gospel Advocate* 1 July 1992:26.

May, Cecil Jr. "Preacher to Preacher." *Bible Herald* 15 Apr. 1992:1469.

Meyer, Jack, Sr. *The Preacher and His Work*. Shreveport, La.: Lambert Book House, 1960.

Schuller, David S. *Ministry in America*. Strommen, Merton P., and Milo L. Brekka, Eds. San Francisco:Harper Row, 1950.

Schuller, Lyle E. *The Multiple Staff and the Larger Church*. Nashville: Abingdon Press, 1980.

Smith, Billy R. "Planning a Year's Pulpit Work." *FHU Lectures* 5 Feb. 1990:225.

Stevens, Eldred N. *The Preciousness of Preaching*. Dallas: (private pub.) Mrs. Eldred Stevens, 1980.

Weed, Michael R., ed. *The Minister and His Work*. Austin: Sweet Publishing, 1970.

Wilson, Herman O. *The Preacher and the Seven Day Week*. Austin: Firm Foundation, 1977.

Winkler, Wendell. "Preacher's Private Life: Study Habits." *FHU Lectures* 4 Feb. 1991:295.

The Man of Compassion
Jeffrey Dillinger

Gospel Advocate, Jan. 1991. The entire issue is devoted to compassion.

Crowell, Mark. "The Glory of Caring" in *Freed-Hardeman University Lectureship Book*. Henderson, TN: Freed-Hardeman University, 1989.

Lucado, Max. *God Came Near*. Hendersonville, TN: Multnomah Press, 1987.

Long-Term Ministry
Paul Watson

Baxter, Batsell Barrett. *Every Life a Plan of God*. Abilene: Zachary Associates, 1983.

Blackwood, Andrew W. *Pastoral Work*. Grand Rapids: Baker, 1971.

Collins, Gary R. *You Can Make a Difference*. Grand Rapids: Zondervan, 1992.

North, Ira. *Balance*. Nashville: Gospel Advocate Co., 1983.

North, Ira and Stafford North, eds. *At Work for the Master*. Nashville: Gospel Advocate Co., 1963.

Lyles, Cleon. *Bigger Men for Better Churches*. Little Rock: (private pub.) Cleon Lyles, 1962.

McGavran, Donald and Win Arn. *How to Grow a Church*. Ventura: Regal Books, 1973.

Towns, Elmer. *The Ten Largest Sunday Schools*. Grand Rapids: Baker, 1969.

The Preaching Pen
Basil Overton

Word Origins And Their Romantic Stories, by Dr. Wilfred Funk; Bell Publishing Company, New York, 1978.

Write Better, Speak Better, by the Readers Digest Association, Inc.; Pleasantville, New York and Mortreal; 1985.

The Chicago Manual of Style; The University of Chicago Press, Chicago and London; 13th edition; 1982.

Webster's New Biographical Dictionary; Merriam Webster, Inc., Springfield, Massachusetts; 1983.

RSVP - Reading, Spelling, Vocabulary, Pronunciation, by Norman Lewis; Amsco School Publications, Inc., 315 Hudson Street, New York, NY 10013; 1984.

Spell It Right, By Harry Shaw; Barnes and Noble Books, New York, Hagerstown, San Francisco and London; 1965.

A *History Of The English Language*, by Albert Baugh; Appleton-Century-Crofts, Inc., New York; 1935.

Roget's II, The New Thesaurus, by the editors of The American Heritage Dictionary; Houghton Miflin Company, Boston; 1980.

Encyclopedia of 7700 Illustrations, by Paul Lee Tan, Th.D.; Assurance Publishers, P.O. Box 753, Rockville, Maryland 20851.

Gems From Greek, by Basil Overton; Quality Publications, P.O. Box 1060, Abilene, Texas 79604-1060; 190 pages; 1991.

The Preacher as a Man of The Word
Earl D. Edwards

Errett, Isaac. "What Are the Duties and Authorities of the Christian Ministry?," *Millennial Harbinger*: 1856, pp. 619-21.

Goodpasture, B.C. "Paul's Charge to Timothy." *Great Preachers of Today*. Edited by J.D. Thomas. Vol., 12, Abilene, Tx.: Biblical Research Press: 1967.

Logan, Samuel T., Jr., ed. *The Preacher and Preaching*. Phillipsburg, N.J.: Presbyterian and Reformed Publishing Co., 1986.

Osburne, Carroll D. "The Authority of Titus. *Firm Foundation*: 1980, pp. 294-299.

Pitt-Watson, Ian. *A Primer for Preachers*. Grand Rapids: Baker Book House, 1986.

Roberts, J.W. "The Located Preacher." *Firm Foundation*: 1953, pp. 1-2.

Sanders, Ed. "Evangelistic Authority." Harding College Preachers' Forum, cassette tape, Harding College, Searcy, Ar., 1973.

Spain, Robert Carl. *Epistles of Paul to Titus and Timothy*, vol. 4 in the *Living Word Commentary*, Everett Ferguson, ed., Austin: R.B. Sweet Co., 1970.

Stott, John R.W. *Between Two Worlds*. Grand Rapids: William B. Eerdmans, 1982.

Yeakley, Flavil Jr. *Church Leadership and Organization*. Arvada, Colo: Christian Communications, 1980.

Waddey, John. *Preaching to Preachers About Preaching*. Winona, Ms. Choate Publications, 1977.

Willimon, William H. "Preaching: Entertainment or Exposition?," *Christian Century*: Feb. 28, 1990.

The Preacher in His Study
Shawn D. Mathis

Blackwood, Andrew W. *Expository Preaching for Today.* New York: Abingdon-Cokesbury Press, 1953.

—. *Preaching from the Bible.* New York: Abingdon Press, 1941.

Brooks, Phillips. *Lectures on Preaching.* New York: E.P. Dutton and Company, 1877.

Jowett, J.H. *The Preacher: His Life and Work.* 1912. Grand Rapids: Baker Book House, 1968.

Logan, Samuel T., Jr., ed. *The Preacher and Preaching.* Phillipsburg: Presbyterian and Reformed Publishing Company, 1986.

Morgan, G. Campbell. *Preaching.* London: Marshall, Morgan, and Scott, 1955.

Phelps, Austin. *The Theory of Preaching.* New York: Charles Scribner's Sons, 1903.

Wood, A. Skevington. *The Art of Preaching: Message, Method, and Motive in Preaching.* Grand Rapids: Zondervan Publishing House, 1963.

Preaching's Place in Christian Doctrine
Duane Warden

Achtemeier, Elizabeth. *Preaching as Theology & Art.* Nashville: Abingdon Press, 1984.

Buttrick, David. *Homiletic: Moves and Structures.* Philadelphia: Fortress Press, 1987.

Carson, D. A. and Woodbridge, John D., eds. *Scripture and Truth.* Grand Rapids: Baker Book House, 1992.

Craddock, Fred. *Preaching.* Nashville: Abingdon Press, 1985.

Greidanus, Sidney. *The Modern Preacher and the Ancient Text: Interpreting and Preaching Biblical Literature.* Grand Rapids: William B. Eerdmans Publish Company, 1988.

Kearley, F. Furman; Myers, Edward P.; and Hadley, Timothy D., eds. *Biblical Interpretation Principles and Practice: Studies in Honor of Jack Pearl Lewis.* Grand Rapids: Baker Book House, 1986.

Stott, John R. W. *Between Two Worlds: The Art of Preaching in the Twentieth Century.* Grand Rapids: William B. Eerdmans Publishing Company, 1982.

Sweazey, George E. *Preaching the Good News.* Englewood Cliffs, N.J.: Prentice-Hall, Inc., 1976.

The Preacher: A Man of Balance
Clarence DeLoach, Jr.

Bailey, Raymond. *Jesus the Preacher*. Nashville: Broadman Press.

Baxter, Batsell Barrett. *The Heart of the Yale Lectures*. New York: The MacMillan Co.

Broadus, John A. *On the Preparation and Delivery of Sermons*. New York: Harper & Bros.

Fleming, Ralph Turnbull. *A Minister's Obstacles*. Westwood: Revel Co.

Gibbs, Alfred. *The Preacher and His Preaching*. Topeka: Walterick Publishers.

Holland, Thomas. *Preaching: Principles and Practice*. Brentwood: Pennman Press.

Knox, John. *The Integrity of Preaching*. Nashville: Abingdon Press.

Pattison, T. Harwood. *The Making of the Sermon*. Philadelphia: The American Baptist Publication Society.

Robertson, A.T. *The Glory of the Ministry*. Grand Rapids: Baker Book House.

Stott, John R.W. *Between Two Worlds: The Art of Preaching in the Twentieth Century*. Grand Rapids: Eerdmans Publishing Co., 1982.

Use of the Old Testament in Preaching
Terry Briley

Achtemeier, Elizabeth. *Preaching from the Old Testament*. Louisville: Westminster/John Knox, 1989.

Baker, David L. *Two Testaments, One Bible: A Study of the Theological Relationship Between the Old and New Testaments*. Rev. ed. Downers Grove: InterVarsity Press, 1991

Fee, Gordon and Douglas Stuart. *How to Read the Bible for All Its Worth*. 2nd ed. Grand Rapids: Zondervan, 1993

Greidanus, Sidney. *The Modern Preacher and the Ancient Text: Interpreting and Preaching Biblical Literature*. Grand Rapids: Eerdmans, 1988.

Hill, Andrew E. and John H. Walton. *A Survey of the Old Testament*. Grand Rapids: Zondervan, 1991

Johnson, S. Lewis, Jr. *The Old Testament in the New*. Grand Rapids Zondervan, 1980.

Kaiser, Walter C., Jr. *Toward an Old Testament Theology*. Grand Rapids: Zondervan, 1978.

Kaiser, Walton C., Jr. *The Uses of the Old Testament in the New*. Chicago: Moody, 1985.

Pratt, Richard L., Jr. *He Gave Us Stories: The Bible Student's Guide to Interpreting Old Testament Narratives*. Brentwood: Wolgemuth & Hyatt, 1990.

Stuart, Douglas. *Old Testament Exegesis*. Philadelphia: Westminster, 1980.

Use of the New Testament in Preaching
Burt Groves

Banowsky, William S. *The Mirror of a Movement*. Dallas: Christian Publishing Company, 1965.

Guild, Claud A. *Training Men to Preach*. Fort Worth: The Manney Company, 1968.

Meyer, Jack Sr. *The Preacher and His Work*. Shreveport: Lambert Book House, 1960.

Ramsey, Johnny. *Back to Bible Preaching*. Arlington: Johnny Ramsey, 1971.

Stevens, Elred. *The Preciousness of Preaching*. Dallas: Mrs. Elred Stevens, 1980.

Warren, Thomas B. *The Bible Only Makes Christians Only and the Only Christians*. Jonesboro: National Christian Press, Inc., 1986.

Warren, Thomas B. and Elkins, Garland, editors. *God Demands Doctrinal Preaching*. Jonesboro: National Christian Press, Inc., 1978.

Whitten, Eddie, editor. *The Validity of the Restoration Principle*. Mesquite: Biblical Bookshelf, 1989.

Woodson, William. *Jesus Christ the Son of God*. Nashville: Gospel Advocate Company, 1973.

Workman, Gary, editor. *The Restorer*. Mesquite: Rowlett Church of Christ (periodical).

McDONOUGH CHURCH OF CHRIST
P.O. Box 1290
McDonough, Georgia 30253
(404) 954-1337